JOHN STEINBECK and EDWARD F. RICKETTS

The Shaping of a Novelist

The mind must be regarded as dictating the course of world building; without it there is but formless chaos.

SIR ARTHUR EDDINGTON

The Nature of the Physical World

JOHN STEINBECK and EDWARD F. RICKETTS

The

Shaping

of

a Novelist

by Richard Astro

THE UNIVERSITY OF
MINNESOTA PRESS, Minneapolis

*The University of Minnesota Press gratefully acknowl-
edges the support for its program of the Andrew W.
Mellon Foundation. This book is one of those in whose
financing the Foundation's grant played a part.*

Library of Congress Catalog Card Number: 73-87252

ISBN 0-8166-0704-4

Quotations from the following works of John Steinbeck are reprinted by permission of The Viking Press, Inc., Elaine A. Steinbeck, William Heinemann
Ltd, and Curtis Brown Ltd: *America and Americans,* copyright © 1966 by
John Steinbeck; *Bombs Away,* copyright 1942 by John Steinbeck, © 1970
by Elaine, Thomas, and John Steinbeck IV; *Burning Bright,* copyright ©
1950 by John Steinbeck; *Cannery Row,* copyright 1945 by John Steinbeck,
© 1973 by Elaine, Thomas, and John Steinbeck IV; *Cup of Gold,* copyright
1929, © 1957 by John Steinbeck; *East of Eden,* copyright © 1952 by John
Steinbeck; *The Forgotten Village,* copyright 1941, © 1969 by John Steinbeck;
In Dubious Battle, copyright 1936, © 1964 by John Steinbeck; *Journal of a
Novel,* copyright © 1969 by the Executors of the Estate of John Steinbeck;
"The Leader of the People" from *The Red Pony,* copyright 1938, © 1966 by
John Steinbeck; *The Pearl,* copyright 1945 by John Steinbeck, © 1973 by
Elaine, Thomas, and John Steinbeck IV; *Log from the Sea of Cortez,* copy-
right 1941 by John Steinbeck and Edward F. Ricketts, © 1969 by John
Steinbeck, © 1969 by John Steinbeck and Edward F. Ricketts, Jr.; *The
Moon Is Down,* copyright 1942 by John Steinbeck, © 1970 by Elaine,
Thomas, and John Steinbeck IV; *The Pastures of Heaven,* copyright 1932,
© 1960 by John Steinbeck; *Sweet Thursday,* copyright © 1954 by John Stein-
beck; *To a God Unknown,* copyright 1933, © 1961 by John Steinbeck;
Tortilla Flat, copyright 1935, © 1963 by John Steinbeck; *Travels with
Charley in Search of America,* copyright © 1961, 1962 by The Curtis Pub-
lishing Co., © 1962 by John Steinbeck; "The Vigilante" from *The Long
Valley,* copyright 1936, © 1964 by John Steinbeck; "The White Quail" from
The Long Valley, copyright 1935, © 1963 by John Steinbeck; *The Wayward
Bus,* copyright © 1947 by John Steinbeck; *The Winter of Our Discontent,*
copyright © 1961 by John Steinbeck. Quotations from *Viva Zapata!* and
unpublished manuscripts by John Steinbeck have been made by permission
of Elaine Steinbeck.

The quotation on page 7 from *Between Pacific Tides,* Third Edition, by

Edward F. Ricketts and Jack Calvin, revised by Joel W. Hedgpeth (Stanford: Stanford University Press, 1952), has been reprinted with permission of the Publishers. Quotations from the unpublished manuscripts of Edward F. Ricketts have been printed by permission of Edward F. Ricketts, Jr. Quotations from "The Green Lady" have been printed by permission of Webster F. Street. Quotations from letters from the following people have been used by permission of the writers: Richard Albee, Nathaniel Benchley, Jack Calvin, Pascal Covici (permission by Pascal Covici, Jr.), Joel W. Hedgpeth, Frank Lloyd, Edward F. Ricketts (permission by Edward F. Ricketts, Jr.), John Steinbeck (permission by Elaine Steinbeck), and Webster F. Street.

For Betty with love

Prefatory Note

*I*n the text of this book, many individuals and agencies are identified by initials. Correspondence between two parties is identified by a hyphen (-). Personal interviews between the author and other individuals are identified by a slash (/). The initials in the text refer to the following people or agencies.

Albee. Richard Albee (friend of Steinbeck and Ricketts)
RA. Richard Astro
AB. Alan Baldridge (Librarian, Hopkins Marine Station)
ROB. Robert O. Ballou (Steinbeck's early publisher)
NB. Nathaniel Benchley (writer, friend of Steinbeck)
TB. Anthony J. Berry (owner and captain of the *Western Flyer*)
LRB. Lawrence R. Blinks (oceanographer, Hopkins Marine Station)
BNP. Bureau of Naval Personnel
VB. Verner Bogard (University Apparatus Company, Berkeley, California)
RLB. Rolf L. Bolin (oceanographer, Hopkins Marine Station)
JC. Jack Calvin (writer, naturalist, co-author of *Between Pacific Tides*)

JOHN STEINBECK and EDWARD F. RICKETTS

Ca.   Joseph Campbell (mythologist, critic)
EG.   Ellwood Graham (artist, Carmel, California)
FPH.   Floris P. Hartog (editor, Stanford University Press)
JWH.   Joel W. Hedgpeth (marine biologist, naturalist)
HK.   Herbert Kline (film producer and director)
FL.   Frank Lloyd (friend of Steinbeck and Ricketts)
ML.   Margery Lloyd (friend of Steinbeck and Ricketts)
R & TL. Ritch and Tal Lovejoy (friends of Steinbeck and Ricketts)
GEM.   George E. MacGinitie (oceanographer, friend of Ricketts)
HM.   Hattie MacGinitie (friend of Ricketts, co-author with husband, George MacGinitie, of a book on the seashore of the Pacific Coast)
MM.   Manuel Madinabeitia (regional director of a large fish export company, La Paz, Baja California Sur, Mexico)
MO.   McIntosh and Otis (Steinbeck's literary agency)
EO.   Elizabeth Otis (Steinbeck's literary agent)
EFR.   Edward Flanders Ricketts
EFR, Jr. Edward F. Ricketts, Jr. (Ricketts' son)
RR.   Richard Rodgers (composer)
VS.   Virginia Scardigli (schoolteacher, friend of Ricketts)
AS.   Antonia Seixas (friend of Ricketts and Steinbeck)
SUP.   Stanford University Press (publisher of *Between Pacific Tides*)
CS.   Carol Steinbeck (first wife of John Steinbeck)
ES.   Elaine Steinbeck (third wife of John Steinbeck)
JS.   John Steinbeck
WFS.   Webster F. Street (Monterey attorney, friend of Steinbeck)
FS.   Frances Strong (Ricketts' sister)
GV.   Gilberto Valdivia (retired professor, La Paz, Baja California Sur, Mexico)
RW.   Robert Wallsten (friend of Steinbeck)

Acknowledgments

*L*ike any writer of applied criticism, I owe my first acknowledgment to the authors of the primary material, John Steinbeck and Edward F. Ricketts, whose writings about man and the world in which he lives provided the impetus and the direction for this volume. Scholarly debts are cited in notes, but I wish to pay particular tribute to Warren French, Joseph Fontenrose, Tetsumaro Hayashi, and Peter Lisca, whose studies of various aspects of Steinbeck's writing have been invaluable. To that wonderfully unique maverick marine biologist, Joel W. Hedgpeth, whose suggestions are responsible for many of the insights in this volume, my debt is personal as well as scholarly. And I am deeply indebted to Edward F. Ricketts, Jr., for providing me with his father's unpublished essays, journals, and correspondence as well as various suggestions and tidbits of information. I owe a similar debt of gratitude to Elaine Steinbeck for her many insights into her husband's life and work.

I wish to thank all of those individuals who have taken the time to write and/or talk with me about Steinbeck and Ricketts: Alan Baldridge, Nathaniel Benchley, Anthony J. Berry, Lawrence Blinks, Rolf Bolin, Mrs. William Brown, Jack Calvin, Joseph Campbell,

JOHN STEINBECK and EDWARD F. RICKETTS

Ellwood Graham, Herbert Kline, Gustav Lannestock, Frank and Margery Lloyd, Manuel Madinabeitia, George and Hattie Mac-Ginitie, Elizabeth Otis, Richard Rodgers, Virginia Scardigli, Antonia Seixas, Gwendolyn Steinbeck, Fred and Frances Strong, Gilberto Valdivia, Robert Wallsten. And I want to convey special thanks to Richard Albee for his valuable insights into organismal philosophy and to Webster F. Street, who always has been a help and a delight.

I am indebted to the Oregon State University Research Council for a grant which permitted me to do the seed work for this study, to the College of Liberal Arts at Oregon State University for research leave time, and to Vice President Roy A. Young, Dean Gordon Gilkey, and Walter C. Foreman, chairman of the Department of English, for their continuing support of my research. I would also like to thank the National Endowment for the Humanities for a grant which enabled me to carry out and complete the major portion of my research. The findings of this study do not necessarily reflect the views of the Endowment.

To the many undergraduates who helped me travel down new paths of Steinbeck research, my thanks and my apologies. I am indebted to my typists, Marci Godshall, Kathy Duncan, and Marilyn Barton, and to Cliff and Donna Dalton who watched over Ben. I also want to thank my colleagues Robert Frank and Peter Copek, who commented on the findings in my manuscript.

Most importantly, I want to thank my wife, Betty, who has lived with this project for a very long time. She typed and proofread, edited, criticized, and indexed. She willingly traveled with me on many research trips and patiently endured my absence from home on others. Without her continuing assistance, this book would not exist except in the mothballs of memory.

R. A.

Corvallis, Oregon
May 1973

Table
of Contents

JOHN STEINBECK and EDWARD F. RICKETTS

The Shaping of a Novelist

Steinbeck
and Ricketts:
An Overview

John Steinbeck's finest writing contains a compelling representation of nature and the land, and a sincere admiration for the simple people and the guileless human virtues as opposed to the mean pursuit of monetary wealth. In such memorable novels as *The Grapes of Wrath*, *Cannery Row*, and *Tortilla Flat*, Steinbeck's unadorned and objectively clear prose style presents, evaluates, and ultimately gives meaning to uniquely beautiful descriptions of the land and the people on it.

But while most readers have acknowledged Steinbeck's descriptive genius and have commented upon the excellence of his prose style, many have coincidentally lamented "the destructive effect of his love of philosophizing," which reduces his otherwise substantial talent to sentimentality in that his ability to depict nature and the natural man is "in his best books watered down by tenth-rate philosophizing and, in his worst books, is overwhelmed by it."[1] Even Steinbeck's most sympathetic critics have admitted that the novelist is an incurable amateur philosopher whose shifting philosophical point of view leads him into impossible thematic paradoxes so that the "central theses of his [Steinbeck's] novels are not likely to carry complete conviction, whatever his narrative

3

and poetic skill," because his is "an inadequate philosophy for a novelist."[2]

Earlier studies of Steinbeck's philosophy of life have been short-sighted and incomplete. Despite some apparent contradictions, Steinbeck's world-view contains a meaningful statement about the human condition which is consistent with his major talent for depicting nature and man. And until Steinbeck's view of man and the world is stated clearly and honestly, there is no way of assessing properly the full measure of his contribution to American letters.

In all fairness to previous Steinbeck scholarship, it must be said that many of the flawed conclusions by the critics resulted from their being forced to operate without many indispensable facts about the writer and his work. More often, though, the problem lies in the writers' limited horizons, because most critics carry out their investigations within the constricted framework of literary patterns and traditions. In some cases, this approach may be sufficient, but with Steinbeck it is disastrous. The serious reader of Steinbeck's work must be prepared to examine the vast horizons of science in general and marine biology in particular, and so most Steinbeck critics face a task foreign to their dispositions and backgrounds.

It is here that we must turn to Edward Flanders Ricketts (1897–1948), the marine biologist who owned and operated the Pacific Biological Laboratory on the Monterey waterfront, and who, as later chapters will point out, serves in varying degrees as the source of Steinbeck's personae in six novels and novelettes (*In Dubious Battle, The Grapes of Wrath, The Moon Is Down, Cannery Row, Burning Bright,* and *Sweet Thursday)* and in one short story ("The Snake"). No analysis of Steinbeck's world-view, his philosophy of life, can proceed without a careful study of the life, work, and ideas of this remarkable human being who was Steinbeck's closest personal and intellectual companion for nearly two decades.[3]

Ed Ricketts was born and grew up on the northwest side of the city of Chicago. After a year at Illinois State Normal University, one stint as an accountant for a Texas country club and another as a member of a New Mexico surveying party, and a tour of duty in the army, Ricketts enrolled at the University of Chicago, which he attended sporadically between 1919 and 1922. Ricketts took classes in German, Spanish, philosophy, and zoology, but the most important thing that happened to him at the University was his exposure to the person and ideas of W. C. Allee, the brilliant ecological theorist whose ideas about the universality of social behavior among animals, and whose theory of social transition in which any given animal (including man) behaves differently in a group than as an individual (later recorded in Allee's classic treatise on the subject, *Animal Aggregations* [1931]), made such a deep and lasting impression on the young Ricketts, that years later, Jack Calvin, Ricketts' collaborator on *Between Pacific Tides*, could write: "We knew W. C. Allee from Ed's conversations, discovering later that all of his former students got a holy look in their eyes at the mention of his name, as Ed always did. It was later, too, that we realized that almost to a man Allee's students approached or achieved greatness of mind. Probably a minute number of teachers have ever so stimulated their students to think for themselves" (JC-RA, 7/14/69).[4]

Ricketts left Chicago without taking a degree, but he did take with him the ideas of his greatest teacher, and they remained at or near the matrix of his philosophical and scientific consciousness throughout the rest of his life.

Ricketts came to California in 1923 with A. E. Galigher, his roommate at Chicago, and the two opened a biological supply house in Pacific Grove. Galigher left shortly thereafter for Berkeley, and Ricketts assumed complete ownership of Pacific Biologicals, which remained his home until his death in 1948.

According to Steinbeck, he and Ricketts met in a dentist's waiting room in 1930. Supposedly each had heard of the other, and they struck up an immediate friendship. According to virtually everyone who knew Steinbeck and Ricketts and is willing to talk about the friendship, theirs was a very unique relationship. Steinbeck felt extremely close to Ricketts and needed and desired his companionship, and Ricketts poured out to Steinbeck what, for lack of a better term, must be called love. For a time, Steinbeck and Ricketts were integral members of a larger group of friends who lived an ostensibly bohemian existence, bound together by their communal poverty which they combated, as Jack Calvin points out, by "stealing vegetables for our communal stews" (JC-RA, 7/14/69). The suggestion, however, that Steinbeck and Ricketts lived lackadaisical and carefree lives during the thirties misrepresents the facts. For while they worked hard at enjoying themselves and drank goodly quantities of cheap wine, Steinbeck labored long to the end of becoming a good writer and Ricketts diligently studied what he called "the good, kind, sane, little animals,"[5] the marine invertebrates of the west coast of North America

Frances Strong, Ricketts' sister, has observed that "the intertidal animals possessed him" (FS/RA, 3/20/71). He spent much of his time (and nearly all of his money) on collecting expeditions as far north as Sitka and Juneau, Alaska, and as far south as Enseñada, Mexico. He read extensively in his field. When the famous Cannery Row fire of 1936 gutted his lab, he compiled a list of possessions destroyed, listing the value of his bound volumes at $2,000.00, a weighty sum at the time, and stating that "I had probably the finest library outside of Stanford and U.C. on the marine ecology of the Pacific Coast."[6]

The published result of Ricketts' many years of reading and collecting appeared in 1939, titled *Between Pacific Tides* (Stanford University Press). The book, as Joel Hedgpeth suggests, "had its origins as a sort of cottage industry among a group of people at Pacific Grove during the Depression."

Ed's friends, who enjoyed going with him on low tide collecting trips, encouraged him to write all these things up. In the beginning it was to be a little book for beginners, and Jack Calvin, a struggling free-lance writer of Sunday school stories and the like, would help make the writing intelligible for the layman. Calvin would also take the photographs, and his brother-in-law, Ritchie Lovejoy, would prepare some drawings. The scope of the book grew and by mid-1930 there was enough of it to send to publishers for consideration.[7]

An Overview

In the end, although he shared authorship with Calvin, who by the time the book was published had moved from Pacific Grove to Sitka, Alaska, *Between Pacific Tides* was, as former Hopkins Marine Station oceanographer G. E. MacGinitie indicates, "essentially Ed's alone" (GEM/RA, 9/3/70).

Between Pacific Tides is a readable, professional account of the habits and habitats of the animals living on the rocky shores and in the tide pools of the Pacific Coast. As Steinbeck noted in his foreword to the third edition of *Tides*, the book

is designed more to stir curiosity than to answer questions . . . There are good things to see in the tidepools and there are exciting and interesting thoughts to be generated from the seeing. Every new eye applied to the peep hole which looks out at the world may fish in some new beauty and some new pattern, and the world of the human mind must be enriched by such fishing.[8]

Contrary to the usual phylogenetic method of depicting marine invertebrates, the treatment in *Between Pacific Tides* is, at the authors' insistence, "ecological and inductive: that is, the animals are treated according to their most characteristic habitat, and in the order of their commonness, conspicuousness, and interest."[9]

Ricketts' and Calvin's efforts paid off. *Between Pacific Tides* has become a definitive sourcebook for studying marine life on the Pacific Coast and is still used at oceanographic research centers from Scripps to Friday Harbor. "There are many reasons for this sustained popularity," Hedgpeth notes, "but perhaps the chief one is that people want to know about sea-shore animals, and no one else has presented this information in terms of the way of life— the ecology, if you will—of the sea-shore in such a readable manner."[10]

Between Pacific Tides seethes with the authors' sense of joy, of genuine good feeling at the prospect of the fullness of life on the rocky shores and in the tide pools. "Everywhere," note Calvin and Ricketts, "there is color, life, movement."[11] As later chapters will show, this same celebration of nature's plenitude is a hallmark of Steinbeck's greatest fiction. The presence of the ideas of W. C. Allee is very apparent in *Between Pacific Tides*. Several times

7

Ricketts and Calvin refer to Allee directly. When, for example, the authors note that the intertwining habit among brittle stars is so pronounced as to "lead us to the borderline of the metaphysical," they recall that "Allee found that aggregations have a distinct survival value for their members, bringing about a degree of resistance to untoward conditions that is not attainable by isolated individuals."[12] The whole ecological approach of the book is largely the result of the impact Allee's ideas made on Ricketts at Chicago. And when Ricketts and Calvin discuss the occurrence of a certain kind of chiton in a variety of habitats, they cite Allee's belief that "if the search is long enough, one can turn out very nearly any animal in any environment, however far-fetched" in an effort to show inherent liabilities of the ecological method.[13]

Besides being one of the few scientific books which views the seashore as an interrelated whole rather than a place where one can see a random sampling of animals at low tide, *Between Pacific Tides* differs from most scientific books on the subject in that Ricketts portrays himself as "a generalizer—with an eye for particulars, to be sure, yet interested in all that went on along a coast of more than a thousand miles."[14] *Between Pacific Tides* shows Ricketts building what he loved to call "the toto-picture" as he worked to develop a "unified field hypothesis" about the littoral of the Pacific Coast. Using the scientific method tinged with a personal brand of metaphysics, Ricketts and Calvin proceed from observation to speculation and ultimately to hypothesis, and this, says Steinbeck, "is the creative process, probably the highest and most satisfactory we know."[15]

Less than a year after the publication of *Between Pacific Tides*, Ricketts began planning his next venture, a handbook of the marine invertebrates of the San Francisco Bay region. This time his collaborator was not to be Jack Calvin, but John Steinbeck. Steinbeck's biographers have barely mentioned the novelist's par-

Edward F. Ricketts at the Great Tide Pool,
Pacific Grove, California

ticipation in this project, noting only that the two explored the littoral north of San Francisco in 1939. But according to Ricketts, the idea of a collaboration was Steinbeck's. "John has suggested that we do it together, and offer the result to SU [Stanford Unisity] Press and to Viking, highest bidder" (EFR-VB, 11/30/39). Proceeding with Steinbeck's encouragement, Ricketts worked out a format for the collecting, and he developed organizational procedures for the writing of the text.

The San Francisco Bay book was never completed, but Ricketts' unpublished essays and notes about the venture show the kind of ideas the two men exchanged and the role Ricketts felt that Steinbeck could play in the project. The handbook, to be written largely by Steinbeck, was, according to Ricketts, "specifically designed for beginning biology classes but will be written and ordered so that it may be used by the sea coast wanderer who finds interest in the little bugs and would like to know what they are and how they live. Its treatment will revolt against the theory that only the dull is accurate and only the tiresome, valuable."[16]

Ricketts charted the text, which would total 200–250 pages and would be divided into three sections: the first, a series of essays on "some biological and general principles," for which Ricketts notes Steinbeck had already written some 3,000 words, and himself, 5,000. Steinbeck did write a preface for the handbook, although the manuscript runs somewhat less than 2,000 words. Affirming that their study will be associational rather than phylogenetic, Steinbeck's preface insists that to study seashore life by an isolated analysis of one marine organism is as pointless as trying to study family life in New York City by examining only one family. The second section of the Bay Area handbook was to be a detailed account of 100–150 animals; the third a selected bibliography, "fairly well annotated." Apparently Steinbeck was to play a large role in the second section as well as in the first, for Ricketts insists that "Jon can make better descriptions than have ever been made."[17] Ricketts states that he will "select out and list the 50 or 100 most common animals, take Jon out into the field, show him the animals in the field (bring them in alive), have him describe them, together (maybe, maybe though) with any others that particularly catch his eye (any that he *must* describe)."[18]

Ricketts' zoological preface to the handbook and his random notes about the project contain speculations consistent with the scientific-philosophic premises about life which underlie *Between Pacific Tides*. As in *Tides*, Ricketts is struck by the fullness of life in the intertidal zones: "In the SF Bay region, as along ocean shores all over the world, animals and plant life are almost everywhere. The most barren looking shore is actually heavily populated, and here, as elsewhere in the sea, wherever you go down to the shore, you'll find something."[19]

Discussing the ecological method to be used in the handbook, Ricketts states that "ecological arrangements cannot yet, probably cannot ever, achieve the finality so characteristic of the taxonomic order," and yet the sensitive collector, "the nostalgic layman who respects Novalis' dictum, 'Philosophy is properly homesickness, the wish to be everywhere at home,' " will find this method "certainly more interesting."[20] When one considers, Ricketts suggests, the molding of and influence on the communities of the littoral by "exposure to or protection from wave shock," by "vertical position in the intertidal zone," and by the "type of bottom," he will grasp "the whole idea of inter-relation [which] seems actually to be pretty much the keynote of modern holistic concepts, wherein the whole consists of the animal or the community *in* its environment, the notion of relation being significant."[21] This holistic way of viewing life, gleaned in part from the lectures of W. C. Allee and evident in *Between Pacific Tides*, is the cornerstone of Ricketts' world-view and is a central thematic strain in Steinbeck's greatest fiction.

Ricketts' notes for the San Francisco Bay project also point to his growing belief in the parallel behavior patterns of animals and men, a notion that many critics have discerned (and soundly condemned) in Steinbeck's fiction. Ricketts observes that "the laws of animals must be the laws of men," and he insists that life in the tide pools affords the observer an unmasked replica of man's social structure.

11

JOHN STEINBECK and EDWARD F. RICKETTS

A study of animal communities has this advantage: they are merely
what they are, for anyone to see who will and can look clearly: they
cannot complicate the picture by worded idealisms, by saying one
thing and being another; here the struggle is unmasked and the beauty
is unmasked.[22]

Despite the fact that the San Francisco Bay Handbook was never
completed, Ricketts' work on the project helped pave the way for
his next enterprise with Steinbeck, the 1940 collecting expedition
to the Gulf of California which resulted in their subsequent collaboration on *Sea of Cortez: A Leisurely Journal of Travel and
Research* (1941).

In terms of its scientific value, critical opinion on this book,
which Ricketts called "a dual structure of thought and beauty,"[23]
was mixed, but largely favorable. Among the most disparaging
remarks are those by John Lyman, who notes that the authors
say a great deal about the Panamic character of the Gulf's fauna,
but they really give "only the bare lists of forms taken at each collecting station."[24] Steinbeck, incidentally, sent Ricketts a copy of
Lyman's piece, writing in the margin that "this is the review of a
completely humorless man and moreover something of a prig."

More approvingly, Joel Hedgpeth, in a review for the San Francisco *Chronicle*, admits that this "first general account of the fauna"
of the region is "not much more than an outline." But he attributes
this to "our incomplete and haphazard knowledge of the fauna of
our own backyard" and insists that the scientific appendix which
forms the second half of *Sea of Cortez* "will hearafter be indispensable for students of marine invertebrates of the Gulf of California."[25] Similarly, Rolf L. Bolin, whose name appears in the narrative portion of *Sea of Cortez* (though he jokingly points out that
Steinbeck spelled it wrong), says it is a good book and a great aid
to people going to the area to collect (RLB/RA, 10/8/70).

Whatever its scientific merits, *Sea of Cortez* has been hailed by
nearly all of Steinbeck's critics as a major statement of the novelist's basic beliefs; it "stands to his work very much as *Death in the
Afternoon* and *Green Hills of Africa* stand to that of Heming-

12

way."[26] It is most important, therefore, to dispel certain myths which have grown up around *Sea of Cortez* by examining the facts about the Gulf of California expedition and by noting how the book was written.

It is generally assumed that "Steinbeck wrote the first part, the narrative of the trip— published separately in 1951 as *The Log from the Sea of Cortez*—and Ricketts wrote the second part, a phyletic catalogue."[27] Most critics also believe that the material for the narrative came from two journals, one written by Ricketts and the other by Steinbeck.

Neither assumption is correct. There were two records kept during the voyage, but neither was written by Steinbeck. Rather, they were kept by Ricketts and by Tony Berry (captain of the boat which Steinbeck chartered for the trip), and Steinbeck composed the narrative almost entirely from Ricketts' journal. In a joint memorandum (presumably written by Ricketts) to Pascal (Pat) Covici and to the editorial board of the Viking Press (the book's publisher), the authors state:

Originally a journal of the trip was to have been kept by both of us, but this record was found to be a natural expression of only one of us. This journal was subsequently used by the other chiefly as a reminder of what actually had taken place, but in several cases parts of the original field notes were incorporated into the final narrative, and in one case a large section was lifted verbatim from other unpublished work. This was then passed back to the other for comment, completion of certain chiefly technical details, and corrections. And then the correction was passed back again.[28]

Additionally, the Steinbeck-Ricketts memorandum challenges the idea that *Sea of Cortez* is two books. Rather, as Ricketts wrote in a brief statement he titled "Morphology of the *Sea of Cortez*," "the structure is a collaboration, but mostly shaped by John. The book is the result."[29]

Steinbeck defended the collaborative nature of *Sea of Cortez*. For example, Covici suggested to Ricketts that "no matter how much John helped in writing your section or you his, it is still unquestionably obvious that the writer of 'The Sea of Cortez' is not the author of the appendix" (PC-EFR, 5/20/41), and advised that the title page of the book read,

The Sea of Cortez
By John Steinbeck
With a scientific appendix comprising materials for a source-book on the marine animals of the Panamic Faunal Province.
By Edward F. Ricketts

Steinbeck objected. "This book is the product of the work and thinking of both of us and the setting down of the words is of no importance," insisted the novelist. "I not only disapprove of your plan—but forbid it." Covici consented, but not without a final word of protest. "It shall be done as you and Ed say, but be it on your heads. I still think you are wrong."

Surely in your introduction you could give Ed full credit for his ideas and the help he undoubtedly was to you, and Ed in turn could honestly tell of the inspiration and assistance you were to him in his end of the job. Neither of you could then be accused of assuming the other's particular talent. However, it is your book and I shall do as you say. (PC-JS, 5/22/41)

Unfortunately, these facts have been overlooked too often, with the result that Steinbeck's novels have been interpreted according to premises stated in *Sea of Cortez* believed to be his, but actually developed by Ricketts. The most obvious example involves the important Easter Sermon on non-teleological thinking which was written not by Steinbeck, but by Ricketts (he had been making notes for the essay before 1940) and is the "large section lifted verbatim from other unpublished work" which is discussed in the Steinbeck-Ricketts memorandum.[30] In a letter to mythologist Joseph Campbell, Ricketts noted that early drafts of the essay on non-teleological thinking (and two other essays) which "pretty well sum up the world outlook, or rather the inlook, that I have found developing in myself more and more during the years," were completed by the middle of 1939 (EFR-JC, 8/25/39). And Ricketts even told Campbell that Steinbeck, with the help of Paul de Kruif, tried without success to get the piece on non-teleology published in *Harpers* (EFR-JC, 10/7/39).[31]

14

Turning from the question of authorship to the details of the trip itself, it is imperative to recognize that although both men worked hard to organize the expedition, Ricketts, not Steinbeck, was the driving force behind the project. Steinbeck was already a writer of some reputation and wealth, and by subsidizing the venture, he enabled the marine biologist to carry out the second stage of his research of the North American littoral.

Webster Street, a close friend and Monterey attorney who accompanied the crew as far as San Diego, helped Steinbeck charter the *Western Flyer*, and the novelist ordered the necessary supplies (which included a copy of Allee's *Animal Aggregations*). Ricketts prepared the collecting materials and obtained clearances from Mexican officials. And on March 11, 1940, Steinbeck, Ricketts, and the crew of the *Western Flyer* (which included Steinbeck's wife, Carol, though she is never mentioned in the *Log*) departed Monterey Harbor, returning on April 20.[32]

Steinbeck and Ricketts worked hard at collecting and preserving specimens, and although they did drink a goodly amount of beer and claimed to be taking a leisurely trip, their pace was far from lackadaisical. Almost immediately after the expedition ended, Ricketts began identifying and classifying specimens, following what he once called "the elaborate protocol of biological nomenclature." Meanwhile, Steinbeck, working with Ricketts' notes spread out before him in the studio of Ellwood Graham, a local artist whom he had commissioned to paint his portrait, shaped the narrative.[33]

Steinbeck stopped work on *Sea of Cortez* during the summer of 1940 when he returned to Mexico with producer-director Herb Kline to work on *The Forgotten Village*, a documentary film about a small Mexican village's fight against disease and outworn medical practices. Ricketts joined Steinbeck in Mexico City, where he played tourist, did a creditable amount of drinking, and, as he wrote Ritch and Tal Lovejoy of Pacific Grove, actually worked on several of the shooting sequences in Steinbeck's film (ERF-R and TL, 7/6/40). Herb Kline notes that Ricketts "asked very intelligent 'whys' as to methods I used as a director and made some valuable suggestions to both John and myself" (HK/RA, 2/27/71). But Klein, who recalls "how much fun Ed was to be with and what a fine mind he had when we got into serious discussions going to and from the filming," also remembers that "Ed's mind then, like John's, was also on *Sea of Cortez*" (HK/RA, 2/27/71). As soon as the filming of *The Forgotten Village* was finished, the pair returned to Pacific Grove and to work on the Gulf of California materials.

According to Rolf Bolin, who helped with the identification of specimens, the putting together of the book had its grand and funny moments (RLB/RA, 10/8/70). One only has to consider the species source of Steinbeck and Ricketts' remarks about the *Proctofilus winchelli*, or notice the reference to the authors' need for a second aquarium "because the first was such that the fish could see out but we couldn't see in" to sense the genial humor and aura of good feeling that runs through the narrative.

The "events" reported in the *Log* (there were, the authors note, no "adventures") actually took place, and in many instances Steinbeck transferred items directly from Ricketts' notes into the final text. It is significant, for example, that the dates and times of events in the published narrative correspond precisely to the chronology in Ricketts' log, since Berry's precise Pilot House Log Book reveals that both accounts are often several hours off. The discussion of navigation (Ch. 5 in the *Log*) is an abbreviated version of what Ricketts called "the world within the horizon," and most of the scientific speculation and the collecting data are taken from Ricketts' journal. The details of the "borrego" hunt in the mountains near Puerto Escondido (Ch. 16) are drawn from Ricketts' account, as are many of the incidents which tell of the contact between members of the crew and the Indians of the Gulf.[34]

Finally, those sections of the *Log* which challenge the value of social progress are taken almost directly from Ricketts' journal. In his log, Ricketts comments about "the genial and slow paced kindness of the Mexicans," and he notes that "many people here have done things for us, even casually, that have no reference to material remuneration or to social, political or financial advancement for them."

16

PILOT HOUSE LOG

DATE_____19

FORM 10

TIME BY CLOCK	NAME OF HEADLAND OR PLACE	TIME ON COURSE		PILOT HOUSE COMPASS
		HOURS	MINUTES	
	April 9, 1940			
8:30 A	Left anchorage for Shrimp Fishing Boats			
	There are 12 Jap Boats here			
	all big boats, They are sure killing			
	a lot of other fish John and Ricketts went aboard			
1:10 P.M.	Started for Tobis Island Anchorage			
	On the way we tried to Spear			
	at least 50 Manta Ray. Lost			
	all our Harpoons.			
6:10 P.M	Dropped anchor.			
	April 10, 1940			
10. AM.	Still on anchor. The Specimen			
	hunter went to the Ester Lagoon			
	Early this morning, not back yet.			
12:05 AM	Left anchor for Aguabomba			
9:15 P.M	Dropped anchor in 10 fathoms of			
	Water. Figure we are about			
	5 miles off shore. off Aguabomba			

Courtesy Tony Berry

A page from Captain Tony Berry's Pilot House Log Book

I thot what a true thing that was, and what a commentary on the whole non-western character which emphasizes the spiritual values of real friendship btwn men for instance, as aginst the European-American insistence on material values. Not many American people have as many or as true friendships as those people up on the mt. near Loreto had for each other, not many Americans put as much into their friendships nor know so much about them.[35]

But, says Ricketts, the "spiritual values of real friendship" will eventually be undermined by "the virus of civilization, the most obvious indices of which are good roads and power hookups and maybe canned foods."[36]

Passages such as these occur often in Ricketts' notes, and it certainly seems feasible that the presence of these sentiments in the published narrative is not attributable to Steinbeck's diminishing commitment to social action as some critics have suggested,[37] but rather to a personal commitment to respect the views of his best friend.

While Steinbeck drew heavily from Ricketts' journal in shaping the final chronicle, he omitted or minimized many things and exaggerated others. Absent from the *Log* are accounts of the all-day "turtle dinner" with the Japanese in Guaymas, of Tiny's fateful prize fight in Guaymas in which he was soundly trounced by the local champion after training all day on Bacardi, and of the rough weather on the trip home. According to Berry, Steinbeck greatly amplified the problems caused by the infamous Hansen Sea Cow, and he deliberately played down the extensive beer drinking on board (TB/RA, 7/23/70). The reasons for the many omissions, magnifications, and understatements are, of course, subject to question, but perhaps some clue can be gleaned from Steinbeck's remark to Berry when, after the book was published, Berry asked Steinbeck: "John, why didn't you tell it true?" and Steinbeck simply answered, "for Ed" (TB/RA, 10/8/70). *Sea of Cortez* stands as it is because of Ed Ricketts' belief in the importance of the work and thinking he and Steinbeck had done in the Gulf.[38] In addition to its value as a scientific record, it contains the central tenets of many of Ricketts' beliefs about life (some of which

Steinbeck shared, others he rejected), and it is a sincere statement of Steinbeck's affection for his greatest friend.

The publication of *Sea of Cortez* on December 6, 1941, marked the high point of a close personal and intellectual relationship which had flowered for over a decade. But neither Steinbeck nor Ricketts had time to relish the fruits of their collective labor because Pearl Harbor was bombed the day after the book was published and both were soon involved in the war effort. Steinbeck performed a variety of services for the military, ranging from the writing of a propagandistic treatise entitled *Bombs Away* (1942) to plotting a "foolproof" scheme of dropping counterfeit money behind enemy lines which, by inflating the German mark, would help the Allies win the war.

Ricketts became interested in the strategic importance of biological information about the South Sea Islands under Japanese mandate, the fauna of which he had been studying for several years. The pages of his notebooks for 1942–1944 are filled with reading notes on various aspects of life on these islands, and include scientific accounts of the South Sea coral reefs as well as reflections on the history of Japanese colonialism.

Ricketts took this work quite seriously, and at one point even contemplated a possible book or a series of essays on the mandated islands.[39] On September 24, 1942, he met with officers from Naval Intelligence, told them of his findings, and proffered his services. He even applied for a commission, listing John Steinbeck among his references. But the Navy ignored Ricketts' request, and shortly thereafter the Army drafted him. Initially, Ricketts annoyed about being drafted, but assigned to duty at the Monterey Presidio where he could keep essentially his own hours, his resentment faded.

Actually, Ricketts' schedule was sufficiently lax to enable him to continue his studies of marine invertebrates at the lab (which in the meantime had fallen on bad times and was being subsidized by Steinbeck). At the same time, he continued to work on articles about the mandated islands and labored sporadically on two philosophical essays, "The Philosophy of Breaking Through," and "A

Spiritual Morphology of Poetry," both of which are crucial to an understanding of his world-view. Military duty did put a stop to extensive collecting trips, however, and while his notebooks mention a ten-day trip to Enseñada in April 1942, a lamprey collecting expedition in California's Eel River a month later, and a two month's sojourn to Puget Sound that summer, there is no mention of any further trips until his discharge in 1945. But even before the end of the war, Ricketts was planning what he projected would be his greatest venture to date: a comprehensive study of the marine invertebrates of the northernmost coast of North America to be called "The Outer Shores."[40]

Meanwhile, Steinbeck returned from the European War Zone and wrote *Cannery Row*. The book made Ricketts a public figure, and while, as George MacGinitie insists, he never considered himself a celebrity (GEM/RA, 9/3/70), he was forced to contend with the curious sightseers who would peer through the windows of the lab, and with groups of well-intentioned graduate students from nearby Hopkins Marine Station who came in search of the kind of parties that Steinbeck immortalized in his novel.

Ostensibly, Ricketts took this attention and activity in stride. Ellwood Graham recalls a day when he and Ricketts were drinking beer at the lab, and a snoopy tourist whom Ricketts had hesitantly admitted inquired about a large tissue-like cloth which decorated one of the walls. Grinning, Ricketts announced, "that, madam, is the foreskin of a whale," and the embarrassed guest picked up her belongings and hurriedly left (EG/RA, 10/8/70).

There is evidence, however, that Ricketts was afflicted by his life as a public figure, and in a notebook entry titled "Program 3-16-46," he advises himself to "be affable but not voluble, perfectly civil and friendly, let there be whatever warmth there is but make no specific attempt to convey it," and not to take "more than one or two drinks in an afternoon or during an evening." He also decided to limit himself to "intercourse not oftener than twice a week" and hoped his income might enable him to undergo psychoanalysis the following year.[41]

Despite some developing personal conflicts, Ricketts' enthusiasm for his work grew markedly during the years following the war. He made two major collecting expeditions to the west coast of Vancouver Island and to the Queen Charlottes during the summers of 1945 and 1946, detailed records of which appear in journals kept during the trips. Ricketts viewed the Vancouver Island–Queen Charlottes venture as another collaboration with Steinbeck which would result in the final portion of a trilogy (the first parts were *Sea of Cortez* and *Between Pacific Tides*); his plan was that they would travel together to the Queen Charlottes during the summer of 1948, and that Steinbeck, with the help of Ricketts' field notes from the earlier trips, would write a narrative similar to the *Log* portion of *Sea of Cortez*.

Ricketts worked diligently on his research of the fauna of Vancouver Island and the Queen Charlottes. In 1947, he applied (unsuccessfully) for a Guggenheim Grant "to make available to laymen, students and scientific workers, detailed ecological and biological information on the great faunal provinces of the Pacific Coast of the Bering Sea." And during the planning stages of the 1948 trip, he wrote to Antonia Seixas that "I feel better every week about the next book, 'The Outer Shores.' That survey work, and the total into which it fits, goes very well" (EFR-AS, 2/4/48).

Moreover, Ricketts was convinced of Steinbeck's commitment to the project. The final entry to the 1946 field notes reads: "Well Jnny boy, this is it, this is 30. The trips of 1945 and 46 are over, it's yr bk now and god bless you."[42] And in April 1948, he told an old friend, Virginia Scardigli, that "Jn and I are going to do the next book together; he's going up N with us this summer. And he'll finance my share of it. To be paid back from royalties" (EFR-VS, 4/9/48).

Appearances seem to indicate that Steinbeck at least considered making the 1948 trip with Ricketts. He says as much in "About Ed Ricketts" and in a letter dated April 14, 1948, to Ritch and Tal Lovejoy. And during that same month, he wrote Ricketts that though their trip would interrupt work on his new novel (*East of Eden*), it would be a good thing since it would give him time to think more about what he wanted to do in that book.

There is, however, some evidence which suggests that Steinbeck was not as excited about "The Outer Shores" as Ricketts assumed. Clearly, it was Ricketts who provided all of the impetus for the project. More and more, Steinbeck had grown to dislike joint writing efforts of any sort, and in 1951 he told Covici that "there are no good collaborations,"[43] since a good writer "always works at the impossible . . . in utter loneliness a writer tries to explain the inexplicable."[44] This is not to suggest that Steinbeck looked back with disfavor on his other work with Ricketts. Indeed, Elaine Steinbeck, the novelist's widow, has noted that he always loved to think of himself as an amateur marine biologist, and that until he began work on *East of Eden*, he talked more about the *Log* than any other book he had written (ES/RA, 3/24/71). At the same time, there is some doubt whether Steinbeck was really interested in the Queen Charlottes expedition or in doing anything with Ricketts' field notes from his earlier trips. Edward F. Ricketts, Jr., who accompanied his father on the 1945 and 1946 trips, at the time questioned Steinbeck's interest in the project (EFR, JR/RA, 10/7/70).

It is, of course, impossible to define precisely Steinbeck's feelings toward the 1948 trip. It seems, though, that he would have gone, if only because of Ricketts' zeal for the project. In any event, Steinbeck never had to make a decision about "The Outer Shores," for on May 7, 1948, Ricketts drove his old Packard into the Del Monte Express. He was rushed to a hospital where a splenectomy was performed, but internal damages were too extensive, and on May 11, 1948, Ed Ricketts was dead.

Steinbeck, hearing about the accident at his home in New York, was crushed. Nathaniel Benchley, the novelist and Steinbeck's close friend, remembers "the night John left for California; we went to the Colony for dinner (I believe) and John got drunk and weepy and said that the greatest man in the world was dying and there was nothing [that] could be done about it" (NB-RA, 3/19/71). And acquaintances in Monterey recall that when Steinbeck arrived for the funeral he acted as if the flesh had been torn from his body.

An Overview

The circumstances surrounding Ricketts' unusual accident are slightly mysterious. The people who were at Ricketts' laboratory that day believed that the marine biologist was simply preoccupied when he left in his old car. Others have suggested, however, that he had been depressed over the disintegration of an affair with a woman, and that he may have committed suicide—a possibility which, according to Rolf Bolin, Steinbeck firmly dismissed (RLB/RA, 10/8/70).

Whatever the case, Ricketts' journals for 1945–1948 reveal that while he may have suffered from reverses with women and from attacks of what he called "nostalgia," his life had not lost its perfume. Dr. Lawrence Blinks of the Hopkins Marine Station recalls that Ricketts' enthusiasm for his work continued unabated until his death (RLB/RA, 10/8/70). In September 1946, Ricketts wrote Steinbeck, telling him that he was "interested now more than ever in comparing the action of human society as is—and how it got there—with the presence of societies in the tidepools" (EFR-JS, 9/15/46), and the conclusion of his Guggenheim proposal records his belief that "The Outer Shores" may shed light "on the social problems of Homo sapiens by a consideration of the social adaptations achieved on a number of humbler group levels." Ed Ricketts, Jr., observes that at the time of his death Ricketts was in the process of working out an arrangement with Stanford University for a new and better equipped laboratory (EFR, JR/RA, 10/7/70), and a discussion in his notebooks for 1947–1948 of a new interest in desert fauna suggests that his scientific horizons were expanding rather than diminishing.

These same notebooks also contain evidence of Ricketts' quest to explore new metaphysical vistas. References to completing the essays on "Poetry" and "Breaking Through," to translating the poetry of the mandated islands, and to working on a series of music graphs clearly indicate Ricketts' continuing interest in his work. Moreover, as Alan Baldridge, chief librarian of the Hopkins Marine Station, points out, the years between 1945 and 1948 saw Ricketts increasingly involved in the problem of the depletion of the sardine industry on the Monterey Peninsula (AB/RA,

23

10/8/70). Sardine notebooks kept during these years indicate that Ricketts was working on a large project tentatively titled "The California Sardine: An Ecological Picture" in which he saw "the desirability of putting together the whole picture, with no axe to grind" (EFR-RL, 10/22/46). In 1946, he planned another article on the sardine for *National Geographic*, and the March 7, 1947, edition of the Monterey *Peninsula Herald* carried a long piece by Ricketts entitled "Science Studies the Sardine," in which the biologist carefully analyzed what conservation methods might be implemented to save the sardine industry.

Similarly, in the field notes for "The Outer Shores" Ricketts extolls the beauty of Vancouver Island and the unpopulated collecting locales in the Queen Charlottes, and condemns those who wish to contaminate them with industry. These notes also discuss the ecological framework of the proposed book on the Queen Charlottes, and Ricketts' scientific horizon expands as he moves beyond the mere cataloguing of the beasts of a given region, and beyond even Shelford and Allee's (aggregations of species) and MacGinitie's (natural history) definitions of the ecological method, to formulate a new and even more holistic definition of ecology based on the application of vector analysis, in which the "relationship" is "the fundamental unit of ecology."[45] A true scientist who respected Eddington's dictum that "in each revolution of scientific thought new words are set to the old music,"[46] Ricketts never discredited but rather built upon the ideas of his predecessors. In ecology, as in all things, Ricketts stressed "the value of building, of trying to build whole pictures,"[47] and there is nothing in the writings of his final years to suggest that his interest and enthusiasm had in any way diminished.

Edward F. Ricketts was a highly complicated individual. Throughout his life, a devoted and highly rational biologist who sought to uncover scientific truths, he had at the same time a variety of eccentricities. He was afraid of rats, and his analysis of the thyroid-neurosis syndrome in the essay on non-teleological thinking was personal. But as Joel Hedgpeth notes so succinctly, he was a man "full of love with such an extraordinary and gentle humor, and such a gift for friendship" (JWH/RA, 7/15/70).

And yet, while a good friend and a sociable companion, the unique nature of his thinking (probably his most complex attribute) stimultaneously set him apart from even his closest friends; so much so, in fact, that even Steinbeck, who stated that "knowing Ed Ricketts was instant" and insisted that for eighteen years "I knew him better than I knew anyone," was forced to concede that "perhaps I did not know him at all."[48]

It remains to discuss in detail Ricketts' world-view and to see how it and the marine biologist's person turn up in Steinbeck's fiction; to see just how Steinbeck understood Ed Ricketts and how he agreed with or rejected the ideas of this unique human being who was the novelist's closest friend during the two decades of his greatest work.

A Morphology
of Breaking Through

*E*d Ricketts' world-view resembles that portrayed by Steinbeck in many of his novels, short stories, and works of nonfiction. It should not be assumed, however, that the marine biologist served as a pipeline from which Steinbeck drew all of his ideas, though there have been suggestions that this was the case. Jack Calvin has observed that "Ed was a reservoir for John to draw on," and that "in Ed he found an endless source of material—or call it inspiration, if you like—and used it hungrily" (JC-RA, 7/14/69). Frank Lloyd, a long-time Carmel resident and a friend of Steinbeck and Ricketts, suggests that the novelist's "interest in all things biological was due in large part to Ed—upon which he romanticized freely" (FL-RA, 3/10/71). And Calvin and Lloyd believe that the fact that Steinbeck wrote little of consequence after Ricketts' death was a matter of cause and effect. "The fountain," says Calvin, "had been turned off" (JC-RA, 7/14/69). Finally, Joel Hedgpeth notes that "a lot of people who were there [in Monterey, Carmel, and Pacific Grove] at the beginning of the relationship still resent Steinbeck as an exploiter of Ed," and Hedgpeth suggests that Steinbeck and Ricketts were part of a larger group which was "a whole greater than the sum of

26

its parts and out of it made Steinbeck a great writer—for a while at least. And he was part of it anyhow. This would explain why Steinbeck had no clear ideas of his own. He was the instrument of the group" (JWH-RA, 7/24/70).

Viewed in perspective, however, whereas it is clear that Ricketts had a profound effect on Steinbeck, he was not the novelist's alter ego. As Herb Kline has noted so succinctly, "Ricketts' premises about the world do have validity, but they cannot be applied as a straightjacket by which to evaluate Steinbeck's accomplishments as a writer." Indeed, asserts Kline, "don't try to pigeonhole a John Steinbeck to fit an Ed Ricketts theory" (HK/RA, 2/27/71). In short, the intellectual side of the Steinbeck-Ricketts relationship is a highly complex matter, and it is necessary to identify those issues on which the two men disagreed as well as those occasions on which Steinbeck simply fictionalized the philosophical premises of his best friend. A few words of caution must be interposed before this investigation can begin. For one thing, it must be pointed out that Ed Ricketts' writing is often clumsy and oblique, and in the three philosophical essays which contain the germinal concepts of his scheme of being ("A Spiritual Morphology of Poetry," "The Philosophy of Breaking Through," and "Non-Teleological Thinking"), the style is very awkward and in places the syntax breaks down. As a matter of fact, Ricketts occasionally acknowledged the defects in his style. When, for example, he sent drafts of two of his essays to Antonia Seixas in 1940, he insisted that while "lots of work went into them," there is "some inaneness still, and a little poor writing is still left" (EFR-AS, 10/21/40).

Beyond the syntactical problems and the bad writing, the Ricketts essays (as well as his Sea of Cortez log and his Vancouver Island–Queen Charlottes journals) reflect the author's confusion about the precise meaning of philosophical terms. Ricketts developed his own private usages for such words as *holistic, emergent, participating,* and *non-teleological,* and "the whole Cannery Row affair would have benefitted from a member who was either a philosopher or a student for holy orders to argue for precision of language" (JWH-RA, 8/13/70).

27

JOHN STEINBECK and EDWARD F. RICKETTS

Ricketts' semantic confusion is largely responsible for the paradoxes and incongruities in his world-view. And yet the central theses of Ricketts' scheme of being, however paradoxical, seem quite reasonable. Affirming that the philosopher cannot hope to explain the many contradictions in the world unless he is inextricably involved in them, Ricketts is not a dogmatist proffering final explanations of everything within the creation. Rather, his is a philosophy of understanding and acceptance in which he seeks to unify experience, to relate the unrelatable so that even nonsense wears a crown of meaning.

Ricketts' unique philosophical perspective reflects his basic world-view, which is ecological and holistic, and in which, through the study of relationships, he sought to grasp and understand the totality of things. Engaged in what could be called "an appreciative response to reality," Ricketts' search for order was a religious quest in the spirit of Havelock Ellis' definition of the religious spirit as "the art of finding our emotional relationship to the world conceived as a whole." In its emotional approach to reality, Ricketts' world-view breathes the spirit of the *Phaedrus* and Aristotle's *Ethics* and finds an understanding response in Goethe, Wordsworth, and Whitman.

As a scientist in the tradition of W. C. Allee, Ricketts worked toward what, in his Sea of Cortez log, he called "a unified field hypothesis" in which "everything is an index of everything else."[1] Appropriately, he defines ecology as "the study of relationships, of living relationships" and he concludes:

I got to thinking about the ecological method, the value of building, of trying to build, whole pictures. No one can controvert it. An ecologist has to consider the parts each in its place and as related to rather than as subsidiary to the whole.[2]

Often, however, Ricketts' relational view of the world becomes panpsychic in the tradition of Novalis and Hermann Hesse and leaves Allee far behind. In such cases, he reaches for an extraphysical interpretation of the cosmos and states his cardinal principle of unity in terms more mystical than scientific. He renounces the need for precise explanations of all the mysteries in the crea-

28

tion; rather, he merely accepts and reveres them as mysteries which form an integral part of an all-embracing scheme of being in which everything is inherently related to everything else. Convinced that all knowledge is relational and that to understand nature means to discern the relationship of its constituent parts, Ricketts combines science and mysticism to show that the totality of life is more wonderful than even most biologists have realized.

In "About Ed Ricketts," Steinbeck states that Ricketts' "thinking was as paradoxical as his life. He thought in mystical terms and hated and distrusted mysticism" (xi). Actually, Steinbeck either avoids or misunderstands the philosophical implications of Ricketts' scientific-mystical mode of perceiving reality. For as Bertrand Russell has pointed out in *Mysticism and Religion*, mysticism may be a creed or simply an attitude toward life. And Ricketts' mysticism, firmly grounded on a naturalistic, scientific base, is of the latter type and suggests an approach toward a perception of reality which does not ignore but rather builds upon the analytic and discursive methods.

As a scientist striving to fathom the controlling laws of nature, Ricketts found it necessary to escape from what Eddington calls "the cut-and-dried framework into which the mind is so ready to force everything that it experiences."[3] "The whole picture should be stressed," says Ricketts, "because too often (in zoology as in other fields) what are thought of as disciplines operate chiefly as biases—prescribed ways of thinking and of doing, into which the professional may retreat when shocked or challenged by some anomaly."[4]

Ricketts was horrified at the growing tendency toward scientific specialization; he believed that so-called experts who carefully localize their interests so that they can boast that they know *one* thing well really have no organon at all. They are, according to Ricketts, vegetables planted too long in one soil which secrete toxins and inhibit their own prosperity. And Ricketts believed that any kind of intensive specialization, vegetable or intellectual, is self-defeating in that it destroys the dynamic unity in nature.

Ricketts explains his holistic world-view throughout his writings.

In "The Outer Shores," he speaks as a scientist in the tradition of Lyman Abbott's *The Theory of an Evolutionist* by incorporating the fact of evolution as a base on which to build a holistic super-structure. Nothing that "the only clear-cutness you can get in an evolutionary picture is if you can get your knife of time to cut across the tree after the forks have been thoroly established," Ricketts points out that because any given cross section may appear muddled to "we who are in it," the observer will "either go crazy, or glimpse the underlying structure." "We must either understand nothing," insists Ricketts, "or thru the muddle come to grips with one of the most ultimate and fundamental ideas: that of essential unity."[5]

Similarly, in the zoological preface to the San Francisco Bay Area handbook, Ricketts discusses the intricate relationship between marine invertebrates and their environment, and he concludes that "this whole idea of inter-relation seems actually to be pretty much the key-note of modern holistic concepts, wherein the whole consists of the animal or the community *in* its environment, the notion of relation being significant."[6]

It is, however, in the published narrative of the Gulf of California expedition that the most articulate statements of Ricketts' holistic world-view appear. And because Steinbeck shaped this theme so eloquently in the *Log* (there are at least a half dozen statements about the holistic approach to life in the published narrative for every one in Ricketts' journal) and because it appears in so many of his works of fiction, one may assume that Steinbeck shared the marine biologist's passion for "whole pictures."

In *The Log from the Sea of Cortez*, Steinbeck and Ricketts note that in viewing marine life in the Gulf they sought to "bring order to a subject previously unordered," and through their search they emerge as holistic semi-scientists (as distinct from scientific specialists driven into particularization), quasi-Darwinian naturalists attempting to impose order on chaos by seeking the meaning of the whole from an inspection of the parts.

We must have time to think and to look and to consider. And the modern process—that of looking quickly at the whole field and then diving down to a particular—was reversed by Darwin. Out of long long consideration of the parts he emerged with a sense of the whole.[7]

Ricketts and Steinbeck took as much time as they could "to think and to look and to consider." Slowly, they realized that the chaos confronting current scientific thinking was the result of science's attempt to separate men and animals from the whole, to isolate the instincts and faculties of living beings from their environment.[8] Instead, they argued,

all life is relational to the point where an Einsteinian relativity seems to emerge. And then not only the meaning but the feeling about species grows misty. One merges into another, groups melt into ecological groups until the time when what we know as life meets and enters what we think of as non-life: barnacle and rock, rock and earth, earth and tree, tree and rain and air. And the units nestle into the whole and are inseparable from it. (216)

The *Log* also contains Ricketts' and Steinbeck's belief about universal plenitude—the idea, originally developed by Ricketts in his analysis of groups of ubiquitous marine invertebrates in *Between Pacific Tides*, that everything which might possibly exist in the cosmos does indeed exist. "It seemed to us that life in every form is incipiently everywhere waiting for a chance to take root and start reproducing; eggs, spores, seeds, bacilli—everywhere. Let a raindrop fall and it is crowded with the waiting life" (1964). And in the introduction to the Annotated Phyletic Catalogue, the authors state that because of the increasing scope and energy of many marine biologists, "more and more ranges will be extended in both directions, so that the *qualitative* zoogeographical records of the future will read, almost literally: 'everything—everywhere.' "[9]

Ricketts' and Steinbeck's belief that everything is everywhere in a full and ordered scheme of being leads them to the borderline of the metaphysical as they celebrate their holistic world-view in tones more religious than scientific.

And it is a strange thing that most of the feeling we call religious, most of the mystical outcrying which is one of the most prized and used and desired reactions of our species, is really the understanding and the attempt to say that man is related to the whole thing, related inextricably to all reality, known and unknowable. (216–217)

31

This unity represents the quintessence of understanding and is what the novelist and the marine biologist gleaned from their experiences in the tide pools of the Sea of Cortez. Slowly, almost imperceptibly, they learned the truth of William Emerson Ritter's dictum that there is "no way of conceiving of a true universe, a state of things that is unified through and through, if the human spirit is not inseparably and essentially identified with it all."[10]

Actually, the most emotionally charged passages in the *Log* and those which obviously gave Steinbeck a good deal of pleasure in shaping are those in which he and Ricketts ponder individual scenes of great natural beauty and then extend their horizons to marvel over a full and ordered scheme of being. Believing that the universe is an evolving rhythmic unity, Steinbeck and Ricketts share "a feeling of fullness, of warm wholeness, wherein every sight an object and odor and experience seems to key into a gigantic whole" (121). Much of this enthusiasm for the fullness of nature is Ricketts' and is related philosophically to his holistic world-view. In the spirit (and words) of the German mystic, Jacob Boehme, Ricketts believes that "the whole outward visible world, with all its being is a signature, or figure of the internal spiritual world; whatever is internally, and however its operation is, so likewise it has its character externally."[11] Accordingly, in "A Spiritual Morphology of Poetry," Ricketts insists that the type of poetry which leads the reader into a state of "deep participation" and enables him to tie together internal and external reality, "must involve the 'signature of all things' . . . the beauty of all things as vehicles for breaking through."[12]

The pages of "The Outer Shores" are filled with Ricketts' descriptions of the beauty of even the most forbidding aspects of life on Vancouver Island and in the Queen Charlottes. Commenting on the rugged but "fantastic" west coast of Vancouver Island, Ricketts notes that while aboard ship he loved to "go out in the rain and wind and see that fantastic coastline go by. I get a curious feeling that's a combination of fear of the sea and of seasickness, and cold, and liking of the sea and its animals and loving that lovely difficult west coast; it's very exhilerating; you have to be alone.[13]

Elsewhere, Ricketts describes with great feeling the locale around Clayoquot, British Columbia, an area as tranquil as the coastline is harsh and austere: "But withal it's certainly a lovely place of green gold hummingbirds, I never saw so many in my life before, and thrushes always singing, and rhododendrons in bloom until you can't see over them, and white sea gulls flying by the black mountains."[14]

In his Sea of Cortez journal, Ricketts is entranced by the natural beauty of Puerto Escondido where he and Steinbeck were taken by Srs. Madinabeitia, Pérpuly, and Valdivia on a pack trip into the mountains of the Baja.

We 6 rode until too steep, then led horses to flat, maybe 1500' up, near 300–400' drop waterfall. (Little water, but good pools). And such an oasis around it; known probably and loved for hundreds of years. Fresh and cool, green; the shadow of a rock in a weary land. Or rather in a fantastic land since the plains and hills over which we came were rich with xerophytic plants, cacti, mimosa, brush and small trees with thorns.[15]

This celebration of nature is reflected throughout the published *Log* and suggests that Steinbeck was also moved by the beauty of natural life in the Gulf. Commenting that "the abundance of life here gives one an exuberance, a feeling of fullness and richness," the authors celebrate even the vicious process of natural selection, "this ferocious survival quotient [which] excites us and makes us feel good" (58). Entranced by "the incredible beauty of the tide pools, the brilliant colors, [and] swarming species" (59), Ricketts and Steinbeck slip into a new frame of reference and develop their "unified field hypothesis" in which all the many aspects of natural life in the Gulf, the beautiful and the ugly, the magnificent and the grotesque, are vehicles by which the authors arrive at their holistic world-view in which "everything is an index of everything else."

It is, of course, one thing to propose a holistic world-view in which "the signature of all things" is an index of the relatedness of everything in an ordered cosmos. It is something else to prove that

Edward F. Ricketts, about 1936

this unity exists or even to suggest an approach by which man can achieve an understanding of the whole. There are those who insist that Steinbeck "is never able rationally to prove that the unity about which he speaks exists at all."[16] Other critics have attempted to rescue Steinbeck by suggesting that the doctrine of non-teleological thinking is a coherent method by which man can perceive the whole. But considering that the essay on non-teleological thinking was written by Ricketts, one cannot help but conclude that it really does not provide simple solutions to serious questions about Steinbeck's idea of cosmic unity.

Put simply, Steinbeck and Ricketts did not agree completely on the means by which this unity might be perceived. It thus seems necessary to take up the ideas of each on the subject independently. The current discussion is concerned chiefly with Ricketts' world-view; Steinbeck's approach to the cosmic whole will be taken up in the following chapter.

In his philosophical essays as well as in his scientific writings, Ricketts consciously worked toward a definition of a method by which man might recognize and understand the relatedness of all living things. And it is Steinbeck who provides the best key to a definition of Ricketts' method when he observes (in "About Ed Ricketts") that the marine biologist was "walled off a little, so that he worked at his philosophy of 'breaking through,' of coming out through the back of the mirror into some kind of reality which would make the day world dreamlike. This thought obsessed him" (liii). The crucial words here are *breaking through,* which Steinbeck defines as the means by which Ricketts pursued his passion for "going home." Actually, what Ricketts meant by *going home* was his quest to follow the dictum of the German Romantic, Novalis, whose metaphysic Ricketts (apparently using Thomas Carlyle's translation) interpreted as "homesickness, the wish to be everywhere at home."[17]

The method by which Ricketts sought to go home, to achieve what he called "the deep thing," was his highly complex philosophy of breaking through. Taking the title from Robinson Jeffers' "Roan Stallion" ("Humanity is the mould to break away from, the crust to break through, the coal to break into fire"), Ricketts defines breaking through as an inner coherency of feeling and thought which leads man into a "deep participation" and enables him to tie together apparently unrelated pictures and see that "the whole is more than the sum of its parts"; to achieve that integrative moment of living in which one understands things "which are not transient by means of things which are."[18]

In "The Philosophy of Breaking Through," Ricketts follows Whitman's exhortation in "Out of the Cradle, Endlessly Rocking" ("Taking all hints to use them, but swiftly leaping beyond them") by discussing four incidents which served him as vehicles for "breaking through." The first dates to his childhood in Chicago and concerns a time when he befriended some neighbors whose tavern had burned down. Convinced all along that he was a snooty and remote person ("in the slums, but to our notion not of them"), Ricketts recalls his sudden change of heart toward people he formerly felt were beneath him.

For the first time, and in the glow of that supposedly destructive fire, we children had become more than ourselves. For those few minutes we were really living, deeply and widely, we were "beyond things"; things had a new meaning, more significance, so that the former values must have seemed dwarfed and strange if we had stopped to think of them.[19]

Ricketts also recalls a woman who, seeing her injured husband lying on the ground before her with a skull fracture, fought off hysteria by intoning the words, "dear boy." "Suddenly," says Ricketts, "I found myself living the whole picture," and noting parallel scenes in Steinbeck's *The Pastures of Heaven* and Hemingway's *To Have and Have Not*, he points out that the words *dear boy* were obviously "the outward and visible signs of an inward and spiritual grace—vehicles on which something beyond was integrally riding."[20]

Ricketts then passes on to a discussion of the essential goodness of his first marriage, despite "all that hectic time of trouble and doubt," and finally to a discussion of the changed behavior of a miner's wife who for years had been repelled by her husband's untidiness, but who suddenly "broke through into illumination" after he had been rescued from a serious mine disaster.

She was actually less blind than at any time in her life, only now she saw things in their relation to a far larger picture, a more deeply significant whole. She genuinely liked him she realized now, neither in spite of nor because of it; it was sufficient simply to face the fact that that trait was him whom she loved.[21]

"It's all part of one pattern," says Ricketts. "The burned saloon, the broken head, the departing wife, and the entombed miner"; it is in moments like these that man can break through the "tragedy that breaks man's face and a white fire flies out of it . . . These break, these pierce, these deify." This motif, stated so explicitly "and with that exact economy of words which we associate with scientific statement" by Jeffers in "Roan Stallion," leads the marine biologist "to call this thing 'breaking through,' and to regard the cognitive considerations of it as 'the philosophy of breaking through.'"[22]

The ability to break through, notes Ricketts, comes only through intense struggle, and "few glimpse the 'white fire' through and beyond the tragedy with which they are chiefly engrossed."[23] But, Ricketts hastens to add, although great struggle is one of the "commonest concomitants to a great emergent," the act of struggle alone is no certain index of breaking through. For not only must the search be filled with integrity, but the actual breaking through must come in its own time. Quoting Maeterlinck's advice in *Wisdom and Destiny*, "Let us wait till the hour of sacrifice sounds; till then, each man to his work," Ricketts suggests that although man is forced to live in constant insecurity and cannot place a valid a priori evaluation on anything, "insecurity may well be only a symbol of the eternal struggle" by which he may ultimately break through.

Ricketts believed that most men are plagued with clay feet, so that few can achieve the "inner coherencies of both feeling and thought" and communicate their understanding of "the deep thing" which is "nameless, outside of time" and "near immortality." Indeed, Ricketts often believed that he too had clay feet, and he was frustrated by his own inability to communicate "the deep thing."

Re my concern over the deep thing in sex or love or friendship or thinking or aesthetics not being communicated: It gives me a feeling of waste, of futility when I have this spark and cannot communicate it. And then I get frustrated and negativistic. Now I suppose I have to work that out so that I myself am not constricted or diminished by not being able to "get across."[24]

Ricketts tried long and hard to work it out; he struggled to find a means by which he could communicate "the deep thing." The method he selected is what he inappropriately called non-teleological or *is* thinking, the precepts of which are defined in the essay

37

of the same name which appears almost verbatim in *The Log from the Sea of Cortez.*

Generally speaking, Ricketts viewed non-teleological thinking as an avenue by which man can approach an understanding of the whole.

The whole picture is portrayed by *is,* the deepest word of deep ultimate reality, not shallow or partial as reasons are, but deeper and participating, possibly encompassing the Oriental concept of "being."[25]

Nevertheless, while Ricketts proposes a means to a perception of the whole through his doctrine of *is* thinking, his explication of this concept suffers from a rather awkward use of philosophical terminology, a fact which Ricketts himself admitted.[26] In philosophy, teleology is an argument which proceeds on the principle of causal or ethical finality and which reasons from the rational order of the world to the necessity that it be grounded in some form of purposive intelligence. In other words, a teleology supposes that things exist for some purpose. But Ricketts disregards this wider meaning and defines teleological thought as the preoccupation with "changes and cures" by men, who, "in their intolerant refusal to face things," often substitute "a fierce and sometimes hopeless attempt to change conditions which are assumed to be undesirable in place of the understanding-acceptance which would pave the way for a more sensible attempt at change if that still seemed desirable."[27] By insisting that teleological thinking is associated only with the evaluation of causes and effects and their relative purposefulness—with an end pattern of what "could be" or "should be," Ricketts unfortunately isolates part of the concept of teleological thinking from its total philosophical and etymological context.

Despite the ambiguity created by Ricketts' terminology, what he really seems to be talking about in his discussion of non-teleological thinking is an open approach to life by the man who looks at events and accepts them as such without reservation or qualification, and in so doing perceives the whole picture by becoming an identifiable part of that picture.

Strictly, the term non-teleological "thinking" ought not to be applied to what I have in mind, because it involves more than thinking, the term is inadequate. *Modus operandi* might be better—a method of handling data of any sort . . . The method extends beyond thinking, even to living itself; in fact by inferred definition it transcends the realm of thinking possibilities, it postulates "living into."[28]

Ricketts insists that the non-teleological method of thinking, in addition to being more ultimate than the teleological method, is capable of "great tenderness, of an all-embracingness" which comes with the love and understanding of instant-acceptance: "*what* they are is unimportant alongside the fact that they *are*. In other words, the 'badness' or 'goodness,' the teleology of the fears [is] decidedly secondary."[29] Moreover, says Ricketts, this "non-causal or non-blaming viewpoint seems to me to represent very often the 'new thing,' the Hegelian 'christ-child' which arises emergently from the union of two opposing viewpoints, such which comprises infinity in factors and symbols might be called mystic."[30]

In short, Ricketts reconciles opposites by extending his concept of unity to include all phenomena, whether understandable through sensory knowledge or through mystical or intuitive insight. He thinks of the world in scientific and mystical terms as a cosmic whole in which everything is inherently related to everything else. And through his doctrine of non-teleological thinking, he combines scientific observation with intuitive insight to realize his conception of "the deep thing."[31]

Ricketts' reliance on intuition is a reflection of his highly intuitive nature. In an unpublished abstract of Jung's essay "Psychological Types" (in *Contributions to Analytical Psychology* [1938]), in which he interprets Jung's definition of intuition as "a perception by way of the unconscious" which is "possibly the most proximate way to transcendent function," and Jung's definition of thinking as "the function of intellectual cognition," Ricketts calls himself an intuitive-thinker and notes that such people have "atypical emergent functions" in that they are "concerned with the inner world of spiritual (to them) realities."[32]

As a biologist, Ricketts is of course intrigued by existing parallels between animal and human societies; he maintains that "who would see a replica of man's social structure has only to examine the abundant and various life of the tide pools" since the two contrasting principles of tide pool life (Allee's concept of animal aggregations and Cabrera's law of ecological incompatibility) operate in human societies as well. But he never loses sight of what he defines as man's distinct cosmic consciousness by which the individual can, if he will, engage in the grand and lonely quest to break through his own projections to transcendent participation.

Seeking a discipline where he feels a few men have achieved an "emergent-consciousness," Ricketts turns to poetry and traces the four successive growth stages of what he calls "the spiritual morphology of poetry." On the lowest plane, Ricketts places the "naive poets," whose poetry "involves a simple and fresh statement of the joy of existence, in the love of landscape, God, home, wife, country, friend . . ."[33] Ricketts insists that most Western poetry falls into this category, "all the pastorals, prayers, hymns, love songs, songs of patriotism, drinking songs, most of the ballads and simple tales."[34] "Naive poets," notes Ricketts, "have axiomatic definitions of right and wrong," their main function is to extol; they aren't even aware of the clay feet which bind most men.

The second stage of poets, whom Ricketts calls "sophisticated," are united "in recognizing and bewailing the ubiquitous clay feet" and "are much confused by the problem of right and wrong." But while Ricketts insists that these poets, unlike the naive poets, may be conscious in an individual sense, they have nothing to offer beyond such romantic substitutions as "Arnold's classicism," "Yeats' fairy realm," and "Swinburne's mythology"—which are "fundamentally evasive."[35]

On the third plane are "a comparatively few mellow poets" who "are also banished from the garden," but who, unlike the sophisticated poets, "catch glimpses of a new promised land, a heaven far greater than the Eden which is all its inhabitants can know."[36] Including in this category such poems as Whitman's "Out of the Cradle, Endlessly Rocking," Jeffers' "Night" and "Roan Stallion," and the Sanskrit "Black Marigolds," Ricketts observes that these poets reflect a heightened consciousness which arises "particularly through the very clay feet of bitter grief, war and death which the sophisticated poets excoriated or morbidly embraced," and which enables them to move non-teleologically toward " 'The Tower beyond Tragedy,' beyond right and wrong to an acceptance of what is.' "[37]

In the highest category, Ricketts places "the all-vehicle mellow poet," who is in and speaks out of "the heaven glimpsed by his predecessors." Noting that no poet has ever emerged fully from "that distant land," except for mystics "who are rarely formal poets," Ricketts insists that when such a poet appears, "everything will be related and known, it will be recognized that 'that's the way things really are.' In that journey the writer will have led the reader also deeply home."[38] These poets will recognize "the beauty of all things as vehicles for breaking through: In that 'all-consciousness,' there is no right and wrong, all things are 'right' including both right and wrong; and there are no clay feet although the poet will know deeply about the things we called clay feet." Unlike the third group who "move to the tower beyond tragedy," for the all-vehicle mellow poet there is no tragedy at all. Quoting Blake's statement in the "Vision of the Daughters of Albion ("All that lives is holy," which is one of the most important lines in Steinbeck's *The Grapes of Wrath*), Ricketts insists that these poets can achieve a "creative synthesis," "an emergent viewpoint" as they live into the whole and know that " 'it's right, it's alright,' the 'good,' the 'bad,' whatever *is*."[39]

Ricketts' doctrine of breaking through, his effusive statement of the means by which man can penetrate beyond the ubiquitous clay feet to an apprehension of "the deep thing," is the philosophical cornerstone of his world-view. And yet it is difficult to understand fully what Ricketts actually meant by such phrases as "holistic tenderness" and an "emergent thought and feeling." Joseph Campbell, who accompanied Ricketts and Jack Calvin on a collecting expedition to southeast Alaska in 1932, pointed out after reading the essays on poetry and breaking through that Ricketts should define and discuss these and other terms more adequately so that the reader "will not be left to work the meaning for himself."[40]

41

Indeed, it is questionable whether Steinbeck ever really understood the entire structure of Ricketts' doctrine of breaking through. And yet Ricketts firmly believed that the novelist, in his best work, had worked toward a statement of "the deep thing." In his journal for 1947, Ricketts wrote that "the real unified field hypothesis" is "the deep thing, that I pursued in non-teleological thinking, the lack of which . . . Jeffers regrets, the breaking thru into which that Jeffers & Miller & occasionally Jn [John] extol."[41]

Jeffers, Miller, and Steinbeck—a select cast indeed. Certainly Ricketts' quest to break through to "the deep thing" which he approaches through non-teleological or *is* thinking can be shared only by the mellow minority; apart from a few mystics, nearly all men do have clay feet which bind them to the day-to-day struggle for survival.

Progress and the Organismal Conception

*I*n his non-teleological quest for the deep thing, for what he called "an indescribable and unnamable quality of life" which is "the most desirable thing in the world,"[1] Ricketts ignored the more mundane problems of existence which enslave most men and limit their vision. Supported by the principle that man's highest function is to uncover his emotional relationship with the world as a whole, Ricketts' world-view tends toward a quiescence which is given to overlooking moral imperatives.

For Steinbeck, however, Ricketts' monistic approach to life, while interesting and containing a substantial measure of truth, ignored man's common human needs and so was socially flawed. Throughout his career as a writer, Steinbeck maintained a deep concern for man's blunders as a social animal. He nearly always retained the broad view, the sensitive insight of the acute, sympathetic observer, and he developed in his writing a series of remedies for the evils he saw in the world and thereby added fresh truths in the endeavor.

Both men were grounded in the traditions of scientific naturalism and drew their responses from the natural environment. But whereas Ricketts was neither an unhinged Werther nor a rebelli-

43

ous Prometheus, but a man who viewed the everyday world with "understanding-acceptance" as a vehicle to break through to the deep thing, Steinbeck's Promethean impulse and his conviction that man is a creature of earth, not a heaven-bound pilgrim, led him to attack passivity and develop corrective means to deal effectively with the burdensome problems of human existence.

Before one can talk with any real clarity about this crucial difference in thinking between Steinbeck and Ricketts, it is necessary to examine Steinbeck's world-view and determine how it differs from Ricketts'. Certainly, as the evidence from Steinbeck's "shaped" version of Ricketts' Sea of Cortez notes indicates, both men were holistic, inductive thinkers. Moreover, there seems little doubt that Steinbeck drew heavily from the marine biologist's view of the cosmos as an integrated whole. But though the novelist was developing his beliefs along lines paralleling Ricketts', the ideas of the two men were by no means identical.

It has often been assumed, for example, that Steinbeck's interest in science in general and marine biology in particular is attributable solely to Ricketts. Actually, Steinbeck's interest in the seashore dates to the summer of 1923 when, at the urging of his sister Mary, he enrolled for the summer course at the Hopkins Marine Station in Pacific Grove. Steinbeck took the class in general zoology from C. V. Taylor, a student of Charles Kofoid at Berkeley. As a member of the zoology faculty of the University of California, Kofoid undoubtedly had come under the influence of the ideas of William Emerson Ritter, whose doctrine of the organismal conception of life formed the zeitgeist of the department at that time. And so Ritter's ideas were transmitted via Kofoid and Taylor to the impressionable Steinbeck, who years later told Hopkins professor Rolf Bolin that what he remembered most from his summer at the marine station was Ritter's concept of superorganism (RLB/RA, 10/8/70).

Ritter's doctrine of the organismal conception is based upon his belief that "in all parts of nature and in nature itself as one gigantic whole, wholes are so related to their parts that not only does the existence of the whole depend upon the orderly cooperation and interdependence of its parts, but the whole exercises a measure of determinative control over its parts."[2] This idea of wholeness involved Ritter's recognition that every unit of existence, from the lowest levels of cellular biology to the upper reaches of human psychology, "exists and is possible only through the existence of parts, or elements."[3] Each unit is a unique whole, the necessary parts of which "contribute their proper share to the structure and the functioning of the whole."[4]

Convinced that the only unit of life is the organism, Ritter examined evidence from the discipline of cellular biology and found that wholes (or organisms) arise not from the establishment of elementary units to form a new whole, but rather from a differentiation of protoplasm in which wholes are divided into newly formed parts. And surveying the fields of genetic, respiratory, and neural biology, Ritter concluded that individual chromosomes, respiratory tissues, and nerves result from differentiation aimed at a further definition of the organism. It is the duty of the true naturalist, claims Ritter, to take as his life's work the task of understanding the organismal basis of living nature. And since "one's ability to construct his own nature from portions of nature in general is a basic fact of his reality,"[5] man can grasp the essential principle of the organismal unity of life and, at the same time, know himself more fully. This, says Ritter, is "man's supreme glory"; not only "that he can know the world, but he can know himself as a knower of the world."[6]

That Steinbeck embraced Ritter's organismal conception of life is subtly apparent in several of his novels and short stories. It is most evident, however, in *The Log from the Sea of Cortez*, in passages which were written by Steinbeck, since they do not appear anywhere in Ricketts' journal. Observing that "there are colonies of pelagic tunicates which have a shape like the finger of a glove," Steinbeck remarks that "Each member of the colony is an individual animal, but the colony is another individual animal, not at all like the sum of its individuals" (165). Steinbeck notes that the strange union implied in the organismal conception of tunicate life might have been called a mystery by the early Church,

45

but he suggests that the thinking man will realize that the individual tunicate and the colony are "two animals and they aren't alike any more than the cells of my body are like me. I am much more than the sum of my cells and, for all I know, they are much more than the division of me" (165). "There is no quietism in such acceptance," insists Steinbeck, "but rather the basis for a far deeper understanding of us and our world" (165).[7]

Ritter's organismal conception, his idea that the whole is more than the sum of its parts and that these parts arise by a process of differentiation from the whole, is an entirely different idea from Allee's carefully controlled thesis that there exists in nature a tendency for organisms to cooperate for the purpose of ensuring their own survival. Allee's work at Woods Hole convinced him that "the social medium is the conditon necessary to the conservation and renewal of life."[8] At the same time, however, Allee found that the principle of cooperation which is present in biotic as well as in chemical relationships is not a conscious process. Indeed, when Allee turned from the lower animals to man, he concluded that the so-called altruistic drives in man "apparently are the development of these innate tendencies toward cooperation, which find their early physiological expression in many simpler animals."[9]

It is not difficult to see that Allee's doctrine of the automatic process by which animal aggregations form and function would appeal to the particular cast of Ricketts' thinking. From the sciences, Ricketts could extract portions of reality for purposes of controlled observation which enabled him to see "the toto-picture" in terms of certain relations. The fact of relation, not its conscious purpose, was that Ricketts gleaned from his study of Allee's work on animal aggregations; relations, Ricketts felt, permitted him to envisage the world with a fullness that far exceeds the circumscribed perspective of the discursive thinker. For Ricketts was a "naturalistic mystic," in Gerald Birney Smith's sense of the term— that individual who, through strenuous effort and unfailing devotion to the facts of science, finds his kinship with the cosmic whole documented by the truths of nature. He viewed reality in synthesis, and he used Allee's laboratory studies to verify his sense of the built-in relationships in the cosmic environment. Finally, Ricketts' insights into Allee's studies were properly non-teleological in that meaning remained ambiguous as far as practical use was concerned.

Organismic biology, on the other hand, is teleological and goal-directed and furnished Steinbeck scientific reinforcement for many of the observations he was coming to make about human life. Indeed, one of the basic premises of the organismal conception is that since given properties of parts are determined by or must be explained in terms of the whole, the whole possesses or is capable of directiveness. In short, "the whole acts as a causal unit . . . on its own parts."[10]

Statements about the directiveness of the organismic whole turn up in passages in the *Log* which do not appear in Ricketts' Gulf of California notebook. Commenting on the fullness of life in San Carlos Bay, Steinbeck observes that the fish in their millions followed a distinct pattern with respect to speed and direction. The novelist flatly rejects the idea that each fish is an isolated individual, and in language paralleling Ritter so closely that coincidence seems unlikely, he defines the organismal conception and the theory that wholes direct the actions of their constituent parts.

And this larger animal, the school, seems to have a nature and drive and ends of its own. It is more than and different from the sum of its units. If we can think in this way, it will not seem so unbelievable that every fish heads in the same direction, that the water interval between fish and fish is identical with all the units, and that it seems to be directed by a school intelligence. (240)

Ritter posits the belief that there is "no way of conceiving a true Universe, a state of things that is unified through and through, if the human spirit is not inseparably and essentially identified with it all."[11] And like Whitehead, from whose *Science and the Modern World* he chose the epigraph for his famous essay on the organismal conception, Ritter felt it was the duty of the two most important disciplines of human inquiry, science and philosophy, to work toward an expression of a unified world-picture and end the divorce of science from our aesthetic and ethical experiences."[12]

Appropriately, Steinbeck turned to philosophy to verify his emerging ideas about the unifying principles of existence, and he began reading the works of those philosophers who seemed to portray a scheme of being congruent with Ritter's organismal conception. Most of Steinbeck's critics, at least those who have labored so long to find a place for the novelist in the mainstream of American philosophic and literary thought, have pointed to his interest in the ideas of such main-line thinkers as Jefferson, Emerson, Thoreau, Whitman, and William James. Often, they have been embarrassed when other critics point out inconsistencies between Steinbeck's philosophy of life and the world-views of his alleged sources. The point, however, is that Steinbeck's familiarity with the ideas of Emerson, Whitman and James is important only secondarily; it is such lesser-known figures as Jan Smuts, Robert Briffault, and John Elof Boodin whose premises about man, nature, and the world Steinbeck learned well and used as the thematic bases of much of his best fiction.

It is not entirely clear how Steinbeck became familiar with the works of Briffault and Smuts. Carol Steinbeck affirms that he had been reading Briffault's anthropological treatise, *The Mothers*, and Smuts' then-popular essay, *Holism and Evolution* (CS/RA, 9/1/71). And, Richard Albee, a longtime friend of the novelist, recalls that many of Steinbeck's group were reading Briffault in the 1930's (Albee-RA, 2/24/73). Steinbeck may have learned of Smuts from Ritter's essay on the organismal conception in which Ritter speaks of Smuts' "penetrating insight" which "leaves no room for doubt that Smuts' general idea is, taken broadly, accordant with that which we are trying to work out in some detail."[13] And Albee recalls a day in Los Gatos when Steinbeck told him he wanted to "go back to Stanford and take some courses, and sit down and read every word Boodin ever wrote" (Albee-RA, 5/9/71).[14]

Taken as a group, Briffault, Smuts, and Boodin are evolutionary thinkers who share John Dewey's feeling that the facts of evolution forced a modesty on philosophy by which it had acquired a sense of responsibility, a new teleology in terms of its usefulness as a method of moral and political diagnosis and prognosis.[15] And each embraces an organic conception of reality which parallels the physical world of process and related behavior described by Ritter.

Organismic philosophy—as portrayed in Smuts' *Holism and Evolution* (1926), Briffault's *The Making of Humanity* (1919), and Boodin's *A Realistic Universe* (1931), *Cosmic Evolution* (1925), and *The Social Mind* (1939)—describes the evolutionary process in terms of "activities within a field" congruent with the operational concepts of the gestalt. It views the cosmos as a sort of superorganism just as Ritter had viewed a combination of individuals as a supercell. This insistence upon the universe as a living whole (particularly apparent in Boodin and Smuts) is based upon insight gleaned from the physical and biological sciences, in which it becomes obvious that reality at a material level is by no means a fortuitous combination of separate elements. Rather, there is a structured whole which prescribes the relations as well as the characters of the individual parts. The overall picture from organismic philosophy is of a universe which is an ongoing configuration in which activity at all levels (organic and inorganic) is integrated in the larger community of life and mind that patterns, controls, and molds the total process.

Such a metaphysic rings with idealism—that is, of constructing an imaginative hypothesis and adapting the postulates of this hypothesis into a consistent fabric. In *Holism and Evolution, The Making of Humanity,* and *Cosmic Evolution,* the authors state that the world has demonstrated an insistent tendency to move toward a renascent idealism based upon a purposive cosmic whole. Indeed, the fact that Boodin posits mind, Smuts mind and personality, and Briffault reason as the guides of cosmic evolution suggests that their world-views are distinctly idealistic.

This emphasis on the role of mind in purposive whole building is central to the world-view of Ricketts as well as of Steinbeck and needs further discussion. In *Holism and Evolution,* Smuts notes that it is the function of the human mind to seek out by a process of synthesis the unity implicit in the creation. For Smuts, mind is "the crowning phase of the regulative, coordinative process of Holism," the source of human individuality and "the chief means whereby organic Holism has developed into human personality."[16] Moreover, says Smuts, while mind is an organic part of the universal Mind, it is simultaneously a subjective entity which "has emancipated itself from the earlier routine of regulation and has assumed creative control of its own condition of life and environment."[17]

Unlike Allee's marine organisms which function automatically for purposes of survival, the human mind makes the regulative function of man conscious and voluntary in that rational purpose, not unconscious cooperation, becomes the principal attribute of human personality. For in man and in man alone, says Smuts, "the individual is going to be universalized, and the universe is going to be individualized, and thus from both directions the whole is going to be enriched."[18]

Smuts recognized, however, that man's mind also could be "a great Disturber." Comparing the "unerring precision" in the regulative social patterns of such highly developed insects as ants and termites with the social disorganization which often results from man's social experiments, Smuts concluded that because conscious ends emerge in which "the pulls in front dominate the pushes behind,"[19] the self can become an anarchist. Nevertheless, asserted Smuts, because "mind on the human level proceeds to create to a large extent the appropriate conditions for its own development,"[20] man, unlike the lower animals, can master his field through knowledge and become an unlimited source of good.

Briffault's doctrine of reason is much like Smuts' idea of mind in that Briffault defines rational thought as the human process of mental digestion, occurring largely through memory, where action is the consequence of feeling and experience. Rational thought, states Briffault, "is responsible for all progress," since human evolution is not anatomical, but psychological, and results from "the whole human environment."[21] But Briffault observes that there rages a conflict between rational and irrational thought. And just as Smuts affirmed that man's mind could effect disorganization as well as unity, Briffault concludes that the evolution of rational thought has been "a contest against non-rational thought."[22]

In *Cosmic Evolution*, Boodin asserts that "we may think of the universe as a sort of organism or superorganism," a rhythmic whole in which "every noble thought and every noble desire comes from above,"[23] and he points out that it is the spirit represented in man by the mind that gives soul to matter and uses matter in an expression of the whole. "The laws of thought are the laws of things," says Boodin[24] (a phrase, incidentally, quoted by Ricketts and Steinbeck in the *Log*), and so it is the human mind alone that can grasp the totality, the unity, and the harmony of things. And not only this, for Boodin, much like Smuts and Briffault, affirms that mind is responsible for man's urge for social creativeness. Actually, Boodin is close here to Bergson's *élan vital*, a notion containing implications Boodin rejected. But the philosopher does claim that there goes along with this genotypic urge for creativeness, a conscious recognition by mind of this vital impulse: "For the evolution of new patterns of society and the mutuality of realization of its members, there must also evolve higher capacities for imaginative sympathy, love and appreciation."[25] Hence, for Smuts, Briffault, and Boodin, man may be differentiated from all other forms of life by his mind (or personality or reason), which enables him not only to "feel" the order in the universe, but to use his vision to benefit the social order.

The tenets of organismic biology and philosophy focus upon two hypotheses which directly concern a comparative study of the world-views of Steinbeck and Ricketts: first, that man, by definition, is a unique creature in a regulated, coordinated scheme of being; and second, that the cosmos and thinking men in the cosmos are goal-oriented—that, as Smuts affirms, "the purposive teleological order is the domain of the free creative spirit."[26]

On the first point, Steinbeck and Ricketts fully agreed. Ricketts, of course, thought of the universe as a coordinate whole, an understanding of which is possible only among men who can break through to a recognition of the deep thing. And Steinbeck, on the basis of his knowledge of the ideas of Ritter, Boodin,

Smuts, and Briffault, and with additional scientific documentation supplied by Ricketts, viewed the universe holistically and distinguished men from lower forms of animal life, a distinction he dramatizes in much of his fiction.

Ironically, however, Steinbeck's critics, noting the novelist's interest in the behavior patterns of colonial animals, have charged that Steinbeck's fictional characters are neither distinct individuals nor even human beings at all; that he views man as he views crustaceans, important only in a biological sense for the manner in which they adapt to their environment. Edmund Wilson's charge that Steinbeck gives the effect of "assimilating human beings to animals"[27] touched off a critical chain reaction which accused Steinbeck of not really understanding man and of being unable to portray him as a complex personality in an even more complex world. Looking closely at the entire catalogue of Steinbeck's work, however, it is clear that he is not a novelist of animality, that while he often thinks of man within a biological frame of reference, most of his characters—and certainly those whom he most admires—are indeed human and are distinctly integrated personalities.

Actually, it is in Steinbeck's additions to Ricketts' Sea of Cortez journal that one finds the novelist's most clearly articulated expression of the principles of organismic philosophy concerning the nature of man. In sections of the *Log* entirely absent from Ricketts' log, Steinbeck observes that man is not a creature of an unknowable pattern of existence, but, by being able to realize "his cosmic identity," he becomes "potentially all things." In a passage resembling Smuts' analysis of man's mind as a potential "great Disturber," Steinbeck describes man as "a two-legged paradox" who "has never become accustomed to the tragic miracle of consciousness."

Perhaps, as has been suggested, his species is not set, has not jelled, but is still in a state of becoming, bound by his physical memories to a past of struggle and survival, limited in his futures by the uneasiness of thought and consciousness. (96)

And yet man, by virtue of his conscious mind, can do more than merely survive; he can, through the use of a "keying-in device," come to learn of his identity as an integral part of the cosmic design and, on the basis of this knowledge, act responsibly for the good of the whole.

At the conclusion of a long discussion by Ricketts based on Boodin's notion that "the laws of thought are the laws of things," in which the marine biologist argues that there is a secondary function of the human mind which enables man to relate the unrelatable and predict the unpredictable, Steinbeck adds the sentence: "And to this secondary type mind might be close by hinge and 'key-in' indices" (257). The vital word here is *key-in*, for Steinbeck uses it in the *Log* (as well as in his fiction and in an important unpublished philosophical paper) to describe the whole-making process. Talking about the schools of fish in San Carlos Bay, the novelist notes that "the larger animal surviving within itself . . . may key into a larger animal which is the life of all the sea, and this into the larger of the world" (241). But whereas individual fish key-into larger wholes simply to survive, the key-ing-in process of the human mind enables man to unify his being with the cosmic whole since (again quoting Boodin) " 'thought and things are part of one evolving matrix, and cannot ultimately conflict' " (257).

In various ways throughout his fiction, Steinbeck disproves the charge that there are no significant differences between his men and his animals. In "Flight," one of the most adroit stories in *The Long Valley* (1938), Pepé Torres' flight into the mountains to escape capture for having killed a man might be interpreted as evidence of Steinbeck's animalism on the grounds that during the course of his journey, Pepé is gradually reduced to the state of an animal. But, though stripped of all his civilized accouterments (horse, gun, and hat), Pepé never becomes an animal.[28] Facing his inevitable death with firm conviction and calm resignation, Pepé displays a quality of understanding which Steinbeck has never attributed to animals in tide pools.

Steinbeck often compares men with animals, and taking the viewpoint of the dispassionate biologist, he notes resemblances between the needs of men and analogous survival drives among the lower animals. But comparisons of similarities should not be confused with precise identification. There are instances in his fiction which might be construed as evidence of Steinbeck's tendency to equate men with animals, but which are really his attempt to use animals metaphorically and for symbolic purposes. For example, the turtle in *The Grapes of Wrath* surely symbolizes the manifold hardships the Joad family will have to endure on their trek west. But never does Steinbeck suggest that the Joads are turtles in the biological sense of the term. Indeed, the vital doctrine of social cooperation which the Joads internalize during the course of Steinbeck's narrative distinguishes their migration from the solitary pilgrimage of the land turtle.

Steinbeck's discrimination between men and the lower animals is most pronounced in his later works, where his deepening investigation of man's moral nature becomes the center of thematic attention. All of *East of Eden* hinges upon a definition of the "Timshel" symbol as meaning "Thou may'st" and the characters' ability to internalize and practice its precepts. Pippin Héristal's internal struggle as king between a desire for power and the moral responsibilities of his position forms the thematic center of *The Short Reign of Pippin IV*. And in *The Winter of Our Discontent*, Ethan Hawley's quest for meaning in a meaningless world—his attempt to find the spiritual in a wasteland—reflects Steinbeck's attention to a distinctly human dilemma. Moreover, the fact that the symbolic affirmation which occurs at the novel's conclusion is achieved at the expense of verisimilitude and is disjointed from the rest of the book points to Steinbeck's strong desire to resolve this uniquely human plight. Indeed, Steinbeck's deepening concern with the problems of man's moral nature was the theme of his Nobel address, in which he affirmed that as a writer he lived to "celebrate man's proven capacity for greatness of heart and spirit," since "a writer who does not believe in the perfectability of man" is not really a writer at all.

But while Steinbeck and Ricketts agree that man possesses unique faculties which set him apart from the lower animals, they differ markedly in their assessment of how these faculties should

best be employed. In short, throughout his career, Steinbeck celebrated man's singular ability to pursue significant goals and achieve
meaningful progress. In even his last work, *America and Americans*, he insisted that "We have failed sometimes, taken wrong
paths, paused for renewal, filled our bellies and licked our wounds;
but we have never slipped back—never."[29] And in a memorable
intercalary chapter in *The Grapes of Wrath*, the novelist cele-
brates his migrants' ability to endure and says that man differs
from any other living being because of his creativity, his ability
to work toward real and sometimes even visionary goals despite
overwhelming obstacles:

The last clear definite function of man—muscles aching to work, minds
aching to create beyond the single need—this is man. To build a wall,
to build a house, a dam, and in the wall and house and dam to put
something of Manself, and to Manself take back something of the wall,
the house, the dam; to take hard muscles from the lifting, to take the
clear lines and form from conceiving. For man, unlike any other thing
organic or inorganic in the universe, grows beyond his work, walks up
the stairs of his concepts, emerges ahead of his accomplishments.[30]

Put simply, there is a wide gulf between Steinbeck's statement
about "the last clear definite function of man" and Ricketts' non-
teleological journey toward a breaking through to the deep thing.[31]
And though it is true that there are characters in Steinbeck's fiction who never move beyond Ricketts' point of "instant-acceptance," it is absurd to believe that the novelist shares the marine
biologist's abhorrence of the teleological.

For Ricketts, the non-teleological method closely coincided with
his vision of the whole picture in which all things, even "dirt and
grief," must be "wholly accepted if necessary as struggle vehicles
of an emergent joy—achieving things which are not transient by
means of things which are."[32] Even what Ricketts calls the "nega-
tion aspects" (night—death—quiet), which, he says, "are so often
considered quietistic by laymen," are symbols of Lao Tse's "path
of no path," of Novalis' indication of the way of inner being.[33]

Actually, Ricketts' quest for the deep thing is closely allied to
the Taoist tradition represented by Lao Tse, to whose works
Ricketts frequently refers. In one unpublished essay written in

August 1942 about Japanese and German patterns of culture, he states that

> Any vehicle for achieving a suprapersonal emergence, an intuitive understanding of the underlying "oneness" of all things, or better, a participation in that universal quality, is a *tao*. The nearest western correlative that comes to my mind is Gerard Manley Hopkins' *inscape*, the opposite of *escape*.[34]

In the way of the tao, the eternal imperfection and incessant troubles of the world of multiplicity are in themselves symbols of a higher reality which is primary, permanent, and omnipresent. And because man cannot fully internalize the absolute for more than a fleeting moment (Ricketts says in "The Philosophy of Breaking Through": "The tao that can be tao-ed can not be the ultimate Tao"[35]), all causal analysis is arbitrary, and no one path of corrective action can justifiably be chosen over another.

Margery Lloyd, a friend of Ricketts during the 1930's, recalls his telling her about the poverty and squalor of Chicago's urban slums shortly after she had finished reading *Studs Lonigan* and was in anguish over Farrell's description of Chicago's south side. Ricketts told her that even dirt and poverty must exist in the larger picture, and to attempt to correct things would be to no good purpose (ML/RA, (3/21/71). Indeed, in the margin of his own copy of *Studs Lonigan*, across from a passage in which a "starved-looking" atheist asks God, "why do you create men and make them suffer and fight in vain, and live brief unhappy lives like pigs, and make them die disgustingly, and rot?" Ricketts noted, "good example of teleological thinking on a very low level."

For Ricketts, the non-teleological approach to life suggests a philosophy of "non-acquisition," a way of life in which the man of vision confidently resigns himself to "the sweet brew of life." This is not a matter of laziness, but an extension of a whole lifestyle by a man who believed in the Chinese proverb "wealth is nothing but manure; the face is worth a hundred thousand pounds."

It is, of course, very difficult for Western man to understand the concept of nonaction, the idea represented by Lao Tse in the *Tao*

Teh King that the worst fault is to want to acquire.[36] And Steinbeck, who embraced a dualistic philosophy of life and consistently put the highest premium upon action, conflict, and change, viewed the ideal of nonaction as one of metaphysical indifference.

Ricketts was very much aware of his conflict with Steinbeck on the issue of purpose and progress, and he spelled out their differences in an essay entitled "Thesis and Materials for a Script on Mexico" (1940) which he considered an "Anti-script" to Steinbeck's *The Forgotten Village* (1940). Early in this work, Ricketts quotes from a 1938 Memorial Day editorial written by the "presumably hard-boiled editor of a very practical newspaper" (the Monterey *Peninsula Herald*) about the virtues of man's suffering and dying for his "traditions, his country, and his love of liberty."[37] Noting that these precepts amount to "spiritual entities" for the editor, Ricketts compares them unfavorably with the "other side," which "in the east even the bravest men are proud to own, [but] is with us rarely discussed by practical men. It is associated too often with feminine traits, with the unconscious—the realm of feeling. The emphasis is on acceptance, on appreciation of what *is* as contrasted with propaganda for change."[38]

Whereas Steinbeck's gospel in *The Forgotten Village* is a plan calling for social action to upgrade Mexico's obsolete medical practices, Ricketts' concern is for "the inward things," the most obvious examples of which are "friendship, tolerance, dignity, or love," and the "larger relationships" between "man and the land, and between man and his feeling of supra-personal participation."[39] Ricketts points out that an emphasis on "change, acquisition, and progress," symbolized by "high-tension lines, modern highways and modern schools," belongs "to the region of outward possessions" as opposed to the more important "region of inward adjustments." He observes that although "in an inward sense, the Mexicans are more advanced than we are," the powerful virus of "the present U.S. mechanistic civilization" can easily corrupt "the deep smile," the rich "relational life" enjoyed by so many Mexican people and by which they have achieved "among their countrymen to the north the reputation for being lazy and careless."[40]

Ricketts' views on the evils of material progress were not limited to the "Anti-script." His opposition to "prosperity" appears throughout much of his Gulf of California log. And in "The Outer Shores," he finds in the faces of the impoverished Indians of Vancouver Island the same deep smile he saw on the visages of so many Mexican peasants in Baja California.

I was walking along the float and I saw one of those things that moves me so much. A young Indian woman, sickish—maybe tb, the rate is said to be high here among the natives—and with an abessed eye, carrying a baby. It was the old business of people in trouble and taking it and being wonderful, "something that happened." I smiled at the woman and really meant it and she smiled back in that wonderful way that Indians do; I havn't ever seen such illumination in a white; just gives you that marvelous sense of contact that transcends language and custom.[41]

In a different vein, Ricketts notes in a letter to Steinbeck on nostalgia (which he considered "the world's most powerful emotion") that perhaps "the best thing is to close the plant and go fishing" (EFR-JS, 8/12/46). And in his essay on Germany and Japan (1942), he contrasts a tribal father with a maladjusted "civilized" young Indian—"we have made a bad American of a potentially good Indian"—and concludes that "it may take generations for the resulting problem to be adjusted."[42]

But it is in the "Anti-script" that his differences with Steinbeck over progress are stated most explicitly, for in defining the thesis and materials for his script on Mexico, Ricketts selected "a motif diametrically opposite to that of John's 'Forgotten Village.'"[43] Ricketts, of course, seeks to preserve "the deep smile" and recommends a non-teleological appreciation of what *is*. But Steinbeck champions material progress and social change in his story of a Mexican village's attempt to combat bacterial disease, a fight which is hindered by the ignorance and superstition of many of its inhabitants. Steinbeck concedes that change will come very slowly since "learning and teaching are slow, patient things," but, speaking through a young Mexican physician, he observes that "the change will come, is coming; the long climb out of darkness. Already the people are learning, changing their lives, learning, working, living in new ways."[44]

Progress and the Organismal Conception

In his "Anti-script," Ricketts observed that "The chief character in John's script is the Indian boy [Juan Diego] who becomes so imbued with the spirit of modern medical progress that he leaves the traditional way of his people to associate himself with the new thing."

The working out of a script for the "other side" might correspondingly be achieved through the figure of some wise and mellow old man, who has long ago developed beyond the expediences of economic drives and power drives, and to whom for guidance in adolescent troubles some grandchild comes (as the young girl to the philosopher in James Stephens' "Crook of Gold"). A wise old man, present during the time of building a high speed road through a primitive community, appropriately might point out the evils of the encroaching mechanistic civilization to a young person.[45]

Steinbeck and Ricketts argued openly about the effects progress might have on rural Mexico. And Herb Kline, the film's producer-director, who worked himself a good deal among primitive peoples, sided with Steinbeck. He remembers with some distaste Ricketts' absorption "with Rousseau and the joys of the primitive man while [that man's] children and wife were dying unnecessarily from the inadequate treatment of witch doctors" (HK/RA, 2/27/71).

Ricketts' and Steinbeck's deep-seated controversy on the issue of progress, overt in the ideological clash between *The Forgotten Village* and Ricketts' "Anti-script," and implicit in most of the writings of both men, is a crucial issue in Steinbeck's fiction because of the novelist's unique handling of Ricketts' gospel of inaction and anti-progress. Indeed, many critics, misreading Steinbeck's fictional intentions, have echoed Donald Weeks' assertion that the novelist idealizes the indolent or animal-like man and adopts "the philosophy of the wino," which, because it requires no more of man than to adapt to his environment, "is nihilistic and lacks any sort of philosophical range."[46]

As a writer, Steinbeck was intrigued by Ricketts' views on progress and social change. But with the sole exception of *The Log from the Sea of Cortez*, in which he allows Ricketts to express his views about progress unchallenged, Steinbeck's primitives, his

escapees, and his visionaries who prefer Santayana's "inward landscape" to the terrain of the real world, while philosophically
interesting, are neither his heroes nor his personae. In viewing
Steinbeck's work in perspective, it becomes increasingly evident
that the novelist carefully and analytically forged his own conception of the human ideal; the vigorously energetic and creative
individual who "walks up the stairs of his concepts" and "emerges
ahead of his accomplishments," that rare man among men to
whom the novelist accords his highest praise and in whom he
places his greatest trust. Indeed, along with his unique ability to
portray nature and the natural world, the manner in which Steinbeck deals with the choice between escape and commitment is his
supreme attribute as a writer: few novelists have ever dealt so
completely and so eloquently with what they regard as the fundamental basis of human character.

The Argument
of Phalanx

*T*here are some striking differences and similarities in Ricketts' and Steinbeck's ideas concerning the relationship between the individual man and the groups or societies in which he functions. Both were interested in the way animals behave within groups, and they wrestled with the possibility that men, like many species of lower animals, may be nothing apart from the groups to which they belong and from which they draw much of their identity. And yet, just as the two agreed that there are fundamental differences between men and animals, so they shared in large measure some very definite ideas about the importance of the individual man as opposed to the individual marine organism.

Ricketts was vitally interested in what happens to the individual man in collective movements, and he notes in a journal kept during his stay at the Monterey Presidio that the forced patterns imposed upon soldiers may result in benefits to those soldiers which outweigh their individual loss of freedom:

What they give up is practically everything they have had or striven for, sometimes even life itself. Often freedom. What they get is in direct ratio to what they give up, because the army forges its deep bond of companionship between men who have lost everything but each other and (deeply, dedicatedly) themselves. And just as many a wife or husband has a greatness in human relation larger than they are themselves, so a rather insignificant soldier can have thrust upon him a great mantle of mass-love. Merely by being a member of a group—a forced member. They don't know it, many are insensitive, not conscious. But they are in it and of it. They are it.[1]

By and large, however, through the highly individualistic Ricketts acknowledges that there are human as well as tidepool societies in which "the individual serves the state, chiefly as a unit or cog in the supra-personal social organization that is the colony," he espouses a clear preference for another kind of society, which is "based on the democratic principle in which the state serves the individual."[2] In his Sea of Cortez journal, Ricketts comments on a group of Japanese fishermen who, at the bidding of the collective Japanese mind, are depleting the shrimp resources of Guaymas while the Mexican Department of Marine watches in helpless dismay. He observes that "there again is the conflict of nations, of ideologies, of two conflicting organisms. And the units in those organisms are themselves good people, people you'd like to know, like the kind young Jap captain."[3]

Similarly, in his "Anti-script" to *The Forgotten Village*, Ricketts wonders why group movements are so inflexible and summarily concludes that whereas the individual, "by intent, discipline and skill" can "walk the knife edge" and channel his "life energy" as he sees fit, "the group, having started in one direction, tends to develop along those lines until it exhibits the law of diminishing returns, or until it contacts powerful opposite influence."[4]

Steinbeck's interest in the relationship between the individual and the group plays a crucial thematic role in much of his fiction and is somewhat more complex and sophisticated than that demonstrated by Ricketts. And yet a cursory reading of the criticism of his work reveals that he has been much maligned for being unwilling or unable to distinguish the individual as a distinct "unit," apart from the interest groups in which he functions. Steinbeck has been condemned for an alleged commitment to collectivism in which "life's fullness is found only in the group and never in the individual."[5]

The Argument of Phalanx

Those who decry Steinbeck's failure to recognize the individual do not seem to understand that the novelist denies that man's participation in a group necessarily negates his individuality. This can happen, of course, and Steinbeck's characters often victimize themselves by selling their souls to collective bodies. The crucial point, however, is that their capitulation to the group is thematically purposeful on Steinbeck's part, and the novelist demonstrates how each character who forfeits his individuality violates his own integrity.

As a student of modern mass movements, Steinbeck examined closely the question whether man can have any individuality apart from the group in which he functions. Similarly, he studied the origin and direction of groups to ascertain why some groups enoble human freedom while others destroy it. When, through Ricketts, he learned Allee's ideas about the automatic behavioral patterns of animal aggregations, Steinbeck wrote a two-page paper on the subject of group behavior, "Argument of Phalanx." According to Richard Albee, to whom Steinbeck gave the paper, it was written in Pacific Grove sometime between 1934 and 1936 and was titled after the use of the term *phalanx* for the battle formations of the Roman legions (Albee/RA, 3/22/71).[6] (The soldier-units in the Roman legions resembled high-domed turtles because of the manner in which they carried their shields above their heads. The colloquial Latin for phalanx is *tortoise*.)

Steinbeck's central thesis in the "Argument of Phalanx" is congruent with the fundamental precepts of organismal biology; that group-man, like any other superorganism made up of smaller units, has a will and a direction of its own. In other words, the whole acts as a causal unit on its own parts, and, as Ritter notes, the "whole is something the original and necessary parts of which are so located and so functioning in relation to each other as to contribute their proper share to the structure of the whole."[7]

As a matter of fact, one of the most useful aspects of the organismal view of life is its ability to explain the behavior of segments of organisms by reference to the organism as a whole, to describe parts of organic structures in their activities as parts by concepts best defined by reference to higher-level phenomena exhibited by the whole. In this process, we "apply to parts concepts defined in terms of phenomena that these parts do not exhibit."[8]

These organismic principles are apparent first on a physico-chemical level, for whereas organisms surely consist of chemical constituents, these constituents are composed in such a fashion that the unit as a whole exhibits properties that are not chemical. On a biological level, J. S. Haldane pointed out as early as 1923 in *Mechanism, Life, and Personality* (a work with which Steinbeck may have been familiar, if not directly, then through his reading of Ritter) "that the living body and its physiological environment form an organic whole, the parts of which cannot be understood in separation from one another."[9] And, if one accepts Ritter's exhortation that there is no proof "that man is apart from nature, is over, against and above nature in such a sense as is held by much of philosophy and especially of theology,"[10] he could inductively conclude (as so many students of human behavior have done) that on a social level, the human group reflects values and exhibits behavior not shared by all of its members; that individuals often behave not as they would like to behave, but rather as the group to which they belong demands.

"We have thought of mankind always in terms of individual men," Steinbeck writes in "Argument of Phalanx."

We have tried to study men and movements of men by minute investigation of individual men-units. We might as reasonably try to understand the nature of a man by investigating the cells of his body. Perhaps if we observe the phalanx, knowing it is a new individual, not to be confused with the units which compose it, if we look back at the things it has done in an attempt to correlate and analyse its habits under various stimuli, we may in time come to know something of the phalanx, of its nature, of its drive and its ends, we may even be able to direct its movements where now we have only great numbers of meaningless, unrelated and destructive phenomena.[11]

Confirming the doctrine of organismal biology that "the organism in its totality is as essential to an explanation of its elements as its elements are to an explanation of the organism,"[12] Steinbeck insists that men must be regarded as "units in the greater beast, the phalanx."

Within the body of a man are units, cells, some highly specialized and some coordinate, which have their natures and their lives, which die and are replaced, which suffer and are killed. In their billions they make up man, the new individual. But man is more than the total of his cells, and his nature is not that of the sum of all his cells. He has a nature now new and strange to his cells.

Man is a unit of the greater beast, the phalanx. The phalanx has pains, desires, hungers, and strivings as different from those of the unit man's as man's are different from the unit cells.[13]

Just as Ricketts suggests that individual soldiers may not comprehend fully what happens to them in the military "whole," Steinbeck observes that the emotions of the phalanx are "foreign and incomprehensible to unit-man."[14] And yet, quoting perhaps the most crucial section of the phalanx paper, "Within each unit-man, deep in him, in his subconscious, there is a keying device with which he may become part of the phalax."[15]

Once he is part of a moving phalanx, his nature changes, his habits and his desires. When the phalanx is in motion, it controls its unit-men with an iron discipline. In phalanx need there can be change of birth rate of the units, of the stature, complexion, color, constitution of the unit. Phalanx resistance to circumstance is far greater than individual man's resistance. Once a man has become a unit in a phalanx in motion, he is capable of prodigies of endurance of thought or of emotion such as would be unthinkable were he acting as individual man . . . All life forms from protozoa to antelopes and lions, from crabs to lemmings form and are a part of phalanxes, but the phalanx of which the units are men, are more complex, more variable and powerful than any other.[16]

Steinbeck's interest in the relationship between the individual and the group was a lifelong passion. And in 1955, two decades after he had written the "Argument of Phalanx," Steinbeck noted in a minor piece entitled "Some Thoughts on Juvenile Delinquency" that "man is a double thing—a group animal and at the same time an individual. And it occurs to me that he cannot successfully be the second until he has fulfilled the first."[17] Most importantly, it is Steinbeck's statement about the unit-man's keying device which bridges the gap between man's double nature;

between the formidable strength of the phalanx and the free, teleologically creative individual. It thus remains to examine in greater detail the nature of this keying device which enables man to recognize his phalanx role and to discover how, through participation as a unit in the group, he fulfills himself as an individual.

Again it is organismic thought—this time the philosophy of Smuts and Boodin—which provides vital answers. Indeed, Steinbeck's thesis as to the means by which the individual must recognize his phalanx role and the way in which his acceptance of this role aggrandizes rather than subverts his individuality so closely resembles the cosmic idealism of organismic philosophy that one might be led to conclude that what Ricketts contributed to Steinbeck's thinking about the group-man was biological documentation rather than initial impetus or ideation.

In Boodin's *Social Mind*, the ideas for which he had been working out in most of his earlier works, the philosopher postulates the notion that man must be understood as existing in a group, consciously pursuing real ends. Boodin believed that the individual mind derives from the society of which it is a part, that minds are organized in a social matrix, and that the group mind (Steinbeck's phalanx) is primary in that organization.[18] Moreover, Boodin opined that the will of any group is not simply a collection of the particular wills of its members: "It has a distinct individuality of its own. Our relation to a group will, whether external or internal, is not a relation to individuals as individuals."[19]

But although Boodin envisaged all meaningful human progress as developing though the organization of men to pursue full collective lives, he was aware that the group, because it forces its will upon its members, can seriously undermine individuality and tend toward impersonalism. In order to avert such a depersonalizing philosophy of life, Boodin was quick to point out that there are men who are able to place an impress of thought upon an entire epoch of humanity. "The great personalities of history stamp upon their social period their creative faith." Whole eras bear the imprint of a creative genius who "directs the stream of history which runs through him and carries him forward."[20] Indeed, while

The Argument of Phalanx

Boodin acknowledged primacy of the group, he simultaneously defended the creative importance of the individual without deifying him. Quite obviously, Boodin dismissed the laissez-faire theory of society in favor of a pattern of social organization dominated by a group consciousness. But he similarly inveighed against the kind of restraint which would be imposed upon the individual by Hegel's *Rechtsphilosophie* or Pareto's notion of forced subjection. In human movements seeking real, measurable ends, some degree of social conformity may be necessary, but it must not inhibit true individual creativity.

Ultimately, the teleological end Boodin seeks in his analysis of the social mind is a universal harmony resulting from the willing union of free minds. Seeking a moral basis for human existence, Boodin posits as an ideal a "panhumanity," a democracy thoroughly congruent with the unity of the cosmic whole. "Human beings who can work together in harmony in larger and larger unities will in the end possess the earth. This, I think is the meaning of the saying 'The meek shall inherit the earth.' "[21]

For Boodin, then, the human mind is born from and enriched by purposive affiliation with the group mind. Moreover, the individual's willing participation in the group is analogous to his recognized participation in the larger cosmic whole. And it is man's mind in synergetic union with the group mind and with the cosmic mind which, as Jan Smuts points out, liberates man and sets him apart from the lower animals. Moreover, says Smuts, in a passage which closely resembles Steinbeck's keying-in argument in the phalanx paper, it is through man's awareness of his "field" ("that area . . . which falls below the 'threshold' of consciousness"[22]) that he synthesizes the present with the past and the future and acts in purposive concord with the society of which he is a part.

Much of Steinbeck's thinking about the group-man grew from his interest in the aggregational patterns of life in the tide pools, and he often draws comparisons between the group-man and the group-animal for purposes of analogy. Never, however, does he say they are synonomous. The *idea* of the group-man is certainly analogous to the *idea* of the group-fish, but, and here Steinbeck moves beyond Ricketts, the purposive, mind-directed objectives of the group-man (in contrast to the chiefly regulative and adaptive behavior of the group-fish) are distinctly human and, in the best of groups, enhance and elevate the self rather than destroy it.

Though detailed analyses of various types of phalanxes in Steinbeck's fiction will be undertaken in subsequent chapters, a few examples are in order here. In "The Leader of the People," originally published as a short story in *The Long Valley*, but now the final section of *The Red Pony*, Grandfather's participation in the movement called westering can in no way be equated with the actions of the group-fish.

We carried life out here and set it down the way those ants carry eggs. And I was the leader. The westering was as big as God, and the slow steps that made the movement piled up and piled up until the continent was crossed.[23]

True, westering was, as Grandfather says, "a whole bunch of people made into one big crawling beast" (180), but it was a uniquely human beast, an energetic force composed of individual men finding personal meaning and direction through joint participation in a concerted effort ("'Every man wanted something for himself, but the big beast that was all of them wanted only westering.'" [180]). Westering, unlike animal migration, had a distinctly human direction; it was a quest by a hungry band of frontiersmen who represent all that Steinbeck loved best in the American past. The impetus behind the westering movement "had its roots not in the flesh but in the human spirit," and it is, in fact, the passing of that spirit of movement from an America in which every frontier has been conquered that Steinbeck laments in "The Leader of the People."[24]

What emerges in "The Leader of the People" is Steinbeck's identification and evaluation of a uniquely human group in which individual purposive goals are realized through collective action. This same belief in the value which can accrue to the individual from group involvement functions on a much larger scale in *The Grapes of Wrath*, in which the Joads, under Casy's guidance, realize that joint participation in a group movement (phalanx) aimed toward an agrarian ideal is necessary not only to ensure biological survival, but also to the moral end of affirming individual dignity. Although at the novel's outset each migrant thinks only of himself or, at best, of his family, and though alone they seem to lack purpose and direction ("The men sat in the doorways of their houses; their hands were busy with sticks and little rocks. The men sat still—thinking—figuring" [7]), by the end of the novel, through a collective venture, the migrants achieve a sense of resolution ("the break could never come as long as fear could turn to wrath" [592]) and an understanding of their own dignity as human beings ("Them's horses—we're men." [592]). And Tom Joad, his character strengthened and his objectives clarified by his ability to key-in to the cosmic whole and by his subsequent participation in the migrant phalanx, emerges as a socially responsible individual who strikes out to spread the gospel of reform.

In "The Leader of the People" and *The Grapes of Wrath*, Steinbeck resolves the apparent paradox of the individual's ostensible inability to maintain his creative individuality within the group, but in *In Dubious Battle* and "The Vigilante" he shows how a different kind of group involvement can result in the destruction of the self. In the first, *Battle*, he deliberately creates "a hero in two persons" (Mac and Jim) who "find their true definition, their very essence, in the fact that they have been freed from themselves . . . because they have voluntarily given up their individualities."[25]

Certainly, the creation of a two-person hero in which each becomes detached from himself is indicative of a loss of individuality. The point, however, is that Steinbeck never applauds this forfeiture of self; he assumes an objective stance in the novel and consciously avoids identification with either Mac or Jim. Indeed, the fact that the Party (to which Mac and Jim belong) seeks to diminish human individuality serves to reinforce Steinbeck's conviction that the dignity of the individual can never be served by a cause whose foundation is based upon a denial of self. Jim Nolan does not become a saint during the course of the novel.[26] Rather, the story of his entrance into and absorption by the Party is attended by his growing lack of vision to the true needs of the striking farmers, which, Steinbeck seems to imply, may well be attributable to his inability to think as an individual about the real needs of individuals.

Hence, while Steinbeck stresses the value of collective action in enhancing individual particularity, he is not so naive as to assert unequivocally that one necessarily leads to the other. He surely realizes that there is more than one type of group-man; that there are creative and destructive phalanxes, and he maintains that man, as a "thinking, figuring" being, must align himself with the group that will safeguard rather than devour his individuality.

A more concise treatment of the group-man is Steinbeck's main thematic concern in "The Vigilante." In this psychological exploration of human behavior, Steinbeck presents in Mike a character who, after participating in a lynch-mob, suddenly feels lost and empty and can understand the reasons for his wife's attack on him.

Then her eyes widened and hung on his face. "You been with a woman," she said hoarsely. "What woman you been with? . . ."
He walked through the kitchen and went into the bathroom. A little mirror hung on the wall. Mike took off his cap and looked at his face. "By God, she was right," he thought. "That's just exactly how I do feel."[27]

Thinking about his participation in the lynching, Mike suddenly views his experience as something unreal and foreign to his basic nature.

Half an hour before, when he had been howling with the mob and fighting for a chance to help pull on the rope, then his chest had been so full that he had found he was crying. But now everything was dead, everything unreal; the dark mob was made up of stiff lay-figures. In the flamelight the faces were as expressionless as wood. Mike felt the stiffness, the unreality in himself, too. (134)

When Mike stops at a bar on his way home, the bartender asks him, "I never been to a lynching. How's it make you feel—afterwards?" (140). Mike replies, "Makes you feel kind of cut off and tired" (140), a statement which reflects Steinbeck's premise that the group-man can alienate man from himself just as surely as it can enoble human dignity.

Edward F. Ricketts at the Great Tide Pool, Pacific Grove, California

JOHN STEINBECK and EDWARD F. RICKETTS

Through his interest in organismic biology and philosophy, his observation of local political events, and his work with Ricketts in the tide pools of the California coast, Steinbeck reached some very definite conclusions about the disposition of the group-animal and the way in which the individual organism becomes absorbed into the group and assumes the group's character. In applying these ideas in his writing, however, Steinbeck voices his preference for groups which heighten the consciousness and increase the freedom of the individual, and he maintains the need to distinguish and celebrate certain types of group-man which preserve rather than decimate individuality. Certainly, Steinbeck and Ricketts believed in the primacy of the collectivity, but they also recognized and accentuated the importance of the creative individual. "Species," Steinbeck and Ricketts note in *The Log from the Sea of Cortez*, are "commas in a sentence"—but to both men they are surely Brobdignagian commas with individual hearts and minds.

It appears then, that the world-views of John Steinbeck and Ed Ricketts, while by no means identical, are quite similar. Both men are naturalists in the sense that they are "sympathetic in their feeling for nature, painstaking in acquiring knowledge of nature," and eager to identify "their whole selves with nature."[28] Both embrace an inductive and ecological approach to the natural world which they study because of their faith in it as that through which their own lives have meaning and worth. And both draw responses from the natural world which lead them to beliefs in higher cosmic principles of order and being. And yet, while Ricketts, by means of his monistic non-teleological philosophy of breaking through, developed a methodology by which he could attain an understanding of the metaphysical whole and acquire a personal emotive relationship with that whole, Steinbeck, by virtue of his interest in organismic biology and philosophy, sought his principle of unity in organic terms—through the concept of the superorganism.

Conclusively affirming that man can know the universe, that he can understand his identity in the cosmic whole, Ricketts and Steinbeck agree that man is unique in the creation, unlike any other form of life, organic or inorganic. They concur that though behavior patterns among individuals often closely resemble the activities of lower animals, the free creative spirit of the individual sets man above and apart. Similarly, both recognize that human groups resemble collections of animals, but they distinguish certain unique qualities in human groups, and Steinbeck, developing this notion in some detail, affirms that the individuality of a person is enhanced, not subverted, when his participation in the group is attended by a recognition of purpose.

Where Steinbeck and Ricketts disagree is on the issue of the proper domain of man's creative spirit. Whereas Ricketts' non-teleological approach to life, which dismisses all analyses of final or efficient causation, makes any goal-oriented activity except the quest to break through to the deep thing fruitless, Steinbeck's dualistic philosophy, which combines empirical realism with a cosmic idealism, is responsible for his deep concern with human problems. A thorough teleologist who rarely loses himself in the intracacies of metaphysics, Steinbeck always identifies reality with the world of experience and could not conceive of man as fore-ordained philosophic dust destined to sit at the feast of the wise. Intrigued, to be sure, by Ricketts' quest to savor the "deep taste of life," to attain what Baker Brownell calls "the integrative moment of living,"[29] Steinbeck consistently championed temporal progress.

Nevertheless, although the novelist advocates a philosophy of action, his view of the larger whole keeps him from falling into the kind of mere partisanship which is an open door to prejudice. Perhaps what he really learned from Ricketts was that action without sight is neither suitable nor adequate. And so, in his best fiction, Steinbeck combines vision and participation and avoids both monistic aloofness and blind political partisanship. Still, at the core of Steinbeck's world-view is his belief that the repudiation of human progress leads not to Tahiti, but to oblivion.

Having determined the essential similarities and differences between the non-teleological quest to break through to the deep thing, and the teleological ramifications of the organismal conception of life; having assessed the general areas of philosophical agreement and disagreement between Steinbeck and Ricketts, it remains to turn to Steinbeck's fiction and examine the formidable impact of Ricketts' person, his ideas, and his imagination on the novelist's management of his fictional material.

The task will not be easy, for there are problems arising from Steinbeck's varied handling of his thematic fabric which changed markedly over the four decades during which he wrote. Indeed, Steinbeck stated publicly that he never repeated himself: "Since by the process of writing a book I have outgrown that book, I have not written two books alike. Where would be the interest in that?"[30] And yet, through an examination of his treatment of Ricketts' person and ideas, we shall see that Steinbeck's fictional canon contains what Emerson points to in "Self-reliance" with his splendid metaphor of the best ship following a zigzag line of a hundred tacks, which when seen from a sufficient distance, straightens itself out; "that beneath the variety, the lack of pattern, there is an harmonious agreement which occurs with a little height of thought."[31]

From Men to Gods

Steinbeck's first novel, *Cup of Gold* (1929), was published before the novelist met Ricketts and thus, in the present context, is as significant for what it does not contain as for what it does. A loosely fictionalized history of the English buccaneer, Henry Morgan, *Cup of Gold* is a weak and inconsequential novel. The story, which is patterned after James Stephens' *Crook of Gold* and the work of Donn Byrne, is contrived, the language is stilted, and Steinbeck's attempt to deal with universal human problems in this eighteenth-century adventure saga by drawing analogies with the Faust theme and the Grail legend results in a weakly conceived book in which the mythical substructure is poorly integrated with the mainline of the narrative.

The plot of *Cup of Gold* concerns a young man, Morgan, who dreams of going to sea and becoming a great adventurer. In a seaport where he is trying to secure passage to the West Indies, he is betrayed and sold as an indentured servant to a severe but easily manipulated colonial planter. Using his position to accumulate knowledge and wealth, Morgan later organizes a pirate brotherhood and becomes a daring and much feared buccaneer. His greatest achievement is his seizure of the city of Panama, once thought impregnable, and the beautiful woman known throughout the Indies as La Santa Roja. But finding that his successes give him little pleasure, Morgan deserts his companions, petitions for and gains a pardon as well as knighthood from the British king, marries a beautiful woman of high society, and retires to Jamaica where, until his death, he serves as lieutenant-governor of that island.

The book failed to sell, and when, after the novelist's popularity was firmly established, Steinbeck was approached about the possibility of reissuing it, he questioned its merits. "I'm not particularly proud of *Cup of Gold*," he wrote to his agents, "Outside of a certain lyric quality there isn't much to it."[1]

This lyric quality is of particular interest here, for despite the fact that the novel's lyricism generally consists of spurious, undirected nervous energy, grandiose archaisms, and a general straining for eloquence,[2] many of the lyrical portions do celebrate nature and depict its effect on man. Passages in *Cup of Gold* demonstrate that Steinbeck was beginning to recognize the intricate relationship between man and his natural environment before he met Ricketts. And while these references are piecemeal and random, and suggest the embryonic state of Steinbeck's thinking, their presence suggests at least that the novelist was likely to be receptive to the professional insight on problems of man's relationship with his environment that Ricketts could provide.

Early in the novel, on the voyage from Cardiff to the West Indies, Morgan is overwhelmed and at the same time inspired by the majesty of nature's power, as he stands alone on the ship's forecastle during a storm at sea:

And in this time Henry exulted like a young god. The wind's frenzy was his frenzy. He would stand on the deck, braced against a mast, face into the wind, cutting it with his chin as the prow cut the water, and a chanting exultation filled his chest to bursting—joy like a pain.[3]

Intent on presenting nature's many moods, Steinbeck also affirms that nature can present itself in a state of unparalleled calm and promote a sense of tranquility in those who view it.

The sea was a round lake of quiet undulation, spread with a silken skin. Slowly, slowly passing to rearward, the water set up a pleasant hypnosis in the brain. It was like looking into a fire. One saw nothing, yet only with infinite struggle could he move his eyes; and finally his brain dreamed off, though he was not sleeping. (52)

Throughout *Cup of Gold*, Steinbeck views the natural world of the West Indies as the unspoiled ideal. When Morgan and his pirates recklessly pillage the peaceful Spanish lands, nature, in the form of howling monkeys, rises up to protest the intrusion: "They howled their indignation and hurled leaves and twigs at the boats. Fourteen hundred outlandish beings had invaded sacred Mother Jungle; the mangiest monkey on earth had, at least, his right of protest" (124).

The scorn heaped on Morgan and his followers by sacred Mother Jungle's monkeys foretells the eventual destruction of the pirate brotherhood. For Steinbeck implies that the buccaneering delights of sack and plunder are inimical to the ecological balance of an area; there is something so very menacing about the threat of a pirate invasion that all the inhabitants of an area flee the onslaught. Conversely, pirates are men and need the products of nature to live, and if their very presence frightens away all living creatures, they paradoxically destroy themselves by eliminating the sources of their own survival. "The men hunted in the jungle, searched through the trees for any living things which might be eaten. Even the cats and monkeys seemed to be leagued with Spain. The jungle was silent and creatureless now. No unit of life was left save the flying insects" (126). And by the time Morgan and his men finally reach Panama, the prize that once seemed so precious no longer is worth the taking.

But while Steinbeck's interest in the relationship between man and the natural environment is apparent in *Cup of Gold*, it is not the focus of the novel. *Cup of Gold* is Henry Morgan's story, a study in the folly of illusion in which Morgan's "exclusive attention to a single purpose [the quest for power] separates him from humanity—the unforgivable sin."[4] For although Morgan achieves his dream of power through violence, it ultimately does him little good. Cut off from his fellow man, Morgan fails in love and happiness and dies a "lumpish man," a fool who wanted something and "was idiot enough to think he could get it" (184).

What is of particular concern here is not so much the specific nature of Morgan's quest (to become the most renowned privateer on the high seas) nor even Steinbeck's conclusions about the illusive folly of power as such (though this theme appears in several of Steinbeck's novels), but rather the reasons which account for Morgan's distorted vision.

Henry Morgan is no ordinary individual. As a child in Wales, his eyes "looked out beyond the walls and saw unbodied things" (4). And when Henry's mother implores her husband to prevent their son from going to sea, Robert Morgan explains that Henry must go. Old Robert knows that

this son of ours will be a great man, because—well—because he is not very intelligent. He can see only one desire at a time. I said he tested his dreams; he will murder every dream with the implacable arrows of his will. This boy will win to every goal of his aiming; for he can realize no thought, no reason, but his own. (12)

It is Morgan's solipsistic world-view, his inability to see the whole which, ironically, will enable him to realize his dreams but will make those dreams worthless. As the young Henry learns from Merlin, the strange mystic seer (the first of several in Steinbeck's fiction), he who seeks material greatness can do so only if he remains a child.

All the world's great have been little boys who wanted the moon; running and climbing, they sometimes caught a firefly. But if one grow to a man's mind, that mind must see that it cannot have the moon and would not want it if it could—and so, it catches no fireflies. (19)

Henry tells Merlin that he must go to the Indies in order to be "whole," since "I am cut in half and only one part of me here. The other piece is over the sea, calling and calling me to come and be whole. I love Cambria, and I will come back when I am whole again" (19). But the whole Henry seeks is not ecological or relational; it is the self-directed dream of wealth and empire that results in temporal power but little lasting happiness. And so Henry becomes "a babbler, a speaker of sweet considered words, and rather clumsy about it" (144). He is a "great" man, but a great fool who "touched all things and watched them pale and shrivel at this touch. And he was lonely" (93).

Morgan's twisted vision resembles that of James Flower, the weak-willed Barbados planter for whom Morgan serves his period of indenture. Both men are failures, and just as Morgan's quest for wholeness fails because of his distorted vision, Flower's "whole life [which] had been a hunger for ideas" (54) is of no value since "his learning formed no design of the whole. He had learned without absorbing, remembered without assimilating. His mind was a sad mass of unrelated facts and theories. . . . James Flower, who had tried to be a creator, became a quiet, kindly little gentleman, somewhat ineffectual and very inefficient" (56). In short, neither the drive for power nor the abstract yearning for ideas is of any consequence unless accompanied by a relational and inclusive understanding.

What is particularly interesting about *Cup of Gold* is Steinbeck's attempt to show that the only plausible alternative to "greatness" is mediocrity. When, for example, Morgan asks Merlin if he ever wanted the moon, Merlin responds that he did, but failing, found a new gift in failure.

I wanted it. Above all desires I wanted it. I reached for it and then— then I grew to be a man, and a failure. But there is this gift for the failure; folk know he has failed, and they are sorry and kindly and gentle. He has the whole world with him; a bridge of contact with his own people; the cloth of mediocrity. (19)

After Morgan takes Panama, he is told by La Santa Roja, the legendary but very sensual woman who served as a symbol for Morgan's quest, "You will take no more cups of gold. . . . You will turn no more vain dreams into unsatisfactory conquests. I am sorry for you, Captain Morgan. . . . All men who break the bars of mediocrity commit frightful sins. I shall pray for you to the Holy Virgin, and She will intercede for you at the throne of Heaven" (162).

Clearly then, while Steinbeck concludes that the solipsistic pursuit of power lacks meaning or purpose, he poses no meaningful alternatives. Midway in the novel, Henry's father visits Merlin and tells him of his son's "success." Merlin comments that Henry must still be a little boy who wants the moon and wonders how long he can stave off manhood. Then, in a passage which anticipates Steinbeck's successful use of the man-animal metaphor in his greatest novels, Merlin asks,

Robert, have you seen those great black ants which are born with wings? They fly a day or two, then drop their wings and fall upon the ground to crawl for all their lives. I wonder when your son will drop his wings. Is it not strange, Robert, how, among men, this crawling is revered—how children tear at their wings, so they may indulge in this magnificent crawling? (108–109)

And yet nowhere in *Cup of Gold* is this "crawling" magnificent at all. Merlin recalls how when "my bitten wings dropped; I was a man and did not want the moon. And when I tried to sing again, my voice had grown husky like a drover's voice . . ." (109) And Robert, who admits that "my youth went out of me sticking to coins" (109), remains jealous of his son who, he insists, "tests his dreams," while "I—God help me!—am afraid to" (12). Finally, Coeur de Gris, Morgan's lieutenant, knows that the quest to conquer Panama will end in a hollow victory, but he wants nothing more for himself than to be a good swordsman and lover, and he really has little identity in the novel apart from his insight into Morgan's frayed dreams.

Cup of Gold is a weak novel for several reasons. But perhaps its greatest failure is Steinbeck's unsuccessful search for options to Morgan's drive for power. What the novelist seems to be doing in *Cup of Gold* is to present in his tale of Morgan an account of the corrupting forces of greed and, through Merlin, Robert Morgan, and Coeur de Gris, to seek out alternative paths of human behavior. We do learn from them that the kind of greatness which results from acquisitive self-interest alienates man from nature and humanity (in short, from an understanding of "the whole"), but their suggestion of the "magnificence of mediocrity" clearly reveals the undeveloped state of the author's world-view.

It is fruitless to speculate how *Cup of Gold* might have differed had the novelist known Ed Ricketts while writing it. All one can say is that *Cup of Gold* fails largely because of its thematic incompleteness, a tendency in Steinbeck's writing which disappeared after his friendship with Ricketts began.

In Steinbeck's second novel, *To a God Unknown* (1933), the impact of the marine biologist's ideas on the novelist's fiction becomes apparent for the first time. And a careful examination of the facts concerning the composition of *To a God Unknown* suggests that by 1932 Steinbeck was already vitally interested in Ricketts' world-view—so much so, in fact, that he altered the entire thematic structure in revised versions of this philosophically crucial novel in accordance with the kind of thinking he and Ricketts were doing.

With the exception of *East of Eden*, no other of Steinbeck's novels was in progress as long as *To a God Unknown* or underwent such extensive reworking. Steinbeck wrote that he "had been making notes for it for about five years,"[5] and there were two earlier versions in addition to the published novel. The first, entitled "The Green Lady" and rejected by several publishers, "had for its protagonist a character who fell in love with a forest, somehow identified with his daughter, and who killed himself by walking sacrificially into that forest while it was ablaze."[6] When a second version, called "To an Unknown God" (1931) likewise failed to find a publisher, Steinbeck wrote his agents that " 'To an Unknown God' should have been a play. It was conceived as a play and thought of and talked of as such for several years. . . . It is out of proportion because it was thought of as two books. I should like to write it again."[7]

There is much more to the story of the composition of this important novel which has heretofore escaped critical attention. Most significantly, "The Green Lady" was not originally a novel, but an unfinished play, written not by Steinbeck, but by his friend Webster F. Street. "In 1927," notes Street, "I was working on a three-act play entitled 'The Green Lady' about a large family that lived in Mendocino County. I couldn't make the Second Act work, so I gave the manuscript to John and told him to do anything he wanted with it" (WFS-RA, 3/26/70). Apparently Steinbeck wanted to collaborate with Street on a novel, but Street did not feel competent and told Steinbeck as much, instructing him to do with "The Green Lady" whatever seemed best. Street did convince Steinbeck to travel with him to Mendocino County; Steinbeck drew much of the material for the plot of his novel from a famous drought in the Big Sur town of Jolon, but the setting of *To a God Unknown* owes much to the lush countryside around the northern California town of Laytonville which Street and Steinbeck visited together.

Street wrote three drafts for the first act of "The Green Lady," "one marked cryptically 'First Draft-Perhaps,' some incomplete copy marked 'Second Draft,' and a third draft consisting of twenty-five pages" (WFS-RA, 4/24/70). There is also a character sketch of Andy Wane and his daugher Susie, the protagonists in Street's play, and some revision notes which were "based to some extent on conversations with John after he had read the character sketch, the second and third drafts of the play, and my notes concerning the general construction of the third act" (WFS-RA, 4/24/70).

What is extant of "The Green Lady" is, in Street's words, a "bulky and jumbled dialogue which runs off in all directions," and which, in retrospect, convinced its author that "I know damn well I had not the slightest inkling of how things would come out" (WFS-RA, 6/30/70). And yet there are things in Street's fragments that made their way into Steinbeck's novel, a fact which Street notes Steinbeck acknowledged "in the inscription on the copy of this book which he gave to me" (WFS-RA, 3/26/70).

Most obviously, the protagonist of "The Green Lady" bears the same last name as the leading character in Steinbeck's novel.[8] Moreover, most of the action in Street's play (as in *To a God Unknown*) takes place on a ranch in the hill country of rural California. Street's Andy Wane is a man in love with a forest near his ranch which he loves as one loves a beautiful woman. When Wane's daughter, Susie, asks about her father's strange fascination for the forest, her mother replies that Andy loves the whole forest, "not trees only, but the whole thing—shrubs an' bushes an' cricks and grass—the whole thing. That's what it is. It ain't only trees—it's ever'thin', I guess. It's a person—a woman."[9] One need only recall how Joseph Wayne is "half-drugged and overwhelmed" by the "curious femaleness" of the forest of Our Lady in *To a God Unknown* to note a striking parallel between the two works.

The plot in Street's play focuses on Andy's strange identification of the forest with his daughter and his selfish refusal to allow Susie to leave the ranch to return to college. Andy regards her as a girl with "an unexplainable wisdom about things, an uncanny power of grasping significances,"[10] and he becomes so intent on keeping her at home that he refuses to sell some timber to get the money necessary for Susie to complete her education. The curtain falls on the first act as a distraught Andy learns that his range is on fire while listening to his angry daughter declare her intention to leave home despite her father's wishes. On the basis of Street's revision notes, we can conclude that Act Two was to reveal that with his forest burned, "Andy has lost the Green Lady and has taken Susie instead." "The last scene in this act must be one in which Andy expresses his true feeling, which is that his feelings toward his daughter are paternal and protective, but selfish."[11] In the last act, Andy was to die in the burning forest. "Andy dies," Street notes, "and sees only green trees."[12]

There are some troublesome hints of incest in the plot of "The Green Lady" which are not easily explained away, despite Street's insistence that Andy's love for his daughter is based upon his identification of her with his burning forest. Street recalls wrestling with this problem unsuccessfully while writing the play, and perhaps for this reason, Steinbeck wisely left the father-daughter relationship out of his novel. Steinbeck wrote his agents in 1932 that he was doing the book over and that it had "a good many characters scraped off."[13]

By 1932 Steinbeck had culled out everything he felt was of value in "The Green Lady," to which he was adding a complex philosophical structure which accounts for the book's importance to serious students of Steinbeck's fiction. It was also at about this time that his friendship with Ricketts began to flourish (they had not met when Steinbeck and Street were working on "The Green

Lady"), and it thus remains to examine Steinbeck's novel to see if and how Ricketts' ideas helped transform Street's fragments into a cohesive, philosophically important piece of work.

To the casual reader, *To a God Unknown* must seem Steinbeck's strangest novel. The plot is highly unconventional, and Steinbeck's hero, unlike most of his leading characters, is most unusual. Upon closer inspection, however, it becomes clear that Steinbeck had no intention of making *To a God Unknown* any more a conventional novel than "The Green Lady" had been a conventional play. When Steinbeck's first effort at revising Street's play was rejected, primarily because of the obscurity of its plot, he told his agents that he would rewrite it, but would not do what his publishers wanted most. "Whether my idea of excellence coincides with editors' ideas remains to be seen. Certainly I shall make no effort to 'popularize' the story."[14] Even after writing the final draft of *To a God Unknown*, Steinbeck was skeptical as to its market value. "It will probably be a hard book to sell. Its characters are not 'home folks.' They make no more attempt at being human than the characters in the *Iliad*. Boileau insisted that only gods, kings and heroes are worth writing about. I firmly believe that."[15] The key words here are *popularize* and *gods*—for Steinbeck could not popularize a story primarily concerned with a symbolic delineation of his developing world-view, and he could not create a believable flesh and blood hero out of a character who is more than flesh and blood.

Philosophy aside, there are descriptive passages in *To a God Unknown* which can please almost every reader. But though the novel is significant as Steinbeck's first successful attempt to evoke and sustain images of life in rural western America, its chief importance lies in Steinbeck's deification of nature and his attempt to create a visionary hero of godlike stature whose perceptions of "the deep thing" enable him to redeem the land and to preserve the natural order.

To a God Unknown begins in rural Vermont just after the turn of the twentieth century; the leading character, Joseph Wayne, is leaving his father's barren rock farm in search of a new and more prosperous life in the coastal valleys of California. Once there,

From Men to Gods

Joseph acquires an acreage in the Valley of Nuestra Sonora (Our Lady), a narrow strip of land bordered on the east by a strange forest (also named Our Lady) and on the west by the coastal mountain range. After Joseph builds his new home and establishes his farm, he writes his brothers in Vermont and urges them to join him as soon as possible. Joseph's brothers agree, and within a short time four families are living on the land originally developed by Joseph.

From the outset, Joseph is intrigued by the density of growth in the nearby forest of Our Lady. He senses "a curious femaleness about the interlacing boughs and twigs, about the long green cavern cut by the river through the trees and the brilliant underbrush."[16] And he sees in the "endless green halls and aisles and alcoves" meanings "as obscure and promising as the symbols of an ancient religion" (4).

Early in the novel, Joseph takes his eldest brother, Thomas, to the mysterious forest, and riding through an open glade, they come upon a moss-covered rock which is "an edifice something like an altar that had melted down and run over itself" (29). Joseph instantly realizes its religious significance: "This is holy—and this is old. This is ancient—and holy" (30). Turning to Thomas, whose fear of the rock prompts him to urge Joseph to return home, Joseph says, "Don't be afraid, Tom. There's something strong and sweet and good in there. There's something like food in there, and like cool water. We'll forget it now, Tom. Only maybe sometime when we have need, we'll go back again—and be fed" (30). Already Joseph has encountered the mysterious presence beyond the protected pale of the civilized boundary. His crossing the threshold is the first step into what Joseph Campbell calls "the sacred zone of the universal source." "The adventure of the hero," writes Campbell, "is always and everywhere a passage beyond the veil of the known into the unknown. . . . yet for anyone with competence and courage [like Joseph], the danger fades."[17]

The mysterious altar of nature is also a symbol of fertility, an image which is reinforced by the presence of the bull standing beside the stream which flows from the rock, whose lashing tail and "long black swinging scrotum, which hung nearly to his knees" (29), deeply impress Joseph with nature's life-giving powers. Nature's abundant fertility is, above all, the primary cause of Joseph's enchantment with the natural life of the Valley of Nuestra Sonora. Realizing that a whole nature must be a fertile nature, Joseph comes to regard his own role in the valley as the protector of the growth of natural things around him.

All things about him, the soil, the cattle and the people were fertile, and Joseph was the source, the root of their fertility; his was the motivating lust. He willed that all things about him must grow, grow quickly, conceive and multiply. The hopeless sin was barrenness, a sin intolerable and unforgivable. (22)

Joseph's wife, Elizabeth, shares her husband's feeling for the essential goodness of nature's altar. And, like Joseph, she recognizes that the rock is a symbol of the earth's fertility, a perception undoubtedly heightened by the psychological implications of her own pregnancy: "And then as she gazed at the rock she saw her own child curled head-downward in her womb, and she saw it stir slightly, and felt its movement at the same time" (99).

In actuality, the forest of Our Lady is, for Joseph and eventually for Elizabeth, the symbolic center of life and meaning in the visible world. Although Joseph agrees to marry Elizabeth in a Monterey chapel in a service he regards as "a doddering kind of devil worship" during which strange sounds of "sunless prophecy" are played by the church organist, he does not feel married until his union with Elizabeth is sanctified by holy nature as the couple rides through the forest on their way home to the Wayne ranch.

Yesterday we were married and it was no marriage. This is our marriage—through the pass—entering the passage like sperm and egg that have become a single unit of pregnancy. This is a symbol of the undistorted real. I have a moment in my heart, different in shape, in texture, in duration from any other moment. Why, Elizabeth, this is all marriage that has ever been, contained in our moment. (52)

Indeed, Steinbeck implies that real marriage, a woman's true loss of her virginity and the unfolding of her potential to become a productive member of the species, must be sanctified not in a sterile church, but rather in nature, itself the seat of cosmic fertility.

As Elizabeth frames her life with Joseph, she begins to share her husband's love of nature and particularly his reverence for the strange rock, so that Joseph approvingly remarks that "She's grown so wise" and "Without any study she has learned so many things" (109–110). When a drought comes and threatens to devastate the valley, Elizabeth senses the urgency of the dilemma and flees to the forest of Our Lady after hearing the altar-like rock "calling" her. Symbolically, though unconsciously, she dies on it, an act which Joseph interprets as her absorption into the natural order. "Joseph lifted his head as though he were listening, and then he stroked the rock tenderly. 'Now you are two and you are here. Now I will know where I must come'" (129).

Following Elizabeth's death, Joseph dedicates his entire being to the preservation of the land into which his wife has passed. Gradually, he undergoes a process of self-annihilation as he removes himself to the "universal source" and comes to think of "the rock no longer as a thing separated from him" (158). And when the drought threatens the Wayne ranch, Joseph dispatches his family to a neighboring valley and goes to live beside the rock, which he recognizes as nature's last line of defense against the forces of sterility. "Here is the seed that will stay alive until the rain comes again. This is the heart of the land, and the heart is still beating" (159).

But the seed begins to wither, the heartbeat flutters, and Joseph shatters the knot of his temporal existence by giving himself to save the land. Joseph transcends life itself and, in so doing, fully understands for the first time his relationship to the cosmic order.

"I should have known," he whispered. "I am the rain." And yet he looked dully down the mountains of his body where the hills fell to an abyss. He felt the driving rain, and heard it whipping down, pattering on the ground. He saw his hills grow dark with moisture. Then a lancing pain shot through the heart of the world. "I am the rain. The grass will grow out of me in a little while." (179)

Joseph, as a part of the whole, sacrifices himself to ensure the harmonious operation of that whole. And the lancing pain which shakes his body a moment before his death is, significantly, a pain which shoots through the "heart of the world" and which immediately alters the course of nature: "And the storm thickened, and covered the world with darkness, and with the rush of waters" (179).

Joseph's self-sacrifice to save the whole makes him, in effect, Steinbeck's Christ of nature.[18] He is, as Rama tells Elizabeth, a godling who is not a man, but who is all men.

I tell you this man is not a man, unless he is all men. The strength, the resistance, the long and stumbling thinking of all men, and all the joy and suffering, too, cancelling each other out and yet remaining in the contents. He is all these, a repository for a little piece of each man's soul, and more than that, a symbol of the earth's soul. (66)

So Joseph, the "symbol of the earth's soul," returns to the earth and, with a single sacrificial act, he saves the entire Valley of Nuestra Sonora.

Much of the story in *To a God Unknown* centers on a series of tensions between Joseph and his three brothers. The novel's title derives from the *Rigveda* ("Who is He to whom we shall offer our sacrifice"—10:121) and from St. Paul's discovery of the altar to the Unknown God in Athens (Acts 17:23), and its meaning hinges upon the various ways in which the Wayne brothers approach the Unknown God.[19]

Benjy, the youngest of the Wayne brothers, is a man motivated entirely by lust. He spends nearly all of his time drinking and seducing women (often other men's wives), and he seeks no further meaning in life than that which can be gathered from a bottle of whiskey. Benjy dies early in the novel, stabbed by Joseph's friend Juanito, who has apprehended him making love to his wife. Actually, Steinbeck rather likes Benjy. He "was a happy man, and he brought happiness and pain to everyone who knew him. He lied, he stole a little, cheated, broke his word and imposed upon kindnesses; and everyone loved Benjy and excused and guarded him" (21). But Benjy's understanding is misdirected and imcomplete, and since the novel is Steinbeck's statement of the manner in which life should be envisioned, Benjy's vision, being the most superficial, must end first.

From Men to Gods

In contrast with the amoral Benjy, who lives only for the flesh, the overly pious Burton lives almost entirely in the spirit. While Benjy defies all sexual restraints, the nonsensual Burton even avoids having relations with his wife.

Burton had embraced his wife four times. He had two children. Celibacy was a natural state for him. Burton was never well. His cheeks were drawn and lean, and his eyes hungry for a pleasure he did not expect this side of heaven. In a way it gratified him that his health was bad, for it proved that God thought of him enough to make him suffer. (20)

Burton is a typical Steinbeck evangelical Christian whose zeal in pursuing the ascetic side of religion inhibits his understanding of life's meaning. One of the basic elements of Steinbeck's worldview is that nature, emblematic of universal plenitude, is intensely fecund. It is precisely this fertility, so vital to Joseph, that Burton considers vulgar and unclean. Hence, when Joseph tells his brother that more than anything else, "I want the land to swarm with life. Everywhere I want things growing up," Burton angrily replies, "You need prayer more than anything. Come to me when you can pray" (23).

In what amounts to a comment on Burton's distaste for nature's fertility, Steinbeck notes in a passage he wrote for *The Log from the Sea of Cortez*, that those who regard reproduction as vulgar are necessarily blind to the "wonder at the structure of life."

If the reader of this book is "genteel," then this is a very vulgar book, because the animals in a tide pool have two major preoccupations: first, survival, and second, reproduction. They reproduce all over the place. (68)

The ascetic Burton is a genteel person; he abhors all of life's processes. When he sees Joseph placing his firstborn into the limbs of an old oak tree (which Joseph calls "the center of the land"), Burton girdles the tree and brings death to nature. Burton leaves the Wayne ranch halfway through the novel and takes his family to live in the evangelist camp at Pacific Grove. Thus, Steinbeck suggests that although Burton, unlike Benjy, will live on, he will never find the meaning of life in his sterile asceticism, by his own choice cut off from an understanding of reality.

Thomas, the eldest of the Wayne clan, finds meaning in a close relationship with animals, and Steinbeck treats him sympathetically and with genuine respect. Thomas is closer to Joseph than are Benjy or Burton, and it is fitting that he remain with Joseph long after his brothers have disappeared, and, at Joseph's request, take the Wayne livestock and Joseph's child out of the Valley of Nuestra Sonora. Unlike Burton, Thomas is intimately involved with natural life on the Wayne ranch.

When Thomas walked through the fields, horses and cows raised their heads from the grass and sniffed the air and moved in toward him. He pulled dogs' ears until they cried with the pain his strong slender fingers induced, and when he stopped, they put their ears up to be pulled again. (19)

But Thomas is also incapable of understanding life as a whole. Thomas is so involved with animals that he has become an animal himself, and his wife, Rama, treats him as one, keeping him clean, fed, and warm.[20] Thomas understands animals perfectly, but he fears the world of men: "he was puzzled and frightened by such things as trade and parties, religious forms and politics. When it was necessary to be present at a gathering of people he effaced himself, said nothing and waited with anxiety for release" (19). Thomas can sense the moment a calf will be born and is always present at a calving in case of trouble, but he cannot even watch a human birth: "I never saw a human baby born. Rama would never let me. I've helped many a cow when she couldn't help herself" (107). Thomas knows and cares for animals and he feels close to Joseph ("Joseph was the only person with whom Thomas felt any relationship" [19]), but he cannot understand his brother's vision.

In addition to the imperfect world-views of Benjy, Burton, and Thomas, Steinbeck presents in Father Angelo, the sternly devout yet tenderly human priest, a further example of an individual's inability to see beyond the restrictive vision of his own interests. Angelo is "a wise and learned man," and is portrayed as sympathetically as any man of religion in Steinbeck's fiction. Nevertheless, his perception is limited by the dogma of his church, so that when Joseph comes to him in desperation and asks him to pray for rain to save the land, the priest reproves an angry Joseph, telling him that the "principal business of God has to do with men . . . and their progress toward heaven, and their punishment in Hell" (172). Joseph realizes the futility of his visit and leaves in disgust.

Despite rebuking Joseph, Father Angelo is visibly "shaken by the force of the man" (172), and he even seems on the borderline of understanding when, in a moment of heresy, he prays for rain which "might come quickly and save the dying land" (172). The priest's obedience to church doctrine prohibits him from openly aiding Joseph, but he does attain a far deeper understanding of Joseph's vision than do Benjy, Burton, or Thomas.

Steinbeck evaluates the main characters in *To a God Unknown* in terms of their perceptions of life, and Joseph is the only figure in the novel whose understanding is limited neither by internal deficiences (Benjy or Thomas) nor by external restraints (Burton and Father Angelo). And though Thomas and Father Angelo admire and try to understand Joseph, neither is equipped to share nor even fully to understand his vision of the cosmic order.

It is here that the impact of Ed Ricketts' thinking on *To a God Unknown* is most evident. For what Joseph really accomplishes in the novel is a successful breaking through to the deep thing. He alone is able to see things in relation to a larger picture, a more deeply significant whole. Unlike his brothers, who are unable to understand transcendence, Joseph breaks through to knowledge beyond the commonplace and, on the basis of that knowledge, acts to save the natural order.

Throughout *To a God Unknown*, Joseph works "to achieve things which are not transient by means of things which are" (the phrase is Ricketts'). During the New Year's festival at the Wayne ranch, he stands apart from an exultant group of dancers and thinks to himself, "We have found something here, all of us. In some way we've come closer to the earth for a moment" (88). Later, he tells Elizabeth that "The dance was timeless . . . a thing eternal, breaking through to vision for a day" (91).

In essence, *To a God Unknown* is Steinbeck's morphology of breaking through, and it is significant that Ricketts considered the novel to be one of the few modern works of literature which concern themselves almost exclusively with a "conscious expression" of "breaking through."[21] Comparing five alternative outlooks on life, four of which are incomplete and unsuccessful, Steinbeck concurs with Ricketts that "many are called but few are chosen."[22] And, by creating as his protagonist a man who is not a man but a godling and a symbol of the earth's soul, Steinbeck shares Ricketts' conviction that "the crust broken through" is not "entirely possible on this earth."[23]

In "The Philosophy of Breaking Through," Ricketts states that "the symbolism of religion, knowledge of the 'deep thing beyond the name,' of 'magic' and of the god within, may ultimately illumine the whole scene."[24] These are precisely the matters which concern Joseph Wayne most, and his strange compulsion to engage in rituals and his susceptibility to religious symbols (the oak tree, the rock, the forest) are best explained as vehicles by which he seeks to arrive at the fountain of life.[25]

It will be remembered that Steinbeck was not at all enamoured with one major implication of Ricketts' doctrine of breaking through—that of the non-teleological approach to life, which the marine biologist believed indispensable to a great emergent. This is certainly true in Steinbeck's political novels, in which purposive, socially directed behavior becomes the chief standard by which the novelist evaluates his characters' actions. But the unusual, almost otherworldly thematic structure of *To a God Unknown* enabled Steinbeck to create a hero whose vision is non-teleological, and while there are goal-oriented considerations which ultimately direct the course of Joseph's actions, he is undoubtedly the most thoroughgoing and accomplished non-teleologist in any Steinbeck novel.

The non-teleological cast of Joseph's thinking surfaces in the way he views events on his ranch with an "understanding-acceptance" which often seems cold and dispassionate (even to Joseph himself). Joseph accepts all things, even the deaths of his wife and brother, as vehicles to an understanding of the whole. After Benjy is stabbed by an irate Juanito, Joseph observes that "Thomas and Burton are allowed their likes and dislikes, only I am cut off." and "I can have no knowledge of any good or bad. Even a pure true feeling of the difference between pleasure and pain is denied me. All things are one, and all a part of me" (61–62).

Later, when Elizabeth slips on the rock and breaks her neck, Joseph "wanted to cry out at once in personal pain before he was cut off and unable to feel sorrow or resentment" (129). But the only words which come from his lips are " 'Good Bye, Elizabeth,' and before the words were completely out he was cut off and aloof" (129). Joseph tells Rama that while he was shaken by Elizabeth's death, his main concern is with "all the things that die," since "there is only one birth and one death" (134). And Rama, recognizing this unique quality in Joseph's thinking, tells him that although he may have loved his wife, "you didn't know her as a person. You never have known a person. You aren't aware of persons, Joseph; only people. You can't see units, Joseph, only the whole." (134).

And yet , while Joseph views people and events non-teleologically, his sacrificial quest to end the drought which has come upon the land demands a deep sense of mission. The novel's mythic structure, in which Steinbeck combines images from Christ's Passion with the myths and rituals of a Frazerian dying king, carries with it a commitment to purpose which extends far beyond a recognition of cosmic unity. Without making a detailed analysis of the mythic structure of *To a God Unknown*, I should like to point out that Joseph is the archetypal hero who, in breaking through the bounding sphere of the cosmos to the ubiquitous world-navel, dedicates and ultimately sacrifices his being to the kingdom of humanity. Joseph places heavy a priori evaluations on things, particularly on the importance of fertility and on the evil of barrenness. Emulating Jesus the guide, the way, and the vision, he does not commit the everyday world to the devil and retire into a heavenly rock-dwelling. Rather, he acts purposively to save the natural order.

Unlike the strange old man at the coast who sacrifices animals simply to achieve a union with nature, Joseph sacrifices himself to save nature. Joseph does try the old man's methods, but for him they are ineffective. " 'His secret was for him' he said. 'It won't work for me' " (178). Salvation as well as union defines Joseph's role in the novel, and his act represents the supreme gesture by the savior of nature whose death re-establishes life.

Steinbeck, though intrigued by Ricketts' doctrine of non-teleological thinking, moves beyond that concept in *To a God Unknown* and completes the nuclear unit of the monomyth. Even at this early stage in his career, before his concern with current social and political problems became dominant, Steinbeck conclusively affirmed that the hero must break through by shifting the spiritual center of his gravity from the pale of self to a zone unknown, but he must simultaneously use the knowledge of his vision to benefit the natural order.

It is little wonder that *To a God Unknown* was five years in the writing. In enlarging Webster Street's loosely wrought play about a man's love for a forest into a comprehensive morphology of breaking through, supported by an elaborate structure of myth and symbol, Steinbeck delineated the thematic base of much of his future writing. *To a God Unknown* is not a flawless novel. There is some bad writing, and Steinbeck occasionally lapses into sentimentality which results from the teleological role of savior he assigns a hero whose character is basically non-teleological. At the same time, it greatly surpasses *Cup of Gold* in characterization, invention, and sweep of imagination, and it clearly indicates that Steinbeck's association with Ricketts was already bearing consequential fruit.

The Pastures
of Pleasure
and Illusion

T*o a God Unknown* contains an explicit statement of Steinbeck's holistic world-view and his clear affirmation of the hero's responsibility to work to benefit the natural order. And yet, the philosophically important novel was a commercial failure. It simply did not sell, a fact Steinbeck anticipated before publication when he wrote that his characters would not be "home folks." "The detailed accounts of the lives of clerks don't interest me much," Steinbeck wrote to his agents in 1933, "unless, of course, the clerk breaks into heroism."[1]

Steinbeck's third novel, *The Pastures of Heaven*, appeared in 1932 (Steinbeck began *To a God Unknown* earlier, but it was published after *The Pastures of Heaven*) and is a book about clerks who don't break into heroism. What seems to interest Steinbeck in this novel is not only the lives of clerks as clerks, but the reasons why most clerks don't become heroes—why, in fact, so few men become Joseph Waynes. Indeed, *The Pastures of Heaven* is proof that Steinbeck's statement about clerks must be qualified. He believed that man's attempt to break through to an understanding of the whole is among the noblest of human endeavors, but simultaneously, he recognized that there are few individuals who can free themselves from their external projections or their internal dilemmas to strive toward a great emergent. In short, Steinbeck recognized that the final responsibility of the novelist is not only to save himself for Time, but to be true to his own time, and thus he felt compelled to examine the lives of everyday people in the everyday world. In so doing, he developed his craft as a master storyteller.

In marked contrast with *To a God Unknown*, the writing in *The Pastures of Heaven* is simple, objective, often moving, and the characterization is superb.[2] But what really gives Steinbeck's novel its particularly human flavor (in contrast with the otherworldly tone of *To a God Unknown*) is the novelist's use of real locations, people, and incidents as the basis for his work. Steinbeck wrote his agents in 1931 that "There is, about twelve miles from Monterey, a valley in the hills called Corral de Tierra. Because I am using its people I have named it Las Pasturas del Cielo."[3]

It has generally been assumed that Steinbeck learned about the Corral de Tierra from stories his mother told of when she, like Molly Morgan in the book, taught school in rural communities.[4] But Jack Calvin affirms that it was not Steinbeck's mother, but a longtime resident of Corral de Tierra, Beth Ingels, who inspired *The Pastures of Heaven*. Calvin even suggests that Steinbeck "stole" Miss Ingels' stories, and he recalls "at my house in Carmel, she spent a long evening telling me in bitter detail about John's 'treachery'" (JC/RA, 3/27/70).

Steinbeck's achievement in structure and characterization in *The Pastures of Heaven* has been acknowledged. What has been overlooked, however, is the book's thematic importance, which consists of the novelist's concrete effort to apply the principles of his view of man and the world (gradually developing through his reading and his conversations with Ricketts) to the temporal problems faced by people Steinbeck knew and heard about. *The Pastures of Heaven* is an ironic novel (as the title suggests), and the irony consists in Steinbeck's conclusion in each of the ten separate yet interrelated stories that while man's highest function on earth may be to break through to an understanding of the cosmic whole and to act to benefit the social order, his fallibility often undermines his potential greatness.

It was noted earlier that while Smuts and Briffault observed that man's mind is, in Smuts' words, "the crowning phase" of the "process of Holism," they concurred that his same mind can also be "a great Disturber." Briffault states, for example, that "the evolution of rational thought" has been "a contest against nonrational thought, against the accumulated force of custom-thought and power-thought."[5]

Appropriately, in *Cup of Gold* Steinbeck presents in Henry Morgan a character whose power-thought turns him into a lumpish fop, and in *To a God Unknown*, he portrays, through the characters of Burton Wayne and Father Angelo, evidence of how obedience to patterns of custom-thought inhibits man's ability to perceive reality.

The episodic structure of *The Pastures of Heaven*, with a complete story every ten or twenty pages, forced Steinbeck to concentrate on a single character in each story and enabled him to work out further his ideas about how man's mind can turn the pastures of heaven into the pastures of deception. The real irony is that while Las Pasturas del Cielo offers its inhabitants the tools to create for themselves full, rich lives, they are unable to make productive use of these gifts, either because they lack the intelligence or because they are so wrapped in illusions and self-deceptions that they are blind to the vaguest sort of reality.

By definition, the impact of Ed Ricketts on *The Pastures of Heaven* is largely indirect. For one thing, Steinbeck was just coming to understand Ricketts' complicated world-view when the book was written. More importantly, the people Steinbeck heard about from Beth Ingels simply could not attain a Ricketts-like vision. Indeed, there is perhaps less of Ed Ricketts in this and in Steinbeck's next novel (*Tortilla Flat*) than in any of the novelist's prewar works after *Cup of Gold*, simply because Steinbeck is dealing in these books with characters whose fallibility, not vision, is the central fact of their existence.

In the tale of Shark Wicks, for example, Steinbeck tells of a simple peach farmer who deludes himself into believing he is a wealthy man and an expert in all things financial. "Gradually his reputation for good judgment and foresight became so great that no man in the Pastures of Heaven thought of buying a bond or a piece of land or even a horse without first consulting Shark Wicks."[6] When Shark's neighbors learn of his poverty, he is so demoralized that he feels he must leave the Pastures of Heaven in order to continue living.

There is an optimistic note in the conclusion to this story, despite the dispatch with which Steinbeck chronicles Shark's demise as a wizard of high finance. For unlike the other characters in the valley whose futures seem promiseless, Shark insists that someday he will succeed. " 'I'll go soon,' he cried. 'I'll go just as soon as I can sell the ranch. Then I'll get in a few licks. I'll get my chance then. I'll show people what I am' " (35). Shark's renewed vigor results from the strength conferred on him by his once-docile wife, Katherine, who grows in strength as her husband weakens.

As Katherine stood in the doorway, a feeling she had never experienced crept into her. She did a thing she had never contemplated in her life. A warm genius moved in her. Katherine sat down on the edge of the bed and with a sure hand, took Shark's head on her lap. This was instinct, and the same sure, strong instinct set her hand to stroking Shark's forehead. (33)

Hearing Shark admit, "I haven't any money. I never had any. . . . Every bit of it was lies. I made it all up," Katherine breaks through to a recognition of her husband's needs.

Katherine stroked his head gently and the great genius continued to grow in her. She felt larger than the world. The whole world lay in her lap and she comforted it. . . .
Suddenly the genius in Katherine became power and the power gushed in her body and flooded her. In a moment she knew what she was and what she could do. She was exultantly happy and very beautiful. (34)

She tells Shark, you've "had no chance" so "we'll sell this ranch and go away from here. Then you'll get the chance you never had," and she dispels her husband's misery and forces him to face life squarely for the first time.

Katherine Wicks is the only character in *The Pastures of Heaven* who, during a moment of crisis, finds herself living what Ricketts called the whole picture. And it is significant that in "The Philosophy of Breaking Through," after Ricketts described the woman in Pacific Grove who broke through to understanding after her husband had fallen off a roof and fractured his skull, he remarked that "there is a similar picture in Steinbeck's 'Pastures of Heaven': the woman who comforted her husband after the loss of his financial-illusion."[7]

In the story of Helen Van Deventer and her mad daughter, Hilda, Steinbeck presents a woman who came to the Pastures of Heaven seeking a fresh start in life and who almost succeeds. Before coming to the Pastures, Helen Van Deventer lived with her husband, Hubert, an amateur hunter-sportsman, in San Francisco. When Hubert dies, Helen, grief-stricken and desiring to remove her mad daughter from the pressures of city life, takes Hilda to live in a section of the Pastures of Heaven significantly named Christmas Valley. Settled in her new home, Helen finds that the peacefulness of the fertile valley begins to diminish the grief of her personal tragedies.

Helen glanced out of her window. The dusk was coming down from the hilltops. Already a few bats looped nervously about. The quail were calling to one another as they went to water, and far down the canyon the cows were lowing on their way in toward the milking sheds. A change was stealing over Helen. She was filled with a new sense of peace; she felt protected and clothed against the tragedies which had beset her for so long. She stretched her arms outward and backward, and sighed comfortably. (59–60)

Gradually, Helen's newly found peace is threatened by the memory of Hubert. Bursting into the room containing Hubert's trophies, which she had hitherto kept locked and curtained, Helen throws open the wide windows, and almost instantly the life outside invades the musty domain of death. In a statement recalling Joseph Wayne's love of a fertile nature in *To a God Unknown*,

Helen gasps: "It's just infested with life . . . It's just bursting with life" (63).

Ironically, Helen's ecstasy is short-lived, since when Hilda runs away, Helen takes the matter of her daughter's madness into her own hands and shoots Hilda with one of Hubert's rifles. Ultimately, then, Helen merely transfers her guilt feelings from the painful memories of her husband's death to the horror surrounding her daughter's murder, and her overall change in the story is negligible.[8] Christmas Valley offers Helen Van Deventer rebirth, a chance for a new life, but Helen, though initially receptive, is unable to accept it.

Whereas nature's serenity attracts Helen Van Deventer, it totally converts Junius Maltby, his son, Robbie, and his hired hand, Jakob Stutz. Once a big-city accountant, Junius moved to the Pastures of Heaven seeking solitude, and he spent idyllic days sitting lazily beside a stream with his son and hired man. As with Joseph Wayne and Helen Van Deventer, it is nature's fertility that particularly commands Junius' attention. " 'But I see,' said Junius. 'You mean that water is the seed of life. Of the three elements water is the sperm, earth and womb and sunshine the mould of growth' " (72). As time passed, Junius became "gloriously happy. His life was as unreal, as romantic and as unimportant as his thinking. He was content to sit in the sun and to dangle his feet in the stream" (72).

Junius fashions himself into a non-teleological thinker. Like Joseph Wayne, he admits to not knowing people and things close to him very well.

I didn't know my wife nor the children very well, I guess. Perhaps they were too near to me. It's a strange thing, this *knowing*. It is nothing but an awareness of details. There are long visioned minds and short visioned. I've never been able to see things that are close to me. (69)

But similarities between Joseph and Junius end here, for whereas Joseph utilizes the non-teleological approach to life as a means of apprehending "the whole," Junius' thinking is trivial. And whereas Steinbeck deifies Joseph, he gently ridicules Junius. Other families in the valley "bought Fords and radios, put in electricity and went twice a week to the moving pictures in Monterey and Salinas," but "Junius degenerated and became a ragged savage" (72). And when Junius and Jacob Stutz philosophize to Robbie about such matters as goodness and evil, right and wrong, and about water being "the seed of life," Steinbeck observes that "thus they taught him nonsense" (72).

Junius is really a weak man, unable to cope with even the simple society of the Pastures of Heaven. When neighbors present his ragged son with a gift package of clothing, Junius breaks down because he cannot cope with their response to Robbie's poverty. Almost immediately, he leaves the valley and takes his son to San Francisco to seek work as an accountant.

Shark Wicks, Helen Van Deventer, and Junius Maltby are by no means the only characters in *The Pastures of Heaven* whose delusions result in their defeat and unhappiness. The lonely Pat Humbert, who "did not often think of people as individuals, but rather as antidotes for the poison of his loneliness" (143), works furiously to remodel his house under the illusory assumption that the attractive daughter of a neighbor will marry him once the remodeling is complete. When he learns that Mae Munroe is engaged to someone else, he is shattered. The good-natured but simple-minded Lopez sisters delude themselves into believing they can establish a successful restaurant if they will only give themselves to customers who buy three of their enchiladas. When the local sheriff breaks up their prospering enterprise, the saddened sisters leave the valley and go to San Francisco to become hard-core prostitutes. And Molly Morgan, the sensitive schoolteacher, flees Las Pasturas del Cielo when she irrationally supposes that an itinerant workman may be her father who deserted her during her childhood.

Human error is also the dominant motif in the Whiteside saga, the longest section in *The Pastures of Heaven*, which chronicles the history of a family through three generations, from humble beginnings to an era of substantial opulence and finally to utter ruin. This story also reflects Steinbeck's burgeoning interest in agrarianism by which he expanded his reverence for nature from the occult forest of Our Lady to the cultivated cotton fields of the San Joaquin.

Richard Whiteside came to California in 1850 in search of gold. Soon, however, Richard became aware that "the earth gives only one crop of gold," and "when that crop is divided among a thousand tenants, it feeds no one for very long. This is bad husbandry" (154). Richard realized that farming was better husbandry, and he rode into the Pastures of Heaven where, like Joseph Wayne in the Valley of Nuestra Sonora, he looked for and received a sign from nature, "an omen to remember and tell the children" that this was the perfect place for his farm.

Richard built his home and established a prosperous farm in Las Pasturas del Cielo which would endure through the ages. "I shall build a structure so strong that neither I nor my descendants will be able to move" (156).

He became a farmer and family man, and under his care the house took shape and "the farm prospered, the sheep and cows increased, and in the garden, bachelor buttons, sweet william, carnations, hollyhocks settled down to a yearly blooming" (158). He had one son, John, who inherited the Whiteside home and farm after Richard's death. Unlike his father, John received no mystical signs from nature, and his interest in farming dwindled to an occasional reading of Virgil's *Georgics* or Varro on farming. "John Whiteside felt his interest in the land lapsing" (171). The sitting room, not the farm, "was the centre of his existence" (168).

He was ambitionless, his farm not only made him a good living, but paid enough so he could hire men to work it for him. He wanted nothing beyond what he had or could easily procure. (170)

John's son, Bill, was even less interested in the joys of farming than his father. John neglected the farm, but Bill turned it into an opportunity for speculative gain which even John could not understand. As Bill grew older, he found farming increasingly unattractive; eventually he moved into Monterey, where he bought a partnership in the Ford dealership. So the Whiteside dynasty came tumbling down. From Richard's love of the land, a love sanctified by nature, to John's armchair interest in farming, and finally to Bill's total abdication of the Whiteside tradition, the agrarian way of life was undermined. The symbolic fire that destroys the Whiteside house at the story's conclusion is final testimony to the defeat of the agrarian ideal. The Whiteside house burns to the ground, and an automobile agency quickly springs up to cover the land with a plague of machines.

The Whiteside farm was founded on Richard Whiteside's oracular vision manifest in a flurry of oak leaves blown in the valley which spoke to Richard "as if from Zeus' oak at Dodona."[9] But the myth is inverted as the founder's descendants fail. Contrary forces are at work. And when John and Bill Whiteside continue to ignore the oracular imperative, they ensure the destruction of the valley's greatest home and farm.

The Pastures of Heaven is also the first work in which Steinbeck's interest in subnormal humanity is evident. In the touching if slightly sentimental tale of Tularecito, the strange cretin whose innocent but destructive actions lead to his confinement in the state mental hospital, Steinbeck presents a character whose subhuman mentality inevitably ensures his inability to survive. Viewed in perspective, however, the strange Tularecito, who claims to be a descendant of a race of earth-people who live below the ground, is really no less successful than most of the other characters in the novel. All are blighted by their fallibility, and the only measurable difference between them is that Tularecito's failure is organic and inevitable whereas theirs are occasioned by their illusions and are thus biologically unnecessary.

Much has been made of the Munroe curse, which provides the unifying link between the various episodes in *The Pastures of Heaven* in that an act by one of the members of the Munroe family is directly or indirectly responsible for the disasters that plague the other valley residents.[10] In view of the character portrayal in the novel, it seems clear that Steinbeck views the curse as a force which ensures the disastrous effects of illusions and self-deceptions as well as the naturalistic doom of the subnormal cretin. Steinbeck seems to say that the characters in *The Pastures of Heaven* fail because they have not "become accustomed to the tragic miracle of consciousness"; they are dreamers whose fantasies are annihilated by the hard facts of reality.

In a very real sense, though, *The Pastures of Heaven* shows Steinbeck's compassion for the plight of ordinary people. Despite revealing their tendencies toward self-delusion, the novelist never openly condemns them or lapses into tirades of abstract moralism. Even the Munroes, who represent the kind of insensitive mediocrity Steinbeck detested,[11] are treated with understanding and civility. Steinbeck was too sensitive an individual and too accomplished an artist to attack people for failing to become heroes, despite the high premium he placed on heroism as he defined it in *To a God Unknown.*

Moreover, in those episodes in *The Pastures of Heaven* which chronicle the demise of inherently decent characters who seek only immunity from the vicious world of material self-interest, one senses a certain ambivalence on Steinbeck's part. He seems to regret that Junius and Robbie Maltby must return to San Francisco; he abhors the traditional codes of sexual morality which drive Rosa and Maria Lopez to prostitution, and he surely laments the fact that civilization cannot tolerate a half-wit like Tularecito who wants nothing more than to look for gnomes under the earth.

Actually, Tularecito is a prototype for the more interesting character of Lennie Small, whose dream of "a little house an' a couple of acres" with "rabbits" is wrecked by the hard facts of existence in Steinbeck's celebrated play-novelette, *Of Mice and Men* (1937). Begun shortly after Steinbeck finished the final draft of *In Dubious Battle, Of Mice and Men* reflects the novelist's awakening political consciousness and, in particular, his interest in agrarian reform as a viable solution to the American economic crisis of the 1930's. But Steinbeck's real subject in *Of Mice and Men* is the frail nature of primeval innocence, a theme which emerges through the author's compassionate treatment of the futile attempt by Lennie and his partner, George Milton, to translate an impossible dream into reality.

George is an itinerant farm worker who, although resourceful, has his freedom limited by his assumed guardianship over Lennie, a retarded child in an oversized man's body. George, who needs Lennie as much as Lennie needs him, struggles to protect Lennie from harming anyone. But the big man's hands, which are not under the control of an adult human conscience, accidentally kill the provocative wife of the boss's son at a ranch where they are employed. Instantly, the pair's happiness is doomed. When Lennie flees the scene of the accident, George overtakes his companion and shoots him in an act of kindness. The story ends with George's accepting the moral implications of his actions as he accompanies Slim, the jerkline skinner, to a local tavern for a drink.

It is possible to read the grim events in *Of Mice and Men* either as tragedy or as dark comedy (the "triumph of the indomitable will [George's] to survive").[12] Both approaches contain a substantial degree of truth, but one must not allow either to obscure Steinbeck's uniquely delicate handling of his fictional materials, which accounts for the book's particular excellence. For Steinbeck neither blames nor accuses in *Of Mice and Men*; he simply tells a story about the way in which "the best laid schemes o' mice an' men gang aft a'gley." The original title of the novelette was "Something That Happened," and while one can read it as simple tragedy, as social protest (against the mistreatment of rootless and helpless farm workers), or on a symbolic level in which the characters can be extended to any symbolic dimension, *Of Mice and Men* is simultaneously a non-teleological tale which simply says, "This is what happened." Viewed this way, "Steinbeck's achievement in *Of Mice and Men* is even more impressive: the hardest task a writer can set himself is to tell the story of 'something that happened' without explaining 'why'—and make it convincing and moving."[13]

With regard to the impact of Ricketts' thinking on Steinbeck's fiction, it would be very convenient if we could say that *Of Mice and Men* is a fictionalized version of Ricketts' doctrine of non-teleological thinking, and that Steinbeck shows he is not concerned with what "could be" or "should be" but only with what "is." But to do so would be to deny the novelist's insistence on the importance of man's voluntary acceptance of his responsibilities, which is based on his belief that man owes something to man. Viewed in perspective, what Steinbeck seems to be doing in *Of Mice and Men* is using Ricketts' ideas about non-teleological thinking not as theme, but as fictional method. He tells the story of Lennie and George from a nonblaming point of view, but never does he suggest the unimportance of the teleological considerations symbolized by Lennie's dream.

Actually, Steinbeck's method in *Of Mice and Men* emerges through the consciousness of Slim, the jerkline skinner and "prince of the ranch," who moves "with a majesty only achieved by royalty and master craftsmen."[14] It is Slim, a character whose "ear heard more than was said to him" and whose "slow speech had overtones not of thought, but of understanding beyond thought" (37), who understands George and Lennie's land hunger but who also knows that the dream must fail. And it is Slim who affirms the need for direct, purposive action by George after Lennie kills Curley's wife. "You hadda George. I swear you hadda" (119).

Significantly, Ricketts observed in one section of his essay on non-teleological thinking that the term *non-teleological* encompassed more than thinking: "*Modus operandi* might be better—a method of handling data of any sort."[15] Indeed, says Ricketts, "the value of it [non-teleological thinking] as a tool in increased understanding cannot be denied."[16] This is the one aspect of Ricketts' notion that particularly appealed to Steinbeck; the use of the non-teleological approach as a means of handling the data of fiction. And Steinbeck is generally at his best when he writes in this manner; when, in such works as *In Dubious Battle*, "Johnny Bear," "The Snake," and "The Leader of the People," but most particularly in *Of Mice and Men*, he achieves what T. K. Whipple calls "the middle distance" in which he places his characters "not too close nor too far away" so that "we can see their performances with greatest clarity and fullness."[17]

As an undergraduate at Stanford, Steinbeck learned from his creative writing teacher, Edith Ronald Mirrielees, that the story-writer's "medium is the spot light, not the search light."[18] And it is the spotlight which illumines the characters and events in *Of Mice and Men*. Unlike *To a God Unknown*, in which Steinbeck's tendency to philosophize seriously mars what is otherwise a highly important piece of writing, the novelist's use of Ricketts' *modus operandi* in *Of Mice and Men* enabled him to avoid pretentious philosophizing while recording his beliefs. And in telling his story about the fractured dreams of mice and men with a precision and lucidity unexcelled in any of his other works, Steinbeck testifies to the fact that Ed Ricketts not only helped teach him how to "live into life," but that he also had a hand in helping him record his observations of it.

Apparently thinking of such characters as Lennie Small and Tularecito, as well as Junius and Robbie Maltby, many critics have commented on Steinbeck's love for his half-wits, children, dockside loafers, and his *paisanos*. Some have even suggested that Steinbeck's admirable characters are all essentially alike; when taken out of pleasant, noncompetitive surroundings and placed in economic situations where they are squeezed rather than tolerated, Steinbeck's dropouts and half-wits become the migrants of *The Grapes of Wrath* or the strikers of *In Dubious Battle*.[19] Steinbeck displays a deep sensitivity toward the ingenuous, guileless individual who draws what he wants from life without involving himself in the petty pursuits which place inhibitions on natural behavior. To assume, however, that Steinbeck's admirable characters are all alike, that only their economic situations change, suggests a serious flaw in thinking, for there are well-defined dissemblances between his vagabonds on the one hand, and his Joseph Waynes and Tom Joads on the other.

In one sense, Steinbeck's simple people, his anti-materialists, serve a single thematic purpose in his fiction, for these free and uninhibited beings act as foils against which the novelist can assess the follies and eccentricities of society. As individual characters, however, Steinbeck's primitives are a diverse group; the only basic quality they share is their native incorruptibility. Most, like Tularecito and Junius Maltby in *The Pastures of Heaven*, Noah Joad in *The Grapes of Wrath*, the *paisanos* in *Tortilla Flat*, Lennie Small in *Of Mice and Men*, and Gitano in *The Red Pony*, live close to nature, and lead decent and certainly tranquil lives as long as they are left undisturbed. Others like Johnny Bear in the short story of the same name, Benjy Wayne in *To a God Unknown*, and Frankie in *Cannery Row* do not live in wholly natural habitats, yet they do share the native simplicity common to Steinbeck's other primitives. Ranging in intelligence from such cretins as Tularecito, Lennie, and Johnny Bear to such intellectually sensitive souls as Junius Maltby, they are alike in their hedonistic, unhurried, and blandly indifferent responses to the acquisitive world around them.

Steinbeck consistently draws his primitives with great warmth and feeling so that they all live and breathe in his fiction. But while he admires their ability to live simply and easily, he realizes their limitations and illustrates how, in the end, they cannot survive in the modern world. And this admission, considering Steinbeck's commitment to a teleological representation of life, hardly qualifies his primitives as ideal men. Of course, Steinbeck never condemns or criticizes from the standpoint of the middle-class American's condescension, which would regard the natural man as quaint but immoral. At the same time, nearly all of Steinbeck's dropouts and primitives are victimized by their own innocence and are undone by an acquisitive society with which they cannot cope. With the sole exception of Noah Joad in *The Grapes of Wrath*, whose destiny is never revealed after he leaves the Joad family in Needles, each either is driven from his leisurely retreat into the fast-paced modern world or is destroyed.

Benjy Wayne is killed by an irate Juanito. George Milton mercifully kills Lennie Small. Johnny Bear, who is a kind of recording device set in operation by a glass of whiskey instead of a nickel, is pummeled by the outraged citizenry of Loma after he divulges a town scandal. Tularecito and a mentally defective boy named Frankie in *Cannery Row* are committed to mental institutions when, in their innocence, they violate the laws of society. And the Lopez sisters and Junius Maltby, though not killed, beaten, or committed to mental asylums, are driven from the Pastures of Heaven into the larger asylum of society.

Shortly after he finished the story of Junius Maltby, Steinbeck's interest in the dropout became so pronounced that he wrote an entire novel to examine what he called "the strong but different philosophic-moral system of these people."[20] Outside of the fact that the characters in *Tortilla Flat* (1935) share life-styles that Ricketts would (and did) find attractive, if not intellectually gratifying, there is very little Ricketts in this book. The Mallorian substructure and the *paisano* stories which were told to the novelist by schoolteacher Susan Gregory (or inspired by the escapades of a famous Monterey dropout, a picaresque remittance man on whom the character of Pilon is based) indicate that Steinbeck conceived *Tortilla Flat* independently of Ricketts. Nevertheless, many of the things Steinbeck says about the *paisano* ethic in *Tortilla Flat* are important for a fuller understanding of the intellectual side of the Steinbeck-Ricketts relationship.

Tortilla Flat has been bitterly criticized because of Steinbeck's alleged idealization of the indolent *paisanos*—his supposed rejection of "Man as Citizen" and "Man as Revolutionary" in favor of "Man as Animal."[21] But a more precise reading of the novel reveals that Steinbeck worked hard to avoid apotheosizing primitive humanity; there is no indication anywhere in *Tortilla Flat* that Steinbeck glorifies *paisano* life in utopian terms. To be sure, he admires the *paisanos'* virtues, particularly their ability to avoid the predatory drives of commercial society. He certainly regards them as natural individuals who, like Junius Maltby, take the time to enjoy life.

Life passed smoothly on for Pilon and Pablo. In the morning when the sun was up clear of the pine trees, when the blue bay rippled and sparkled below them, they arose slowly and thoughtfully from their beds.

It is a time of quiet joy, the sunny morning. When the glittery dew is on the mallow weeds, each leaf holds a jewel which is beautiful if not valuable. This is no time for hurry or for bustle.[22]

Yet, in his examination into the *paisano* ethic, Steinbeck raises penetrating questions about the lasting value of this kind of existence, the answers to which indisputably prove his rejection of their life-style as an avenue to solving the pressing problems of modern life.

Steinbeck begins *Tortilla Flat* by stating that his narrative has a tragicomic theme which is revealed through an examination of how Danny's court, like Arthur's Round Table, forms, flourishes, and dies.

For Danny's house was not unlike the Round Table, and Danny's friends were not unlike the knights of it. And this is the story of how that group came into being, of how it flourished and grew to be an organization beautiful and wise. This story deals with the adventuring of Danny's friends, with the good they did, with their thoughts and their endeavors. In the end, this story tells how the talisman was lost and how the group disintegrated. (1)

Steinbeck liked the *paisanos* and the Mallorian knights too much to condemn either group, but by subtly showing how the actual lives of the men on Tortilla Flat—like the careers of Arthur's knights—run contrary to their legendary lives, Steinbeck is able to elevate Danny and the boys while simultaneously presenting reasons why "the talisman was lost and how the group disintegrated."

In fact, while on the surface *Tortilla Flat* tells of the *paisanos'* riotous escape from civilization and social conventions, it simultaneously tells how this escape results in their defeat as individuals. After Danny and his followers move into the old house which Danny has inherited, they live for several months in glorious indolence. But as the novel progresses, the *paisanos* develop their own "intricate pattern for satisfying wants through socially acceptable channels," and they become as "civilized" as the society they have rejected.[23] Danny becomes listless and he begins to feel his life is losing its meaning.

Where is Danny? Lonely as smoke on a clear cold night, he drifts through Monterey in the evening. To the post office he goes, to the station, to the pool rooms on Alvarado Street, to the wharf where the black water mourns among the piles. What is it, Danny? What makes you feel this way? Danny didn't know. There was an ache in his heart like the farewell to a dear woman; there was vague sorrow in him like the despair of autumn. (165)

The Pastures of Pleasure and Illusion

Danny looks into the "deep, deep water," and he realizes the futility of his existence: "Do you know, Danny, how the wine of your life is pouring into the fruit jars of the gods? Do you see the procession of your days in the oily water among the piles? He remained motionless, staring down" (165). But Danny refuses to surrender passively, and he turns his back on the deep black water, whispering "to the gods a promise or a defiance" (167). He revives himself for one last *paisano* fling, one last party which, says Steinbeck, some dry historian may see as symbolizing the fact that "a dying organism is often observed to be capable of extraordinary endurance and strength" (168).

Steinbeck's depiction of the *paisanos'* last party as the act of a dying organism suggests, of course, the novelist's interest in the organismal conception of life. Indeed, *Tortilla Flat* contains the fullest statement of Steinbeck's organismic world-view to date. "That story of Danny and of Danny's friends and of Danny's house" is the "story of how these three became one thing, so that in Tortilla Flat if you speak of Danny's house . . . you are understood to mean a unit of which the parts are men, from which came sweetness and joy, philanthropy and, in the end, a mystic sorrow" (1).

When things go well for the *paisanos*, the group flourishes and grows "to be an organization beautiful and wise." But when Danny loses his zest for life, the health of the organism deteriorates. Then, at Danny's party, the organism rallies for one last time so that "The whole happy soul of Tortilla Flat tore itself from restraint and arose into the air, one ecstatic unit" (167–168).

Danny dies during the party, and his friends realize that the old life has been irrevocably lost: "Thus it must be, O wise friends of Danny. The cord that bound you together is cut. The magnet that drew you has lost its virtue" (178). Appropriately, they allow the house, once the organismal center of their carefree, leisurely existence, to burn to the ground "in one last glorious, hopeless assault on the gods" (178). And as the flames consume the remains, the *paisanos* go their separate ways; they all realize that their experiment in indolent living has failed to shield them permanently from

111

the reality of the outside world. "Danny's friends still stood look-ing at the smoking ruin. They looked at one another strangely, and then back to the burned house. And after a while they turned and walked away slowly, and no two walked together" (179). Steinbeck likes Danny and his friends, but he recognizes the feeble basis of the talisman of escape. In short, Steinbeck implies in *Tortilla Flat* that there is no inherent strength in the "philosophic-moral system" of the *paisano* organism, nothing that will enable man to achieve and retain more than the most superficial of goals.

The episodic nature of *The Pastures of Heaven* and *Tortilla Flat* suggests Steinbeck's affinity for the short story form during this early stage in his writing career. His first wife, Carol, recalls that Steinbeck reluctantly heeded her advice to tie the various *paisano* stories together, though, she points out, the idea of using the Arthurian round table as the unifying device in the novel was Steinbeck's own (CS/RA, 9/1/71). Actually, salability, the opportunity to try out a variety of techniques, and a feeling of competence based on his instruction from Edith Mirrieless were responsible for Steinbeck's continuing interest in this genre, which peaked with the publication of his only formal volume of short stories, *The Long Valley*, in 1938.

Many of the stories in *The Long Valley* were written long before 1938. *North American Review* printed parts one and two of *The Red Pony* in 1933, "The Murder" and "The Raid" in 1934, and "The White Quail" in 1935. Later in the same year, "The Snake" appeared in the Monterey *Beacon*. Another story, "Saint Katy the Virgin," is mentioned in Steinbeck's correspondence as early as 1932.

It is pointless to seek a unifying thematic thread connecting the eleven stories in *The Long Valley* beyond the fact that all but "Saint Katy the Virgin" are vignettes of life in California's Salinas Valley. Two ("The Raid" and "Breakfast") are preparatory sketches for Steinbeck's most ambitious works, *In Dubious Battle* and *The Grapes of Wrath*. In writing the stories for *The Long Valley*, Steinbeck followed the advice of his mentor at Stanford, who taught him that "a story to be effective had to convey something from writer to reader, and the power of its offering was the measure of its excellence."[24] Thus, what really unifies *The Long Valley* is Steinbeck's ability to communicate to his readers a sense of life lived beyond the confines of their own existence. In each of the sketches in this volume, Steinbeck knew what he wanted to convey and, almost without exception, he does it with power and eloquence.

Several of the stories in *The Long Valley* contain items of particular interest for Steinbeck's world-view and its relation to the person and ideas of Ed Ricketts. Specifically, *The Long Valley* contains Steinbeck's first fictionalized portrait of Ed Ricketts. In "The Snake," Dr. Phillips is a thinly camouflaged Ricketts who lives and works at a "little commercial laboratory on the cannery street of Monterey."[25] And the story of the strange woman who fulfills a morbid psychological need by watching Phillips feed a white rat to a rattlesnake is based, according to Steinbeck, on an incident that actually happened.[26] Webster Street says he was in Ricketts' lab when the incident occurred, and recalls that Ricketts had

two big rattlesnakes in a cage in the lab, and he had a bunch of white rats running around. He went in and got a white rat and put it in the cage. A girl who was one of the dancers from a local vaudeville team that was passing through Monterey was there. She was just fascinated by the whole thing, but she didn't say a word. The little rat went in there, and the snake waited and pierced the rat behind the ear. The snake pulled back and the fang caught and pulled him over to one side. The rat ran around for a little while, unconscious of the fact that he was mortally wounded, and he finally died and the snake took him. The girl never said a word, and when it was over, she just got up and left and we never saw her again.[27]

Street notes that Steinbeck added to the story a series of sexual implications, "which you could not help doing if you had seen that girl," and he observes that the episode reveals Steinbeck's "ability to relate an incident from real life to something he created."[28]

Although Steinbeck's focus in "The Snake" is psychological and appropriately devoted to the strange ophidian female, his characterization of Dr. Phillips is handled sensitively and is essentially honest. Phillips is an intelligent, competent scientist with a deep interest in the life of the tide pools. And Steinbeck's description of Phillips' aversion to "people who made sport of natural processes" (80), since he himself was "not a sportsman but a biologist" who "could kill a thousand animals for knowledge, but not an insect for pleasure" (80–81), is consistent with the novelist's portrayal of Ricketts' professional integrity in "About Ed Ricketts."

More importantly, in his depiction of Phillips' ambivalent reaction to the events in his laboratory, Steinbeck portrays what he regarded as the highly paradoxical nature of Ricketts' thinking. As a biologist, Phillips is repelled by the woman and vows that if she returns, "I will go out and leave her alone . . . I won't see the damned thing again" (86). As a man, however, he is fascinated by the woman and searches for a coherent explanation of what has happened in his lab. Phillips "looked for her when he walked about the town. Several times he ran after some tall woman thinking it might be she. But he never saw her again— ever" (86).

As mentioned before, "The Leader of the People" and "The Vigilante" contain brief and synthesized portraits of differing types of phalanxes (destructive in "The Vigilante," self-aggrandizing in "The Leader of the People"), a fact which is particularly significant since Steinbeck completed these tales at about the same time he was working on his first major political work, *In Dubious Battle*.[29] In "Johnny Bear," a story which, according to Webster Street, grew from observations by Street and Steinbeck of the behavior of a deaf mute in a tavern outside Castroville, California (WFS-RA, 3/26/70), the bar in Steinbeck's narrative is described organismically by a local resident as "the mind of Loma": "It's our newspaper, our theatre and our club."[30]

In a vein resembling Katherine Wicks' breaking through to glory in *The Pastures of Heaven*, two stories in *The Long Valley* deal with "ordinary" people who break through to vision in situations of extreme physical and emotional stress. In "Flight," which in terms of style and structure, may be the most skillfully told tale in the volume, Pepé Torres' growth from adolescence to maturity is chronicled during the course of his flight through the forests and desert mountains south of Carmel. At the outset a "toy-baby" (his mother calls him "a peanut" and "a foolish chicken") content to pass the time throwing his big black knife into redwood posts, Pepé is sent to town by his mother to get a supply of medicine. When, in an irrational moment, he throws his knife into a stranger in a Monterey bar, "he has bid into a man's game and must play it to the end."[31] It is in his moment of crisis, Steinbeck seems to say, that a boy must break through to manhood. As Mrs. Torres explains to Pepé's younger brother, Emilio, "A boy gets to be a man when a man is needed. Remember this thing. I have known boys forty years old because there was no need for a man."[32]

In "The Raid," the neophyte organizer Dick (an early version of Jim in *In Dubious Battle*) achieves manhood when he and his companion, Root, are confronted and savagely beaten by a group of angry vigilantes. The inexperienced Dick, who formerly needed encouragement from the more experienced Root, suddenly becomes a man of purpose whose vision soars beyond the strictures of party ideology. Christ-like, he shouts at his assailants: "Can't you see? . . . It's for all of you. We're doing it for you. All of it. You don't know what you're doing!"[33] And as the final assault comes, Root "caught a moment's glimpse of Dick's face smiling a tight, hard smile" (107).

Ironically, when Dick recovers from his wounds and has time to think about what has happened, he hardens and becomes a doctrinaire apostle of communism. But in his moment of crisis, when the very essence of his being is at stake, Dick breaks through to the larger vision and, in his plea to his assailants, achieves what amounts to a messianic expression.

In sharp contrast with Pepé and Dick, who break through to understanding, the protagonists in three other stories in *The Long Valley* are plagued by illusions and made miserable by personal frustrations so that they closely resemble most of the characters in *The Pastures of Heaven*. "The Harness" is very similar in theme to the story of Pat Humbert. And in "The Chrysanthemums" and "The White Quail," Steinbeck carefully analyzes two women who

115

are so shrouded in self-deceptions that the natural environment in which they live provides no genuine solace for their tormented souls.

Elisa Allen's feeling of identity with nature in "The Chrysanthemums" is undoubtedly sincere, but underlying it are deep-seated sexual frustrations which are the result of her inadequate relationship with her insensitive husband. And when, by the end of the story, Elisa finally realizes her sense of sexual loss which her work in the garden has merely cloaked by a simple transference of sexual energy, she is a defeated individual, "crying weakly—like an old woman."[34] Similarly, Peter Randall's feeling of fulfillment after harvesting a bountiful crop of sweet peas, accomplished only after the death of his cautious and domineering wife, is destroyed when he realizes that his wife still has him in harness. " 'She didn't die dead,' he said thickly. 'She won't let me do things. She's worried me all year about those peas.' "[35]

In "The White Quail," Steinbeck creates a character so engulfed in private fantasies that her perception of nature is a mirror of her own distorted mind. Steinbeck conducts a penetrating exploration of Mary Teller's personality in order to demonstrate that although nature is an inherent source of strength and understanding to the receptive, uncluttered mind, when viewed through the eyes of a disjointed, neurotic individual, it becomes a mere extension of that person's neurosis.

Mary Teller is a superb portrait of a woman whose narcissism is matched only by her all-consuming fear of change and her lack of sexual vigor. Interested only in her trim, changeless, and artificial garden, Mary identifies with the garden and especially with the strange white quail that comes to drink from its artificial ponds.

"Why," Mary cried to herself, "she's like me!" A powerful ecstasy quivered in her body. "She's like the essence of me, an essence boiled down to utter purity. . . ."

The white quail stretched a wing backward and smoothed down the feathers with her beak. "This is the me that was everything beautiful. This is the center of me, my heart."[36]

Identification with nature is nothing new for Steinbeck's characters, particularly when one recalls Joseph Wayne's oneness with the land and the rain in *To a God Unknown*. But Mary, unlike Joseph, creates a false and unnatural nature ("proper fushias and cinerarias" and "potted oak trees"), and her perception of the center of nature and herself (the white quail) is freakish and self-oriented, and is as unreal as Joseph's vision is unencumbered by personal projections and is thus authentic.

Mary regards the mysterious and vitally alive aspects of nature, those with which Joseph seeks communion, as "the enemy," as the "rough and tangled and unkempt" world she cannot face. She identifies her fears with those of her quail being pursued by a cat, and she fears consumption by nature just as Joseph welcomes it. Hence, Mary tells her husband, "Can't you see dear? The cat was after me. That's why I want to poison it" (41). Whereas Joseph sacrifices himself to complete his identification with nature and restore the natural processes, Mary Teller desecrates nature in order to save a distorted vision of herself.

Taken as a whole, Steinbeck's fiction from *Cup of Gold* to *The Long Valley* represents the first segment of his long career in which the novelist developed his craft as a literary stylist while working toward a manageable explanation of various forms of human behavior. The presence of Ed Ricketts' ideas about breaking through and non-teleological thinking achieve substantial expression only in *To a God Unknown*, and Ricketts' person is clearly represented only in "The Snake."

The absence of Ricketts' person and ideas in Steinbeck's other early fiction can be attributed to several causes. As has been pointed out, *The Pastures of Heaven* and *Tortilla Flat* were based on stories told to Steinbeck by other people; *Cup of Gold* was written before Steinbeck and Ricketts met; and sections of *The Long Valley* were based on incidents Steinbeck witnessed or heard about independently of Ricketts. More importantly, with the notable exception of *To a God Unknown*, Steinbeck's main concern in his early California fiction is with simple, ordinary people who have enough trouble just surviving, let alone breaking through to cosmic vision. Undoubtedly, one of the things Steinbeck learned from the commercial failure of *To a God Unknown* was that his world-view was of little literary value unless applied to flesh and blood characters in concrete, human situations. And listening to the stories of his friends and looking around him in the towns and valleys of coastal California, Steinbeck neither heard about nor saw many Joseph Waynes. Rather he found lonely, dissatisfied farmers (Shark Wicks, Pat Humbert, and Peter Randall), illusion-ridden and/or sexually frustrated women (Elisa Allen, Mary Teller, Helen Van Deventer, and Molly Morgan), half-wits (Tularecito and Johnny Bear), and leisure-loving vagabonds (Junius Maltby and the *paisanos* of Tortilla Flat). Steinbeck examined the lives and ordeals of these individuals, and in the process displayed a unique sensitivity toward aspects of the human condition.

Yet, despite Steinbeck's sympathy for his primitives, the novelist's belief that man is capable of more than mere survival, based largely on his holistic world-view gleaned through conversations with Ricketts and through his reading of organismic biology and philosophy, remained constant. Steinbeck's problem was that by writing stories like nearly all of those in *The Pastures of Heaven* and *The Long Valley*, he was simply not giving his characters much of a chance. Indeed, what Steinbeck sacrificed by using the short story format and by concentrating on various types of deviant behavior was a fictional vehicle sufficiently expansive to work out his developing metaphysic.

But even as he was still at work on some of the stories for *The Long Valley*, the deteriorating political and economic situation in California's agricultural valleys, which Steinbeck witnessed with growing horror, provided the category and the imperative. Put simply, California hurt John Steinbeck into his greatest fiction, and in the process, into a comprehensive statement of his and Ricketts' philosophies of life.

In the
Troubled Garden

*U*ntil the publication of *In Dubious Battle* in 1936 and *The Grapes of Wrath* in 1939, many readers had typed Steinbeck a first-rate teller of charming if inconsequential tales. But the novelist's dramatic shift into the arena of political controversy forced a critical reappraisal of his achievements. Many people who earlier dismissed him as a light novelist now shrugged him off as a propagandist, but more astute readers praised *In Dubious Battle* and *The Grapes of Wrath* as highly accomplished works by a writer gifted with a unique ability to deal artistically with the complex political turmoil in California's agricultural valleys.

What is of particular concern here is the fact that Steinbeck's political observations in *In Dubious Battle* and *The Grapes of Wrath* grew largely from his interest in Ed Ricketts' ideas. In these works, which in many ways are the brightest gems in his entire canon, Steinbeck portrays, analyzes, and ultimately accepts or rejects Ricketts' fundamental precepts about man and the world. And the value of the novelist's social message lies in his ability to construct a viable political vision out of the Rickettsian cosmic whole. Neither *In Dubious Battle* nor *The Grapes of Wrath* are proletarian novels in the customary sense of the term; rather, they

119

are serious studies of complicated social and political issues. The real strength of both books is Steinbeck's ability to avoid blind political partisanship, a feat which is attributable in large measure to the heavy impact of Ricketts' ideas.

Completed early in 1935, *In Dubious Battle* deals with the efforts of Mac, a seasoned Party worker, and Jim Nolan, a new and inexperienced Party member, to organize an insurrection among the migratory farm workers in the apple orchards of California's Torgas Valley. Mac and Jim win the respect of the migrant leaders, and with their help and the invaluable assistance of Doc Burton, a concerned observer but not a Party member, they organize the farmers and establish their own camp on the land of a small grower named Anderson. When vigilantes burn Anderson's barn and destroy his crop, the outraged farmer evicts the migrants and the strike appears doomed. Finally, Jim is ambushed and killed, and the novel concludes with Mac dragging Jim's bloody corpse in front of the strikers' camp in a final effort to preserve their will to resist.

In Dubious Battle is a brutal novel, a fact which Steinbeck acknowledged when he told his agents, "I guess it is a brutal book, more brutal because there is no author's moral point of view."[1] Because Steinbeck wanted to portray varying political opinions while avoiding a direct statement of political partisanship, the novelist assumes an objective stance: everything is learned from the actions and conversations of his characters. What emerges is a hardheaded analysis of two inadequate world-views which are unable to deal effectively with the explosive labor problems in California's agricultural valleys. *In Dubious Battle* is Steinbeck's statement of the wrong perspectives, the wrong approaches, and the wrong solutions. The battle is brutal because it is of dubious value, and the futile methods practiced by the leading characters reflect hopelessly muddled social visions and thoroughly unrealistic political objectives.

Steinbeck's "cold prose" and his dramatic presentation of character are especially effective in his depiction of Mac and Jim. For though we are prone to identify with their struggle against the ruthless agri-businessmen of the Torgas Valley, Steinbeck demonstrates that Mac and Jim are obdurate men to whom the human virtues of friendship, tolerance, and brotherly love are platitudes to be voiced when politically expedient, but are actually impediments to the real business of fighting a revolution. Throughout *In Dubious Battle*, the seasoned Party worker, Mac, tells the neophyte, Jim, "Don't go liking people, Jim. We can't waste time liking people."[2] And, when Mac rallies the migrants with Jim's blood-stained body, knowing that the men will be butchered if they resort to violence, it becomes clear that he is manipulating the people rather than helping them overcome their oppressors.[3] Mac and Jim express outrage at the social injustice they see around them, but their real objectives have little to do with helping the exploited apple pickers. Instead they talk of vague "ends" and "great things" which are never clearly defined and are somehow just out of reach.

It is fitting that Steinbeck chose as his epigraph for the novel a passage from Satan's address to Beelezebub in Book I of *Paradise Lost*, for this passage accurately describes Mac and Jim's relentlessly Satanic drive to organize the distressed migrants—even to the extent that on a proletarian level, one reacts to the toughening Jim Nolan in much the same way one reacts to the titanic Satan. As Jim grows progressively more hard-boiled, he becomes an anti-Christ who recognizes that "the field be lost," but nevertheless arms the "innumerable force of Spirits" with the "courage never to submit or yield." Mac and Jim merit a degree of admiration for their refusal to surrender on the plains of Torgas (here, the fact that the Torgas is an apple valley becomes particularly significant), but their Satanic election of violence and their lack of genuine concern for their constituency negate the value of their cause.

One of the means by which Steinbeck rejects all sympathy for Mac and Jim is through his use of the character of Doc Burton as an objective chorus who challenges their inhumanity and their willingness to compromise the strikers' cause by resorting to violence.[4] When, for instance, Mac and Jim insist that "all great things have violent beginnings," Doc Burton comments that "in my little experience the end is never any different in its nature from the means. Damn it, Jim, you can only build a violent thing with violence" (230). It is Burton who identifies Jim as the satanic anti-Christ. Telling him, "you've got something in your eyes, Jim, something religious" which he identifies as "the vision of Heaven" (181, 182), Burton pinpoints Jim's revolutionary fervor as "religious ecstasy" by "partakers of the blood of the Lamb" (231) who lead a group of men who would be God.

Because Burton confronts Mac and Jim and questions their motives and ends, and because on occasion he does seem to speak for Steinbeck, one might assume that the doctor is the novelist's hero in *In Dubious Battle*. But if, contrary to his stated intention that the book contain no author's moral point of view, Steinbeck makes Burton his moral and philosophical spokesman, he violates the self-neutralizing ambivalence by which he maintains a delicate balance between blind political activism and frustrated detachment which is the novel's greatest thematic virtue.

Quite clearly, then, Steinbeck's real accomplishment in *In Dubious Battle* can only be clarified by defining the heretofore misunderstood role of Doc Burton, who is, in fact, modeled directly on Ed Ricketts. For although there are selected instances in the novel in which Burton voices some of Steinbeck's ideas (particularly with respect to his organismic view of life), in the main the novelist uses Burton in order to scrutinize Ricketts' world-view and to analyze the way in which it functions (or fails to function) in a difficult political situation. The result is that while Steinbeck believed that Ricketts' insights could expose the flaws in the closed political system of Mac and Jim's Party, he indicated that Ricketts' world-view, which dismisses any and all analyses of final or efficient causation, is unable to deal with the plight of the politically and economically oppressed. *In Dubious Battle* marks a kind of bottom in Steinbeck's political pessimism. Through Burton he shows that the kind of power which falls into the hands of those who use raw violence is nihilistic and self-defeating. Still, the novelist offers no alternative solutions which might ameliorate the predicament of California's dispossesed agricultural workers.

Burton is certainly a Ricketts-like character. A scientist by training and disposition, he is an introspective man who remains detached from partisan causes in order "to see the whole picture . . . I want to be able to look at the whole thing" (130). Refusing "to put on the blinders of 'good' or 'bad,' and limit my vision" (130), Burton is a non-teleological thinker who accepts what is and strives to understand as much as he can. He calls Mac and Jim "practical men," and he insists that their restrictive, causal approach to life will fail ultimately because of their intolerant refusal to face the whole situation. When, for example, Mac tells Doc that "We've got no time to mess around with high-falutin ideas," Doc responds, "Yes, and so you start your work not knowing your medium. And your ignorance trips you up every time" (133). Indeed, Burton is telling Mac and Jim about what Ricketts felt was the most serious error in teleological thinking.

It considers changes and "cures," what "should be," the presumed bettering of present conditions (often, unfortunately, without achieving more than a most superficial understanding of those conditions). . . . In their intolerant refusal to face things, teleological notions frequently substitute a fierce and sometimes hopeless attempt to change conditions which are assumed to be undesirable in place of the understanding acceptance which would pave the way for a more sensible attempt at change if that still seemed desirable.[5]

And Steinbeck, who learned from Ricketts that action without sight is unsatisfactory, employs the one aspect of Ricketts' doctrine of non-teleological thinking with which he fully agrees to demonstrate the inherent pitfalls of myopic political vision.

At the same time, Steinbeck uses Burton to explain his notion of the group-man to Mac and Jim, an idea, as seen earlier, he developed somewhat independently of Ricketts. And in this one sense, Doc Burton appears less a Ricketts-figure than a mouthpiece for the novelist's social psychology, the basic precepts of which Steinbeck evidently felt needed explicit statement in *In Dubious Battle*. Burton's explanation of the group-man concept is

123

squarely congruent with the novelist's conclusions about the relationship between wholes and their parts which he learned from his study of organismal biology. "A man in a group isn't himself at all," insists Burton, "he's a cell in an organism that isn't like him any more than the cells in your body are like you" (131). Burton believes that the basic unit of life is the organism, and he explains that even Mac might be an effect or an expression of group-man, a newly formed part of a whole established by the process of differentiation aimed at furthering the life of the organism.

You might be an expression of group-man, a cell endowed with a special function, like an eye cell, drawing your force from group-man, and at the same time directing him, like an eye. Your eye both takes orders from and gives orders to your brain. (131)

Convinced that the whole exercises determinative control over its parts, Burton applies the precepts of organismic biology to the study of human movements and concludes: "I want to watch the group, and see what it's like. People have said, 'mobs are crazy, you can't tell what they'll do.' Why don't people look at mobs not as men, but as mobs? A mob nearly always seems to act reasonably, for a mob" (131).

Just as organismic biology is teleological in that the given properties of wholes must be explained in terms of the directive nature of the whole, the detached Burton tells Mac that all social causes are ultimately founded on goals or standards proposed by group-man.

It might be like this, Mac: When group-man wants to move, he makes a standard. 'God wills that we recapture the Holy Land'; or he says, 'We will wipe out social injustice with communism.' But the group doesn't care about the Holy Land, or Democracy, or Communism. (131)

What Burton is really explaining is Steinbeck's phalanx theory. And Steinbeck's statement in the "Argument of Phalanx" that the phalanx forces its units into line under the banners of "Deus Vult," "Break Germany," or "We are ringed with steel" closely parallels Burton's convictions of how group-man rallies its forces under the standards of "making the world safe for democracy" or "recapturing the Holy Land." Similarly, by expressing a strong desire to "watch the group and see what it's like," Burton observes the phalanx,

knowing it is a new individual, not to be confused with the units which compose it . . . if we look back at the things it has done in an attempt to correlate and analyse its habits under various stimuli, we may in time come to know something of the phalanx, of its nature, of its drive and its ends, we may be able to direct its movements where now we have only great numbers of meaningless, unrelated and destructive phenomena.[6]

But despite his insights, Doc Burton is an enigmatic character. He is able to see more deeply than Mac and Jim and can understand Steinbeck's phalanx theory, but his non-teleological refusal to key-into the phalanx and his concomitant aloofness from "the cause" renders him incapable of directing its movements and so enriching the lives of its unit-men.

Jim Nolan does, of course, key-into the strike phalanx. And consistent with Steinbeck's thesis in the "Argument," once he becomes part of the moving phalanx, his nature, his habits, and his desires change. He becomes "capable of prodigies of endurance and thought or of emotion such as would be unthinkable were he acting as individual man."[7] The Party veteran, Mac, recognizes this change in Jim, and tells him, "Jesus, Jim, I can see you changing every day. I know you're right. Cold thought to fight madness, I know all that. God Almightly, Jim, it's not human. I'm scared of you" (249).

The problem with Jim, who claims to be "stronger than anything in the world, because I'm going in a straight line" (249), is that he lacks Burton's larger vision and so fails to use his phalanx experience to fashion his own individuality. Instead, his blind keying-into the "big animal" of the strike is complemented by his growing misconceptions about his own needs and about those of the striking apple pickers. Neither Mac nor Jim recognizes that man, as a thinking, figuring, creative individual, must align himself with the phalanx that will safeguard rather than subvert individualtiy.

Early in *In Dubious Battle*, old Dan, the proud top-faller, points

125

out to Jim that because millions of working stiffs have been exploited beyond all reasonable limits, their need will lead to a new
phalanx movement and to a direct confrontation with the forces
of tyranny.

". . . Only it ain't just in one man. It's like the whole bunch, millions
and millions was one man, and he's been beat and starved, and he's
gettin' that sick feelin' in his guts. . . . I feel it in my skin," he said.
"Ever'place I go it's like water just before it gets to boilin'." (59)

Springing from a deep sense of social injustice extending beyond
the level of human tolerance, the phalanx movement in *In Dubious
Battle* is necessary and inevitable.

Man cannot defy the phalanx without destroying himself. Let a man go
into a wilderness away from all contact with any phalanx and his mind
will dry up, his emotions will leave him, he will become incapable
of ecstasy, his body will grow lean and hungry and at last he will die
of starvation for the food he can only get from participation in the
phalanx.[8]

This is, of course, precisely what happens to Doc Burton, who
denies the phalanx and becomes himself a lonely man, convinced
that because "man has engaged in a blind and fearful struggle out
of a past he can't remember, into a future he can't foresee nor
understand . . . he cannot win over himself" (230). Unable to
provide something of meaning, something of worth to the phalanx
need, Doc becomes "incapable of ecstasy." He tells Mac, "I'm
lonely, I guess. I'm awfully lonely," and he admits, "I'm working
all alone, towards nothing" (232). The doctor becomes so "lean
and hungry" that Mac, who vaguely senses that he may "die of
starvation," suggests to Burton that he needs a woman. And Burton, who knows that his starvation is all too real, tells Mac, "Sometimes you understand too much, Mac. Sometimes—nothing" (233).

Significantly, this exchange occurs during the doctor's final
appearance in the novel, for he soon leaves the strikers' camp to
go to the Anderson ranch and is never seen again. Doc drifts off
into the night, a lonely, defeated man whose defeat is the direct
result of his inability to reconcile his non-teleological world-view
with a teleological program of meaningful social action.

In the Troubled Garden

In demeanor as well as in attitude, the character of Doc Burton is patterned after Ricketts, the first of several Doc's in Steinbeck's fiction modeled on the marine biologist. Steinbeck's description of Burton's large eyes which had "a soft, sad look like those of a bloodhound" (110) resembles his comment about Ricketts' "transcendent sadness" in "About Ed Ricketts." And paralleling his picture of Ricketts in that work is Steinbeck's portrayal of Burton as dedicated to a sensual approach to life, an aspect of his personality which is particularly apparent when he responds to Anderson's pointers with "a sensual pleasure, almost sexual" (132). Mac sums up the difference between himself and Burton when he tells Jim that the pointers are "not dogs to Doc, they're feelings. They're dogs, to me" (132).

Doc's non-teleological approach to life, which dismisses distinctions between good and bad as impediments to clear vision, closely parallels Ricketts' acceptance of all things, even "dirt and grief," as vehicles to a breaking through to the deep thing. And by refusing to do more than understand "the whole thing," Burton (Ricketts) questions the whole idea of direction and purpose, which Steinbeck regarded as "the highest, most complex manifestation of the free, creative, holistic activity of Mind."[9]

In a sense, Burton's relationship with Jim is particularly tragic because Burton is the one character in the novel from whom Jim might learn how to channel his energies constructively.[10] Sadly though, Jim cannot learn from Doc because Doc is an ineffective teacher. Burton is frustrated by his inability to apply the principles of his understanding to concrete purpose. Victimized by his own pessimism, and unable to cope with the ideology of "practical men leading men with stomachs," Doc drifts away into the wilderness. And shortly thereafter, Mac succinctly sums up Burton's tragedy: "Doc was a nice guy, but he didn't get anywhere with his highfalutin ideas. His ideas didn't go anywhere, just around in a circle" (294).

The non-teleological Burton is a dreamer, a mystic and a metaphysician whose desire "to see as much as I can . . . with the means I have" results in his monastic aloofness, which, Steinbeck implies, is as flawed an approach to the daily problems of existence as the political partisanship of Mac and Jim. By contrasting the dehumanizing Party phalanx with the clear-visioned but socially inadequate world-view of Doc Burton, Steinbeck achieves in full measure the self-neutralizing ambivalence which accounts for the novel's structural and thematic greatness.

In order to comprehend fully Steinbeck's efforts to deal critically with Ricketts' person and ideas in *In Dubious Battle*, the novel should be read in conjunction with *The Grapes of Wrath*, for though they are separate works dealing with mutually exclusive characters and situations, *The Grapes of Wrath* is in many ways a sequel to *In Dubious Battle*. If the battle in *In Dubious Battle* is questionable, and if its characters lack perspective or direction, the battle in *The Grapes of Wrath* is completely lucid, and the characters seek and attain intelligible goals. Whereas *In Dubious Battle* ends in self-neutralizing ambivalence, *The Grapes of Wrath* ends in triumph.

This distinction is particularly manifest in the differences between the parallel characters in the two novels. Doc Burton is an incomplete Jim Casy, the clear-visioned preacher in *The Grapes of Wrath*, and if Doc's high-falutin ideas go around in a circle, Casy's doctrines inspire direct social action. Jim Nolan is an unfinished Tom Joad, for although both men are social activists, Tom alone works toward a realistic solution to the migrants' plight.

The Grapes of Wrath is unquestionably Steinbeck's most ambitious as well as his most successful novel; the epic scale on which this story about the struggles of a band of Oklahoma tenant farmers is conceived enables the novelist to say virtually everything he knows and feels about man and the world in which he lives. This is most evident with regard to his basic world-view, for in telling the story of the dispossessed Joads, Steinbeck's belief in an ordered universe in which all living things are inherently related, his reliance upon holistic and organismic thought as a means of perceiving this unity, and his belief that the land is a perpetual source of human enrichment and freedom achieve their finest fictional expression.

It would be a grave error to assume that the person and ideas of

Ed Ricketts serve to organize the entire thematic structure of this gigantic novel. It is, in fact, unlikely that Ricketts assisted Steinbeck at all with the composition of the book. Steinbeck wrote *The Grapes of Wrath* when he was living in Los Gatos, seventy-five miles from Monterey and Ricketts' lab, and Ricketts visited him only occasionally. Actually, Thomas Collins (to whom, along with Carol Steinbeck, the book is dedicated), Eric Thompson and George Hedley (both ministers on leave), and people in the San Francisco Office of the Farm Security Administration provided Steinbeck with much of the material for his novel. Nevertheless, despite the absence of any overt influence, Ricketts' ideas are present in *The Grapes of Wrath*, if in the process Steinbeck transformed and modified them to fit his developing social gospel.

The major portion of Steinbeck's world-view in *The Grapes of Wrath* emerges through the increasing consciousness of Jim Casy, who, like Doc Burton, is loosely patterned on Ricketts. An ex-preacher who abandoned the doctrines of Christianity because of their rigidity and their inability to provide practical solutions to human problems, Casy breaks through to an understanding of the cosmic whole, and through his disciple, Tom Joad, employs the principles of his vision to work to alleviate the plight of the dispossessed migrants. Casy roams the wilderness searching the sun and stars for clues to the meaning of reality. Almost intutitively he arrives at a recognition of the fundamental unity of all life and of his relationship to the world around him which he defines as holy: "I got thinkin' how we was holy when we was one thing, an' mankin' was holy when it was one thing" (110). It is, in fact, Casy's recognition of the inherent relatedness of all men in a unified cosmic whole that he defines as the "Holy Sperit" and which Frederic Carpenter suggests may well be a version of the Emersonian Oversoul floating down to earth in the Oklahoma dust bowl.[11]

maybe that's the Holy Sperit—the human sperit—the whole shebang. Maybe all men got one big soul ever'body's a part of. Now I sat there thinkin' it, an' all of a suddent—I knew it. I knew it so deep down that it was true, and I still know it. (33)

Casy comes to understand what Ricketts claims involves the "Signature of all things," the beauty and unity of all things as vehicles for breaking through. In "A Spiritual Morphology of Poetry," Ricketts states that the poet who portrays this, "the most active, moving, participating message in all western poetry," will recognize the truth of William Blake's conclusion in "Vision of the Daughters of Albion" that "all that lives is holy."[12] And Casy, returned from the wilderness where he learned that he and the hills "wasn't separate no more. We was one thing. An' that one thing was holy" (110), has indeed broken through. Little wonder that Ma Joad, upon first seeing Casy, tells Tom that Casy "looks baptized . . . Got that look they call lookin' through" (127).

Casy reflects that he

heard a fella tell a poem once, an' he says "All that lives is holy." . . . Got to thinkin', an' purty soon it means more than the words says. An' I wouldn't pray for a ol' fella that's dead. He's awright. He got a job to do, but it's all laid out for 'im an' there's on'y one way to do it. But us, we got a job to do, an' they's a thousan' ways, an' we don' know which one to take. An' if I was to pray, it'd be for the folks that don' know which way to turn. (197)

Unlike Burton, whose vision of the whole is never converted into meaningful action, Casy knows that "we got a job to do" and applies the principles of his perceptions to help "the folks that don' know which way to turn." Both men love people and believe in humanity (early in *The Grapes of Wrath*, Casy tells Tom, "I love 'em fit to bust, an' I want to make 'em happy." [32]). But whereas the non-teleological Burton remains detached and ends up "working all alone, toward nothing," the more participating Casy, although at first uncertain about the nature of the task confronting him ("I got the call to lead the people," Casy says early in the novel, "an' no place to lead 'em." [29]), eventually dedicates himself to "go where the folks is goin'."

Gonna lay in the grass, open an' honest with anybody that'll have me. Gonna cuss an' swear an' hear the poetry of folks talkin'. All that's holy, all that's what I didn' understan'. All them things is the good things. (128)

Proceeding from the non-teleological assumption that "no valid a priori ultimate-evaluation can be put on anything,"[13] Casy discards the restrictive moral codes of doctrinal Christianity and concludes that "There ain't no sin and there ain't no virtue. There's just stuff people do. It's all part of the same thing. And some of the things folks do is nice and some ain't nice, but that's as far as any man got a right to say" (32). But as the novel progresses, the non-teleological visionary turns teleological activist. Indeed, so much has been made of Casy's role as a Christ-figure in *The Grapes of Wrath* that this aspect of Casy's character needs no further explanation here, except to point out that Casy's Christ-like demeanor is perfectly consistent with his developing teleological character. By returning from the wilderness, where he learned that isolation dries up the mind and the emotions and renders a man "incapable of ecstasy," Casy becomes a leader in the migrants' fight "for human rights and a twelve-hour day." And his death at the hands of his oppressors (to whom he addresses his symbolic last remark, "You fellas don' know what you're doin'" [527]) serves as a catalyst to unite the Joads with the entire migrant family in the fight for human dignity.

Unlike Burton, whose non-teleological life-style inhibits his ability to act, and unlike Mac and Jim, who are swallowed by a phalanx which maligns rather than aggrandizes individuality, Casy keys-into a phalanx based upon his understanding of the organismal conception of life and his belief in the value of social cooperation. One of the premises the Joads learn from Casy is W. C. Allee's thesis that "the social medium is the condition necessary to the conservation and renewal of life." More than any other character in Steinbeck's fiction, Casy lives the novelist's dualistic philosophy of life, which combines a cosmic idealism with an empirical realism designed to meet contemporary social needs. The teleological end Casy gives his life for is, in fact, a Boodinian panhumanity, a democracy congruent with the principles underlying the unity of all life. Casy insists that if the people work together, they will ultimately prevail, and so he echoes Boodin's dictum that "human beings who can work together in harmony in larger and larger unities will in the end possess the earth. This, I think is the meaning of the saying: 'The meek shall inherit the earth.' "[14]

The phalanx movement Casy comes to understand is the movement from the *I* to the *we*, or what Warren French calls "the education of the heart," which results in a change among the migrants "from their jealously regarding themselves as an isolated and self-important family unit to their regarding themselves as part of a vast human family, that in Casy's words, shares 'one big soul ever'body's a part of.' "[15] At the beginning of *The Grapes of Wrath*, the members of the Joad family are interested only in themselves or at best in the preservation of their family unit. Like Tom Joad, who wants only to "lay his dogs down one at a time," the Joads view their trip to California in terms of personal success. Casy alone sees beyond the moment of the Joads' troubles. It is he who knows that Tom is only one of many migrants who want to lay down their dogs one at a time. It is the non-teleological philosopher turned social reformer who understands what Steinbeck calls the "organization of the unconscious," composed of once self-sufficient farmers who suddenly "obeyed impulses which registered only faintly in their thinking minds" (135). It is Casy who comes to recognize that "need is the stimulus to concept, concept to action"; and it is Casy who intuits and defines the concepts. Indeed, it is Casy who helps the Joads key-into the migrant phalanx. As his perceptions come into focus, Casy observes that all of the folks are "layin' 'em down one at a time," and he tells Tom about the newly-developing phalanx need.

they ain't thinkin' where they're goin', like you says—but they're all layin' 'em down the same direction, jus' the same. An' if ya listen, you'll hear a movin', an' a sneakin', an' a rustlin', an'—an' a res'lessness. They's stuff goin' on that the folks doin' it don't know nothin' about—yet. They's gonna come somepin outa all these folks goin' wes'—outa all their farms lef' lonely. They's gonna come a thing that's gonna change the whole country. (237)

And, at the end of the novel, when Tom strikes out to spread the gospel of reform, he acknowledges that it was Casy who helped him key-into the moving phalanx in which "his nature, his habits and his desires changed."

Guess who I been thinkin' about? Casy! He talked a lot. Used ta bother me. But now I been thinkin' what he said, an' I can remember—all of it. Says one time he went out in the wilderness to find his own soul, an' he foun' he didn' have no soul that was his'n. Says he foun' he jus' got a little piece of a great big soul. Says a wilderness ain't no good, 'cause his little piece of a soul wasn't no good 'less it was with the rest, an' was whole. Funny how I remember. Didn' think I was even listenin'. But I know now a fella ain't no good alone." (570)

Throughout much of *The Grapes of Wrath*, Ma, the strongest of the Joads and "the citadel of the family," regards the pilgrimage to California only in terms of family welfare. Carol Steinbeck calls Ma "pure Briffault" (CS/RA, 9/1/71), in the sense that Ma represents Briffault's thesis in *The Mothers* that "the animal family is a group produced not by the sexual, but by the maternal impulses, not by the father, but by the mother."[16] Ma's "hazel eyes seemed to have experienced all possible tragedy and to have mounted pain and suffering like steps into a high calm and super-human understanding. . . . She seemed to know that if she swayed the family shook, and if she ever really deeply wavered or despaired the family would fall, the family will to function would be gone" (100). At the outset, Ma wants no more than for her family to stick together and for her men to have good jobs, so that "maybe we can get one of them little white houses" (124). She threatens her husband with a jack handle when she feels that the integrity of the family unit is endangered.

All we got is the family unbroke. Like a bunch of cows, when the lobos are ranging, stick all together. I ain't scared while we're all here, all that's alive, but I ain't gonna see us bust up. (231)

Gradually, though, Ma shifts her reference orientation from the family unit to the migrant community as a whole; she accepts Casy's belief in the larger responsibility which extends beyond the family. And she translates this belief into action when, at her unstated suggestion, her daughter gives her own milk to a starving migrant.

133

JOHN STEINBECK and EDWARD F. RICKETTS

Much has been made of the symbolic significance of the indomitable land turtle which moves slowly southwest in *The Grapes of Wrath*. *Tortoise* being colloquial for *phalanx*, it is significant that the chief impediment to the turtle's progress is Tom Joad. And if all of the obstacles the turtle faces represent the hardships the Joads will have to endure on their trek, it is clear that what slows the Joads' movement most is the self- or family-centered orientation of its own members. Tom wants to take the turtle "to my little brother. Kids love turtles" (28). But Casy, who symbolically envisions Tom's later conversion when he will leave to go "off somewheres," knows that "Nobody can't keep a turtle though. They work at it and work at it, and at last one day they get out and away they go—off somewheres" (28). Ironically, Tom laments, "I ain't got no present for the kids . . . Nothin' but this ol' turtle" (34). When the turtle finally escapes and heads southwest again, Tom asks: "Where the hell you s'pose he's goin'? . . . I seen turtles all my life. They're always goin' someplace. They always seem to want to get there" (60). By the novel's conclusion, Tom will know precisely where he and the turtle are going.

By combining a Ricketts-like understanding of the fundamental unity of all life which involves the non-teleological stripping away of the superficial distinctions of good and bad, right and wrong, with a goal-oriented, organismically based gospel of social action, Casy affirms Steinbeck's ringing statement about man's ability to "walk up the stairs of his concepts" and "emerge ahead of his accomplishments." He tells Tom about a fella who rightly concluded that "the on'y thing you got to look at is that ever'time they's a little step fo'ward, she may slip back a little, but she never slips clear back" and "that makes the whole thing right" (525), and so reiterates Steinbeck's most memorable statement about the goal-directed nature of the human animal:

This you may say of man—when theories change and crash, when schools, philosophies, when narrow dark alleys of thought, national, religious, economic, grow and disintegrate, man reaches, stumbles forward, painfully, mistakenly sometimes. Having stepped forward, he may slip back, but only half a step, never the full step back. This you may say and know it and know it. . . . And this you can know—fear the time when Manself will not suffer and die for a concept, for this one quality is the foundation of Manself, and this one quality is man, distinctive in the universe. (204, 205)

The goal-oriented Casy does suffer and die for a concept. He is Steinbeck's greatest hero; the fulfilled Doc Burton, the Ricketts-ian man of vision who, although refusing to assign causes and place blame on people for "doin' what they got to do," converts chaos into cosmos by transforming an understanding of cosmic wholeness into a meaningful program of social and political action.

Little has been said or needs to be said here about Steinbeck's doctrine of agrarian idealism as a viable economic solution to the migrants' dilemma—the notion that being born on the land, work-ing it, and dying on it gives man a sense of self-worth and endows his life with meaning.[17] What must be pointed out here, however, is that Steinbeck carefully fuses his agrarian idealism with the Casy-Ricketts doctrines of social cooperation and the unity of all life. This fusion occurs during Tom's last conversation with Ma, shortly before he leaves the family to spread the gospel of reform. Tom explains his "calling" to Ma, and he concludes, "I been a-wonderin' why we can't do that [unite] all over. . . . All work together for our own thing—all farm our own lan' " (571).

At the beginning of *The Grapes of Wrath*, the frightened ten-ant farmers sit alone in the doorways of their houses, "their hands were busy with sticks and little rocks. The men sat still—thinking—figuring" (7). But with the help of Casy's vision and his Christly self-sacrifice, their needs turn to concepts (unity and agrarian idealism) and concepts turn to action. By the end of the novel, the migrants have keyed-into a moving, self-aggrandizing phalanx, and "the fear went from their faces, and anger took its place. And the women sighed with relief, for they knew it was all right—the break had not come; and the break would never come as long as fear could turn to wrath" (592).

If a gospel of social action programed to relieve the plight of the downtrodden permeates the thematic design of *The Grapes of Wrath*, it overwhelms Steinbeck's next work, the story and accom-panying screenplay for *The Forgotten Village* (1941), which depicts the fight against superstition and disease in rural Mexico. *The Forgotten Village* has already been discussed in regard to Ricketts' "Anti-script." What is of particular concern at this point is why Ricketts should find such great fault with *The Forgotten Village* (the only one of Steinbeck's works with which Ricketts expressed open disapproval) and at the same time applaud *The Grapes of Wrath*, since both contain similar doctrines of social action which are inimical to the marine biologist's world-view. In short, what is the difference between *The Grapes of Wrath* and *The Forgotten Village* which led Ricketts to praise the former without reservation while noting about *The Forgotten Village*, "I don't think it's much good. And I cannot imagine even that the movie from which the scenes and captions are selected is much good" (EFR/AS, 3/7/41).

Many factors are involved. Quite obviously, it is impossible to evaluate a documentary screenplay on the same level with one of the most powerful novels of this century. Long in the writing, *The Grapes of Wrath* is a masterful novel, made remarkable by the author's ability to tell an epic saga while maintaining perfect control over his fictional materials. *The Forgotten Village*, on the other hand, is the result of some hasty writing, for Steinbeck's mind was on *Sea of Cortez* all the time that he was working on the screenplay.[18]

There is also the strong possibility that Ricketts objected to Steinbeck's participation in *The Forgotten Village* project. The pair had just returned from their expedition to the Gulf of California when Steinbeck agreed to return to Mexico to work on the film, and Ricketts would have preferred that the novelist remain in Monterey and complete the narrative while he identified and catalogued the marine specimens they collected on the trip. There is, in fact, evidence that their friendship was strained when Ricketts joined Steinbeck in Mexico for the filming of *The Forgotten Village*. Accompanied by an attractive young woman from Monterey, Ricketts drove Steinbeck's station wagon to Mexico (the car was used in the film, which, by the way, was filmed in the evirons of Patzcuaro), and stayed for a while, "intrigued," as Herb Kline notes, "by the way a director works to get a story onto film" (HK/RA, 2/27/71). But Ricketts, who spent much of his time at the library of the Mexican Academy of Sciences "looking up bibliographic references and abstracting Mexican scientific articles for our forth-coming book [*Sea of Cortez*]" (EFR-R and TL, 6/18/40), felt estranged from the film makers who, Kline recalls, "were following the daily struggle and the joy in our work to get John's story on film" (HK/RA, 2/27/71). "I have seen almost nothing of Jon or Crl." Ricketts wrote to Ritch and Tal Lovejoy.

I am off their list; they are very careful not to invite me over there, especially when they're going to have company, and we have had meals there only a couple of times, and then when Jn Crl are away or scheduled to be away. Such a feeling of coldness and hecticness that I'd prefer not to be around anyway. A new experience for me being the poor cousin. (EFR-R and TL, 6/18/40)

And so there were reasons why Ricketts might react less than enthusiastically to *The Forgotten Village*. But these explanations, while partially satisfying, are not sufficient. Certainly they do not account for Ricketts' decision to write his "Anti-script," in which he takes issue with Steinbeck's central thesis, that marked social change must occur if Mexico is ever to solve its problems of poverty and rural health care.

It is imperative to recognize that Steinbeck had been interested in the subject of rural health for some time. In *Their Blood Is Strong*, published in 1938 by the Simon J. Lubin Society, Steinbeck accused the state of California of failing to provide adequate medical facilities for the influx of migrant farm workers. And according to Carol Steinbeck, Steinbeck had discussed the possibility of doing some writing about rural health with film maker Pare Lorentz, whose *The River* and *The Plow That Broke the Plains* provided Steinbeck with ideas about technique for the intercalary chapters in *The Grapes of Wrath* (CS/RA, 10/1/71). When Herbert Kline approached Steinbeck about doing a film on Mexico and suggested a study of a small Mexican family caught amidst the attempt by the fascist General Almazon of Monterrey to overthrow the progressive Mexican government of President

Cardenas, Steinbeck, though interested, eventually transformed the story into a study of the efforts of rural doctors to cure diseases from which Mexican-Indian peasants were dying.

From the beginning, then, *The Forgotten Village* was constructed with a specific social objective in mind, and reading an early draft of Steinbeck's story, one is struck by the novelist's heavy employment of social propaganda. The protagonist, Juan Diego, grows outraged when his sister sickens and his younger brother dies from a deadly bacterial virus which has polluted the village well. Juan Diego realizes the absurdity of curing microbial infections with witchcraft, and he leaves the traditional way of his people to learn medicine in the capital so that he may one day return to assist in the fight against disease and superstition. Told by a doctor in the Rural Health Service that

Changes in people are never quick. But the boys from the villages are being given a chance by a nation that believes in them. From the government schools, the boys and girls from the villages will carry knowledge back to their own people, Juan Diego. And the change will come, is coming; the long climb out of darkness. Already the people are learning, changing their lives, learning, working, living in new ways. The change will come, is coming, as sure as there are thousands of Juan Diegos in the villages of Mexico. (140–142)

Steinbeck's story ends with the boy proclaiming prophetically, "I am Juan Diego" (143).

There are several clear parallels between *The Forgotten Village* and *The Grapes of Wrath*. Most importantly, the family of Juan Diego is a "personalized group," and it functions in much the same way as does the Joad family in *The Grapes of Wrath*. Paco, Esperanza, Carlos, and Maria are so absorbed into the story's thematic design that "the reader's response goes beyond sympathy for the individuals to moral indignation at their social condition."[19] In the Preface to *The Forgotten Village*, Steinbeck defines his use of the "personalized group."

A great many documentary films have used the generalized method, that is, the showing of a condition or an event as it affects a group of people. The audience can then have a personalized reaction from imagining one member of that group. I have felt that this is the more difficult observation from the audience's viewpoint. It means very little to know that a million Chinese are starving unless you know one Chinese who is starving. In *The Forgotten Village* we reversed the usual process. Our story centered on one family in one small village. We wished our audience to know this family very well, and incidentally to like it, as we did. Then from association with this little personalized group, the larger conclusion concerning the racial group could be drawn with something like participation. (5)

The crucial word here is *participation*. Steinbeck wants his readers to participate with Juan Diego's family, who live "in the long moment when the past slips reluctantly into the future" (9) in order to draw the larger conclusion concerning the racial group as a whole; just as by participating with the Joads the reader can understand the plight of the entire family of California's migrant poor.

But somehow, one does not feel the same way about the Mexican villagers as one feels about the Joads. For whereas Steinbeck demonstrates in *The Grapes of Wrath* how a band of once-thoughtless, impetuous, ignorant people can unite under a banner of human brotherhood to work toward meaningful social reform, the natives in *The Forgotten Village* are "a benighted lot, and the hero must run away to preserve himself."[20] In *The Grapes of Wrath*, the Joads learn that if they work together, they may someday be able to acquire a little parcel of land, thereby regaining their dignity as human beings, which was destroyed when they were tractored off by the Oklahoma land corporations. On the basis of Casy's vision that "all that lives is holy," they struggle to preserve what Ricketts called "the age old relation between man and the land, and between man and man."[21] Casy also teaches the Joads about "the inward things," which Ricketts defines as "the larger relationships, between human society and the given individual," and "between man and his feeling of supra-personal participation from within." As a symbol for an understanding of these "inward things," Ricketts posits what he calls "the deep smile," and one immediately thinks of Ma Joad's "deep smile" when Rosasharn feels a "supra-personal participation from within" and feeds the starving migrant.

There are no deep smiles in *The Forgotten Village*. The rich relational life of the Mexican villagers and the age-old relation between "man and the land, and between man and man" have been replaced by a new zeitgeist which emphasizes what Ricketts calls "the region of outward possessions."[22] The holistic vision, the organismal conception, and Allee's doctrine of social cooperation, so vital to the social gospel of *The Grapes of Wrath*, are absent in *The Forgotten Village*. And Steinbeck's nonblaming portrayal of aberrent human behavior in the earlier work (Uncle John's sin, Noah's decision to leave the family to live by water, etc.) is replaced by his caustic, almost condescending attack on primitive superstition. In short, Steinbeck, the metaphysical visionary and agrarian idealist, becomes Steinbeck the social propagandist. And because the doctrine of medical reform in *The Forgotten Village* is not supported by a network of principles conveying sound philosophical truths, the brunt of Steinbeck's social argument lacks force. This is not to say, of course, that Steinbeck's concern or his compassion diminished between the writing of *The Grapes of Wrath* and *The Forgotten Village*. It simply suggests that his social outlook had narrowed; that in his zeal to bring modern health practices to disease-ridden Mexico, Steinbeck abandoned the eclectic(and largely Rickettsian) social and philosophical vision that distinguishes the thematic design of his greatest fiction.

Steinbeck and Ricketts Go to War

After the bombing of Pearl Harbor, Steinbeck became an ardent supporter of America's participation in the global conflict, and when he offered his writing talents to the State Department, they were quickly accepted.

There is something deeply troubling about this apparent shift in Steinbeck's thinking in the light of the sardonic statements about war's being a regular and observable "murder trait of our species" in *The Log from the Sea of Cortez*, even though the general tone of the novelist's writing about the war indicates that he did not stoop to the kind of sloganeering which urges men to fight for this glory or that. And yet, Steinbeck actively supported a war which just months earlier (in the *Log*) he and Ricketts stated was a conflict which "no one wants to fight, in which no one can see a gain—a zombie war of sleepwalkers which nevertheless goes on out of all control of intelligence" (88).

As is the case with so many of the apparent contradictions in Steinbeck's world-view, the novelist's sudden decision to go to war is best explained through an examination of Ricketts' impact on Steinbeck's thinking, for upon closer inspection, it becomes clear that the quietistic attitude toward war in the *Log* belongs largely to Ricketts and is based upon his cosmic world-view contained in that work. And although Steinbeck put his name to statements about the pernicious nature of "man's murder instinct," the events at Pearl Harbor evidently convinced him that the role of the detached observer was no longer morally tenable.

None but the most devout pacifist could refuse to respond with some measure of patriotism to a frontal attack on one's homeland. And even Ricketts, although in his characteristically detached and non-teleological style, felt compelled to take part in the war. But there are crucial differences between the general character of Ricketts' and Steinbeck's reactions to World War II. An analysis of the war writings of both men not only provides a key to the basic philosophical discrepancies in their thinking, but in one instance shows how, when Ricketts' ideas appear in Steinbeck's fiction without the novelist's qualifying their limitations, they prove fatal to his art.

It has already been indicated that for some years before World War II, Ricketts had maintained a scientific curiosity about the fauna of the Pacific Islands under Japanese mandate. When the war came, Ricketts believed that his knowledge of the tides, reef patterns, and general geography of the islands (reported in detail to the world scientific community by highly articulate Japanese biologists) would be of value to American naval forces planning campaigns in the South Pacific. In a notebook entry made during late April 1942, Ricketts abstracts "an important paper with chart of the [Iwayama] bay," and insists that "all this (and other data) must be available to any raiding party."[1]

During the summer of 1942, Ricketts extended the scope of his reading and made extensive journal entries about the life and thought patterns of the Japanese and German people. He concludes in an essay on war written in August of that year, that while "people must be sick of war," "like poverty we have it with us still," and he identifies himself as "another peaceful American, thrown into this ageless pattern of war too suddenly for comfort," who has sought to work off "my maladjustment by trying to find out how things are in this and other wars."[2] Ricketts retains the non-teleological distance of the disinterested observer by noting that "wars we must have. Or do have anyway. And since having them, we must accept them." But although he admits that his studies of Japan and Germany were originally undertaken "as a cure for that curious malady, the war jitters," he maintains that if his knowledge "may be valuable to others, I cannot see why it shouldn't be shared."[3]

Ricketts' study of Japanese and German character led him to conclude that the principal reason for World War II was the contagious bias of the collectivist power drives currently in vogue in those nations. He points to the "violent idealism," the "jumbled logic" of German and Japanese nationalism, and he contrasts the "food standard" of the West with the "path standard" of the East, noting that these countries have turned from "the way of peace" or "the way of non acquisition" to the "present savage mechanistic drive" in which the old has been "discarded temporarily" while the new absorbs "all the available energy."

In an individual or a nation there are always conflicting polarities. Germany has had her Goethes and her Hitlers. The present Japanese nation must be full of such unresolved conflicts—internationalism defeated by nationalism, but nevertheless producing anti-bodies that make a nation sick and vicious. A good Oriental race has become an inferior Occidental.[4]

By late 1942, Ricketts was convinced that "the key to what the Jap is and what the German is, to what our enemy is most likely to do and how he will do it, and the key to what we best may do after the war, is available right here in this country, in any good library."[5] He concluded that this information needed merely to be selected out and interpreted according to the enemy's psychology, coordinated with our own, and then applied, "supplemented by geopolitical intelligence, to the military problems and to the subsequent international problem facing us."[6]

It was in this spirit of the disinterested observer who had applied his non-teleological understanding to the problems of a very real war, that Ricketts wrote to the Bureau of Naval Personnel in Washington, offering them his services. He stated that he was "much interested in going on with this work" (particularly his studies of the mandated islands) and indicated that "if it seems likely that such service will be of value along the lines suggested, I would want to file an application [for enlistment] right away. I am naturally anxious to see that my particular and highly specialized abilities should be used most appropriately" (EFR/BNP, 9/9/42).

Unfortunately for Ricketts (and, more probably, for the armed forces), the Navy was not interested, and instead, he was drafted into the Army and stationed at the Reception Center at the Monterey Presidio. For a time, Ricketts was bitter, angered by the Army's misuse of its potential manpower. Gradually, however, he came to view not only war but military life itself philosophically and non-teleologically as a means by which man might "escape through war into reality." Assigned to the medical unit at the Presidio, Ricketts treated sick and tired soldiers who had been overseas with kindness and affection, and he noted that they often left his clinic "with their 'souls fed' or with their 'spirits all over heaven.' "[7]

What Ricketts disliked about the Army was its emphasis on a "loud voice" and "aggressive, decisive action, whether right or wrong," behavior he felt was "out of relation to the whole."[8] And yet the non-teleological Ricketts was not opposed to all of the Army's foolishness. Strangely enough, he even found value in "doing an ordered job that has no significance either in itself or in the 1g picture, a job that you don't like and to which you are not adapted . . . with good will. Knowing the work is wasted. And feeling good about it."[9] Ricketts compares this sort of behavior with the Japanese concept of *Bushido*; he suggests that many soldiers have "their morale and their fine efforts blunted by the realization that it's all to no purpose," and he observes that simply "doing it (if you are pledged to do so, or ordered to) and feeling good about it, is a noble thing."[10] Indeed, Ricketts considers that war and armies have become "our common denomination." And since "we are all in this thing together," we have achieved "a democracy of a deep sort."[11]

Ed Ricketts made his peace with war in general and with the Army in particular. He attained the "emergent" vision of the holistic observer and came to realize that in the military, "many men are more deeply into a suprapersonal thing, more supported in a great unconscious father, than they have been ever before in adult life or than they ever will be again."[12] Indeed, Ricketts maintained that military life can forge a deep bond of companionship between men, so that "a rather insignificant soldier can have thrust upon him a mantle of mass love."[13]

Despite his inherent antipathy toward war and toward the nationalistic power drives which spawned the conflict in which he found himself engaged, Ricketts found evidence in his military experiences of what he loved to call "the great continuity." And in a 1943 entry to his Presidio journal, Ricketts notes that Beethoven's music reflects the emergent joy which is the unifying factor in "the great continuity," and which transcends all doubt and conflict. He wishes he could afford to send some Beethoven recordings to Steinbeck, who, "having gone from blind 'going along with' a collective [the war], now should have the quiet and joyful affirmation of integrity that is Beethoven's."[14]

Throughout his essays, Ricketts posits a doctrine of "participation," not in the teleological sense represented by a loud voice and aggressive action, but in the emergent sense which leads to that "indescribable and unnamable quality of life" best described as "an illumination."[15] And in his studies of the mandated islands, in his research on the nationalistic mind-sets of the German and Japanese character, and through his experiences as a member of the medical wing of the Monterey Reception Center Service Command Unit 1930, Ricketts broke through to view even war and military life as parts of the deep thing which is "grandly the same everywhere."[16]

When Ricketts talks about how Steinbeck had moved from "going along with" a collective to the "quiet and joyful affirmation of integrity that is Beethoven's," he places the phrase "going along with" in quotation marks. Near the end of his own Gulf of California log, Ricketts had also set this phrase off in quotes and defined "going along with" as "an articulate expression for a process of relaxation whereby you go along with, rather than fight against, the pace of external events over which you have no control."[17] Moreover, Ricketts notes that one often "goes along with" something while he is "developing a technique of control in the case of events that aren't inexorable."[18]

One could not find a more succinct statement of Steinbeck's response to World War II. Shocked out of reflections about his Sea of Cortez trip by the bombing of Pearl Harbor, and living in New York, 3,000 miles from where Ricketts was developing his own reactions to the war, Steinbeck's war writings reveal that, at least initially, he "went along with" the "pace of external events."

Ironically, Steinbeck's response to the war closely equated his own philosophical convictions about the manner in which unit-men are marshalled into a moving phalanx. By writing the highly propagandistic *Bombs Away* (1942), and talking a lot about the military importance of the mandated islands (apparently he began to think of Ricketts' research on the islands as a joint project, though there is no evidence that he actually did any reading on the subject, much less any abstracting of technical papers by Japanese scientists),[19] Steinbeck keyed-into the specialized artist's role, which is to speak for the phalanx in time of phalanx need. ("In phalanx need there can be change of birth rate of the units, of the stature, complexion, color, constitution of the unit."[20]) Certainly, the Steinbeck who, at the suggestion of General "Hap" Arnold, wrote *Bombs Away* in order to tell people "of the kind and quality of our Air Force, of the caliber of its men and of the excellence of its equipment,"[21] was himself proof that in phalanx need there is a change in the "constitution of the unit."

In *Bombs Away*, which Steinbeck wrote after visiting several Air Force training bases with photographer-flier John Swope, the novelist retains his deep interest in group movement (so evident in *In Dubious Battle*, *The Grapes of Wrath* and "The Leader of the People") by applying the argument of phalanx to the organization of airmen preparing for bombing raids against the enemy. Steinbeck notes that

146

Steinbeck and Ricketts Go to War

The attack on us set in motion the most powerful species drive we know—that of survival. . . . The goal has been set now and we have an aim and a direction, and a kind of fierce joy runs through the country. The President has set an end in production that was almost beyond reason and that end is being reached. (14–15)

In short, the novelist nationalizes his goal-directed vision of the movement from the *I* to the *We* which he portrayed with such conviction in his analyses of the migrant drive toward unity in *The Grapes of Wrath*. But the formula fails to work in *Bombs Away*, possibly because Steinbeck's statements about the means by which individual American soldiers key-into the military phalanx are unsupported by a network of philosophical principles such as those voiced by Casy in *The Grapes of Wrath*. At one point in *Bombs Away*, when Bill, a bombadier cadet, joins the Air Force team, Steinbeck attempts to combine his doctrine of phalanx need with Ricketts' notion of "participation." He points out that at first Bill "disliked the formations," but goes on to show how when

he became precise in his step and carriage he grew to like them; the beat of the step, the numbers of men all acting in precise unison, became a satisfying thing to him. He discovered something he had not learned, which the directionless depression had not permitted him to learn—the simple truth that concerted action of a group of men produces a good feeling in all of them. (49)

Unhappily though, succeeding passages demonstrate that Bill's simple sense of goodwill is more the result of his (and Steinbeck's) willingness "to go along with the collective" than it is a reflection of that "indescribable and unnamable quality of life" which Ricketts calls "participation" and which he believed is manifest in the military's "mantle of mass-love." As a matter of fact, after Steinbeck completed *Bombs Away*, he began to entertain some second thoughts about having written it at all. Shortly before the book was published, Steinbeck told Webster Street that it was a straight recruiting job, and he expressed concern about playing the role of the goat who leads the sheep in, only to step aside himself (WFS/RA, 7/23/70).

147

JOHN STEINBECK and EDWARD F. RICKETTS

The extent of Steinbeck's misgivings about *Bombs Away* is unclear, but it is significant that although he continued to write about the war, the focus and tone of his writings shifted markedly. Nowhere is this departure more evident than in the subject matter of the loosely related series of dispatches he wrote in 1943 as a foreign correspondent for the New York *Herald Tribune*, which were published together in 1958 as *Once There Was a War*. In several of his early communiques, written aboard an American troopship in June 1943, the novelist is still concerned with the argument of phalanx; he points out that need dictates that "men cannot be treated as individuals" so that each soldier in his helmet resembles "a mushroom in a bed of mushrooms."[22] But Steinbeck quickly glosses over the real loss of individuality of men in war, and the remainder of his dispatches stress "human interest," "the hopes, fears, and activities of 'G.I. Joes' under the various conditions of the war."[23]

In 1958, Steinbeck reflected back on his work for the *Tribune*, and he admitted that his accounts and stories, "written in haste and telephoned across the sea to appear as immediacies," were "period pieces, the attitudes archaic, the impulses romantic, and, in the light of everything that has happened since, perhaps the whole body of work untrue and warped and one-sided" (vi). Indeed, the novelist recalls that while the events reported in *Once There Was a War* did happen, many other things that happened were not reported because of "a huge and gassy thing called the War Effort. Anything which interfered with or ran counter to the War Effort was automatically bad" (vii). Noting that "We were all a part of the War Effort," Steinbeck verifies Ricketts' crisp analysis of the novelist's response to the war by affirming that "we went along with it, and not only that, we abetted it" (viii).

Thus, fifteen years after he wrote his *Tribune* dispatches, Steinbeck conceded that he had written about "only a part of the war," and yet he is quick to point out that he fervently believed at that time that "it was the best thing to do. . . . And perhaps we were right in eliminating parts of the whole picture" (xii). Herein, of course, is the basic flaw of *Bombs Away* and *Once There Was a*

War. For the first time in over a decade, the novelist had abandoned the whole picture, the importance of which as a way of seeing the world he learned so well from Ricketts, and the implementation of which as fictional method accounts for the particular excellence of *In Dubious Battle* and *The Grapes of Wrath.* Perhaps Steinbeck's avoidance of the whole picture was necessary with respect to the war effort, perhaps not. Certainly, Ricketts' conclusion that war breeds a democracy of the deepest sort which reflects "the great continuity" makes it clear that "blindly going along with a collective" is not a necessary attitude for the patriot. What is more important, of course, is that however commendable his intentions may have been, Steinbeck's capitulation to the pressures of political expediency had disastrous consequences for his art.

Certainly one cannot fault Steinbeck for not writing a great novel about the war to match the excellence of his fiction about America's dispossessed tenant farmers. Nor can one condemn him for turning from fiction to journalism. But the basic motivation behind *Bombs Away* and *Once There Was a War* resembles (in scope, if not in design) the political ambitions of Mac and Jim in *In Dubious Battle.* With no time for high-falutin ideas, and unwilling to portray the whole picture, *Once There Was a War* and *Bombs Away* fail as art just as Mac and Jim's Party fails as a political machine. And just as one must move from the Party to the developing migrant phalanx in *The Grapes of Wrath* to find a viable solution to the problems of California agriculture, one must turn from Steinbeck to Mailer, Heller, and Vonnegut to read of the true horror of war.

Steinbeck did write one fictional work about and during the war which reflects his continued interest in Ricketts' holistic thinking. This, of course, is his second play-novelette, *The Moon Is Down* (1942); it, too, may have had roots in Steinbeck's dedication to the War Effort,[24] but it moves far beyond the restrictive limits of political propaganda.

Because of the frenzied times in which it was written and staged (the play first opened in Baltimore on March 17, 1942, several months before the publication of *Bombs Away*), *The Moon Is Down* provoked nearly as much controversy as *The Grapes of Wrath*. Angered at Steinbeck's apparent complacency toward Nazism, some critics (including James Thurber and Clifton Fadiman) attacked Steinbeck for his alleged ignorance of the brutality of the German occupation armies. Others defended the novelist, noting that while he may have been too easy on the Nazis, he "portrayed the heroic resistance of a basically peace-loving people with great understanding."[25]

Steinbeck was bothered by the more personal attacks on *The Moon Is Down*, but he did not object to the fundamental controversy over the question whether man should or should not hate blindly. But when the critical dogfight dragged on, Steinbeck grew disgusted, and at one point told Webster Street that the critics had stopped criticizing literature and turned instead to criticizing each other (WFS/RA, 7/23/70).

Efforts to assess the real issues concerning Steinbeck's accomplishments in *The Moon Is Down* were hopelessly lost amid the tumult raised by those critics Steinbeck labeled "Park-avenue commandoes." And these real issues, only obliquely referred to until now, have to do with Steinbeck's treatment of some of the most crucial philosophical concepts developed by him in *In Dubious Battle* and *The Grapes of Wrath*, and by Ricketts in his Gulf of California narrative and in his "Anti-script" to Steinbeck's *The Forgotten Village*. *The Moon Is Down* is not really a war novel, nor is it an antiwar novel. Rather it is a quasi-fictional philosophical debate, cut off by definition from World War II or from any other war. Its failure as art is traceable not to Steinbeck's refusal to polemicize the horrors of Nazism (actually, neither World War II nor the Nazi army is mentioned in *The Moon Is Down*), but rather to his inability to relate an abstract philosophical vision to concrete reality.

Of paramount significance in this regard is the fact that Steinbeck began work on *The Moon Is Down* in the late summer of 1941, before the bombing of Pearl Harbor and just after he had finished the difficult task of shaping the narrative portion of *Sea of Cortez*. Considering the date of the book's publication, early in 1942, it is unlikely that the novelist's sensibilities had yet been shaken by the contagion of war. Ricketts, in many ways Steinbeck's most astute critic, immediately recognized the relationship between *The Moon Is Down* and the *Log*. Writing to Steinbeck's agents in mid-1942 about his ideas for a reissue of the narrative section of *Sea of Cortez*, Ricketts noted that "the philosophical controversy over the 'Moon' would itself center fresh attention on the philosophical ideas expressed in the 'Sea'" (EFR-EO, 6/6/42).

The philosophy implicit in Steinbeck's account of the invasion and occupation of a small Scandinavian village is a carefully worked out fusion of Ricketts' non-teleological gospel of breaking through and his belief in the evils of a mechanized, collectivist state, in conjunction with the novelist's thesis about the different types of group-man. Transforming these notions into a story of conflicting societies (or phalanxes), Steinbeck demonstrates how free men will ultimately prevail over herd-men because they key-into their phalanx and aggrandize their individuality, whereas herd-men live fragmented lives, out of relation to the whole.

The free men in *The Moon Is Down* are the Scandinavian villagers, who unite to frustrate and thwart the ambitions of their stronger captors. Before the invasion, the peaceful villagers were a quiet, self-indulgent lot who were easy prey for the occupation army. Initially, they are astonished at being invaded. Like the dispossessed Oklahoma tenant farmers, who at the beginning of *The Grapes of Wrath* sit alone in the doorways of their houses, "thinking—figuring," the townspeople

moved sullenly through the streets. Some of the light of astonishment was gone from their eyes, but still a light of anger had not taken its place. . . . The people spoke to one another in monosyllables, and everyone was thinking of the war, thinking of himself, thinking of the past and how it had suddenly been changed.[26]

Led by the toughening Mayor Orden and by his close friend, Dr. Winter, the townspeople gradually unite to challenge the invaders. When, midway in the novelette, a villager named Alex

Morden strikes out and kills a captain of the occupation army, an act for which Morden is sentenced to die, Mayor Orden tells the doomed man that "Yours was the first clear act. Your private anger was the beginning of a public anger" (54). By his actions, Alex has in fact "made the people one." And just as the fear went from the faces of the Oklahoma tenant farmers "and anger took its place," the captive townspeople harden so that "the hatred was deep in the eyes of the people" (58).

Dr. Winter, the mayor's confidante, is a loosely fictionalized version of Ed Ricketts. He recognizes the flaws in the teleology of the "time-minded" invaders who "hurry toward their destiny as though it would not wait," and who "push the rolling world along with their shoulders" (3, 4). And discussing the vulnerability of the overly integrated group which attempts to subdue and destroy the free creative human spirit by killing the leaders of the townspeople, Winter articulates Ricketts' non-teleological theory of true leadership, in which it will be found that "the people we call leaders are simply those who, at the given moment, are moving in the direction behind which will be found the greatest weight, and which represents a future mass movement."[27]

Indeed, says Winter, the invaders "think that just because they have only one leader and one head, we are all like that. They know that ten heads lopped off will destroy them, but we are a free people; we have as many heads as we have people, and in a time of need leaders pop up among us like mushrooms" (107). In the denouement of the plot in *The Moon Is Down*, Steinbeck utilizes Ricketts' (Winter's) theory of leadership to thematic advantage; it forms, in fact, the crux of his belief that free men will ultimately overcome herd-men.

Mayor Orden is more than a mayor, he is an "idea-mayor." "He is the people," the invader's Colonel Lanser remarks. "He will think what they think" (33). Significantly, it is Orden who tells Lanser that the invading army has taken on "the one impossible job in the world, the one thing that can't be done. . . . to break man's spirit permanently" (49, 50).

Steinbeck and Ricketts Go to War

Free men cannot start a war, but once it is started, they can fight on in defeat. Herd men, followers of a leader, cannot do that, and so it is always the herd men who win battles and the free men who win wars. You will find that is so, sir. (113)

Finally, it is Orden, who in the moment of his greatest stress (after being arrested and sentenced to die), breaks through to an understanding of his role in the whole scheme of things.

You know, Doctor, I am a little man and this is a little town, but there must be a spark in little men that can burst into flame. I am afraid, I am terribly afraid, and I thought of all the things I might do to save my own life, and then that went away, and sometimes now I feel a kind of exultation, as though I were bigger and better than I am. . . . (108)

The invading army is comprised of herd-men who have sacrificed their integrity as individuals to the kind of national collectivist movement which does not spread a "mantle of mass-love" over its members. Colonel Lanser, the commanding officer of the occupation army, is by disposition a humane, sensitive man who knows that war is treachery and hatred, the torture and killing of innocent men. And yet he fights off his individuality, repeatedly reminding himself that he is a soldier, not allowed "to question or to think, but to carry out orders" (22). And in a crucial passage in which Steinbeck explains how participation in an aggressive army dulls the human spirit, the novelist blatantly injects his own thesis about the dehumanizing effects of blind mob behavior (first developed, it will be recalled, in "The Vigilante") to explain how otherwise sensitive men like Lanser can exist in a completely collectivist state.

In marching, in mobs, in football games, and in war, outlines become vague; real things become unreal and a fog creeps over the mind. Tension and excitement, weariness, movement—all merge in one great gray dream, so that when it is over, it is hard to remember how it was when you killed men or ordered them to be killed. Then other people who were not there tell you what it was like and you say vaguely, "Yes, I guess that's how it was." (22)

Among the officers in the occupation army, only Captain Loft is a true professional, a man with "no unmilitary moments" who lives and breathes his captaincy, and who implicitly believes that

God is "an old and honored general, retired and gray, living among remembered battles and putting wreathes on the graves of his lieutenants several times a year" (20). The others are inherently decent, peace-loving men who, like Lanser, as individual men with memories might reject the military and political pattern which exhibits "an inability to learn, an inability to see beyond the killing which is the job" (49). But, says Lanser, speaking for himself and for the soldiers under his command, "I am not a man subject to memories" (49).

Lanser's officers are men like Major Hunter who would prefer to work at home on his model railroad than serve as a military engineer. They are men like Captain Bentick, "a family man, a lover of dogs and pink children and Christmas" (19), who is forced to order Alex Morden to work and is in turn killed by Morden. And they are men like Lieutenant Tonder, a bitter poet "who dreamed of perfect, ideal love of elevated young men for poor girls" (21), and who is stabbed to death when he tries to realize his dreams with Morden's angry widow. To a man, Lanser and his officers are absorbed in the violent idealism and the jumbled logic of their leader's fierce and contagious bias. They are engulfed in a terrible confusion of ends and means which desensitizes the otherwise sentient Lanser, and which kills Captain Bentick and Lieutenant Tonder.

Just as herd-men cannot for long subdue free men, neither can they overturn the ecological balance of an area without destroying themselves. Here, Steinbeck's attitude is squarely consistent with Ricketts' notion (developed in his "Verbatim Transcription" and included by Steinbeck in the *Log*) that overly collectivized states are mutations of nature, unequipped to cope with natural habitats not tailored for their particularized needs. The occupation army in *The Moon Is Down* disturbs the pastoral tranquility of the Scandinavian landscape. A fully alive and vital nature and a well-disciplined, thoroughly integrated army brandishing high-powered guns and tanks can never coexist for very long. For when the machines of death meet the natural forms of life, death inevitably triumphs. Even the pictures on the walls in the homes of the townspeople reflect the aura of death which surrounds the invading army: "on the back wall were two pictures, one of fish lying dead on a plate of ferns and the other of grouse lying dead on a fir bough" (72).

But nature, in conjunction with the unconquerable spirit of the townspeople, rises up to frustrate the invaders in the form of the seemingly endless snowstorms which bury the village under successive levels of packed snow. Arriving early in the fall, the snows become as threatening to the warm-blooded invaders as their own destructive war machines are to the Scandinavians. Soon after the snows begin, the cold and miserable soldiers find it increasingly difficult to safeguard the operation of the local coal mines which are indispensable to their war effort. Moreover, the snow aids the partisans during the "terrible Easter Egg Hunt" for the sticks of dynamite which they need to continue their struggle against their oppressors.

Gradually, the conquerers themselves become surrounded by a small group of partisans and by the ever-present snow. As winter sets in, the men under Colonel Lanser's command find themselves "alone amid silent enemies, and no man might relax for even a moment. If he did, he disappeared, and some snowdrift received his body. If he went alone to a woman, he disappeared and some snowdrift received his body" (58). By the middle of winter, Steinbeck notes, "the snow was rotten with bodies" (59).

In *The Log from the Sea of Cortez*, Steinbeck and Ricketts affirm that the mutations of the collectivized state and the mechanized army "might well correspond to the thickening armor of the great reptiles—a tendency that can only end in extinction" (88). Unable to adapt to the Scandinavian balance of nature and frustrated by the partisans' will to resist (Steinbeck's decision to name the doctor figure Winter is significant in that it seems to represent his attempt to fuse the opposition forces of man and nature), the invading mutation is doomed to extinction. "The flies have conquered the flypaper," Winter prophesizes as he is being led away to be shot, "The debt shall be paid" (114, 115).

Nearly a decade after he completed *The Moon Is Down*, Steinbeck recalled in "About Ed Ricketts" that "very many conclusions Ed and I worked out together through endless discussion and reading and observation and experiment" (xlv).

> We had a game which we playfully called speculative metaphysics. It was a sport consisting of lopping off a piece of observed reality and letting it move up through the speculative process like a tree growing tall and bushy. We observed with pleasure how the branches of thought grew away from the trunk of external reality. We believed, as we must, that the laws of thought parallel the laws of things. (xlv)[28]

"Once a theme was established," recalls Steinbeck, "we subjected observable nature to it" (xlvi). And then, Steinbeck discusses the paleontological principle that over-armor or overornamentation are symptoms of decay, and he reflects that this "is an example of our game—one developed quite a long time ago" (xlvi).

The discussion of the effects of overornamentation does occur in *Sea of Cortez*, but it also serves as a philosophical base upon which the novelist builds his distinction between creative and destructive phalanxes in *The Moon Is Down*. And herein lies the chief problem with the play-novelette. The long discussions between Mayor Orden and Doctor Winter are a thinly veiled fictional version of Steinbeck and Ricketts "lopping off a piece of observed reality" and letting it "move up through the speculative process like a tree growing tall and bushy." But whereas watching the branches of thought growing apart "from the trunk of external reality" is appropriate in abstract theorizing, in fiction this method of conceptualizing a philosophy of life is aesthetically calamitous. And though Steinbeck does "subject observable nature" to the philosophical conclusions of Orden and Winter, the laws of thought in *The Moon Is Down* do not naturally parallel the laws of things.

In *The Log from the Sea of Cortez*, Steinbeck defines the design of a book as a "pattern of a reality controlled and shaped by the mind of the writer" (1). But in *The Moon Is Down*, Steinbeck loses control of his method (worked to such perfection in *In Dubious Battle* and *The Grapes of Wrath*) by shaping too hard. The leading characters (particularly Orden and Winter) are not really individual men (except as they resemble Steinbeck and Ricketts) but abstract philosophical types. Moreover, the novelist's efforts to corroborate his (and Ricketts') thesis about the survival value of contrasting phalanxes by means of a blatantly schematic portrayal of nature as an active force is so hackneyed, so forced, that verisimilitude is sacrificed and the possibility of fusing an otherwise believable plot to reality is lost.[29] Unlike his California novels and short stories, in which Steinbeck had been able to supplement and qualify his and Ricketts' abstract philosophical notions with feelings and insights gleaned from personal experience, there was nothing in his background or experience to furnish these feelings and insights for *The Moon Is Down*. Instead, Steinbeck's contrived portrayal of nature (particularly his descriptions of the snow) reveals his inability to apply his unique descriptive talents to a landscape with which he was unfamiliar.

In short, despite Steinbeck's efforts to control his pattern of fictional reality, *The Moon Is Down* is little more than a somewhat altered version of Steinbeck (still immersed in the Ricketts materials he used in shaping the narrative portion of *Sea of Cortez*) playing "speculative metaphysics" with his own and Ricketts' ideas. In marked contrast with the efficacious effect of Ricketts' way of seeing on the thematic materials in Steinbeck's greatest fiction, the overpowering force of Ricketts' thinking overwhelmed the novelist in *The Moon Is Down*, with fatal consequences to the quality of his art.

Steinbeck may have realized this himself, and in his next works deliberately decided to detach himself from Ricketts' person and ideas. Certainly, the fusion of their respective world-views in *The Moon Is Down* is not apparent in *Bombs Away* and *Once There Was a War*. Perhaps it may not be entirely fanciful to suggest at least that *Bombs Away* and *Once There Was a War* owe their inspiration not only to the novelist's patriotism, but also to Steinbeck's decision to break from Ricketts and reassert his independence as a writer.

Intimations
of a Wasteland

Despite Steinbeck's early enthusiastic support of the American war effort, there is little question but that the novelist's faith in the human species was sorely tested by his experiences in the European theater. The writer who in 1939 had posited an idealistic theory of agrarian reform as a solution to the economic and political crises in American agriculture was shaken by the irreconcilable fact that hoes and spades had yielded to howitzers and submachine guns. And despite the conviction with which he asserted his belief in the ultimate victory of free men over the herd (*The Moon Is Down*) and with which he reported seeing evidence of man's finest qualities among American soldiers in the most hellish of wartime situations (*Once There Was a War*), by 1944, Steinbeck's interest in and sympathy for the war had worn thin.

In February 1943, the novelist told Webster Street that Ricketts had developed a philosophical pattern of thinking that enabled him to accept the war and write about it without liking it (WFS/RA, 7/23/70). But for a goal-oriented novelist like Steinbeck, non-teleological philosophical patterns of understanding-acceptance were impossible. Moreover, the war had taken a heavy toll on John Steinbeck the novelist. *Bombs Away*, the communiques in *Once There Was a War*, and even *The Moon Is Down* were among his least consequential works to date, and Steinbeck knew it. And so, by 1944, Steinbeck realized that if he was going to reassert himself as a writer of good fiction, he would have to return to the subjects and locales he knew best and had written about most successfully. If Steinbeck's unusually heavy dependence upon Ricketts' thinking which overwhelmed the fictional pattern of reality in *The Moon Is Down* drove the novelist away from any sort of literary involvement with Ricketts' ideas, the artistic inconsequence of his later war writings temporarily sent him scurrying back. Writing to Street in July 1944, Steinbeck discusses his work on a "fun book" that never mentions the war, and he indicates that while he had written many words during the past three years, for the first time in that period he was really working (WFS/RA, 7/23/70).

The result of this "return to work" was *Cannery Row* (1945), a novel Steinbeck described as "a mixed-up book" with a "pretty general ribbing in it."[1] Ostensibly, the theme of *Cannery Row*, which Orville Prescott called "a sentimental glorification of weakness of mind and degeneration of character,"[2] is as foreign to Steinbeck's great political novels as those works are to *Bombs Away* and *Once There Was a War*. But a deeper, more penetrating look at the novel reveals that *Cannery Row* contains Steinbeck's greatest statement of affection for Ed Ricketts as well as the novelist's objective portrayal of the inherent shortcomings of the marine biologist's complex philosophy of life. Steinbeck returns in *Cannery Row* to his most fundamental social and philosophical concerns. It is a book about a real if unusual world and about a wonderful man at the center of that world. But, despite his love for this world and the people who inhabit it, Steinbeck orders his novel to show beyond all doubt that it is as doomed to eventual extinction as the world of Colonel Lanser's overly integrated soldiers in *The Moon Is Down*.

In many ways, *Cannery Row* is a fictional sequel to the *Log* section of *Sea of Cortez* in that Steinbeck applies directly to a work of fiction many of the philosophical premises he and Ricketts developed in the Gulf of California. Most importantly, Doc, the main character of *Cannery Row*, is the most lifelike fictional version of Ed Ricketts in the entire catalogue of Steinbeck's fiction. And even Steinbeck's statement about the manner in which he ordered the fictional pattern of reality in *Cannery Row* resembles the methods he and Ricketts used to collect faunal specimens in the Gulf:

How can the poem and the stink and the grating noise—the quality of light, the tone, the habit and the dream—be set down alive? When you collect marine animals there are certain flat worms so delicate that they are almost impossible to capture whole, for they break and tatter under the touch. You must let them ooze and crawl of their own will onto a knife blade and then lift them gently into your bottle of sea water. And perhaps that might be the way to write this book—to open the page and to let the stories crawl in by themselves.[3]

In his discussion of *Cannery Row*, Joseph Fontenrose concludes that the main issue in the novel is the way in which Steinbeck suggests that man may "savor the hot taste of life."[4] It will be remembered, of course, that "the hot taste of life" was also a central concern in the *Log* where, at the end of the trip, the authors remark that their voyage had "dimension and tone." It was "no service to science," but "we simply liked it. We liked it very much. The brown Indians and the gardens of the sea, and the beer and the work, they were all one thing and we were that one thing too" (270).

It is important to recognize, however, that the pursuit of "the hot taste of life" in *Cannery Row* is Doc's, not necessarily Steinbeck's. For while the author was deprived by definition of a fictional persona in the *Log*, in *Cannery Row* not only could he portray Ricketts' quest for dimension and tone, but at the same time he was able to examine the inherent pitfalls which betray the seeker. In "About Ed Ricketts," Steinbeck recalls that he took the typescript of *Cannery Row* to Ricketts for approval. And he notes that the marine biologist "read it through carefully, smiling, and when he had finished he said, 'Let it go that way. It is written in kindness'" (lvii). Steinbeck surely wrote *Cannery Row* in kindness. And yet beneath the novelist's moving account of Doc and his friends is his penetrating look at the liabilities of a life-style which, because it denies many of the hard facts of existence, is ultimately untenable.

In many ways, Doc is the most loved and gingerly treated character in any Steinbeck novel. A man of broad vision, Doc owns and operates the Western Biological Laboratory on Cannery Row and is the universal man: "his mind had no horizon—and his sympathy had no warp" (17). "He lived in a world of wonders, of excitement. He was concupiscent as a rabbit and gentle as hell" (17).

Like Ricketts, Doc is a dedicated and accomplished marine biologist who studies the "good, kind, sane little animals" in the Great Tide Pool with a unique understanding of the interrelated patterns of animal life. And no wonder, for the Great Tide Pool "is a fabulous place."

when the tide is in, a wave-churned basin, creamy with foam, whipped by the combers that roll in from the whistling buoy on the reef. But when the tide goes out the little water world becomes quiet and lovely. The sea is very clear and the bottom becomes fantastic with hurrying, fighting, feeding, breeding animals. Crabs rush from frond to frond of the waving algae. Starfish squat over mussels and limpets, attach their million little suckers and then slowly lift with incredible power until the prey is broken from the rock. (17)

Doc spends much of his time in the tide pools, where the "smells of life and richness, of death and digestion, and decay and birth, burden the air" (18). Indeed, for Doc, the tide pools are microcosmic emblems of the delicately maintained ecological balance in the holistic order of things where all life forms struggle in the unending fight for survival. Moreover, Doc knows the faunal patterns of the California coast as well as any man.

The sea rocks and the beaches were his stockpile. He knew where everything was when he wanted it. All the articles of his trade were filed away on the coast, sea cradles here, octopi here, tube worms in another place, sea pansies in another. He knew where to get them but he could not go for them exactly when he wanted. For Nature locked up the items and only released them occasionally. Doc had to know not only the tides but when a particular low tide was good in a particular place. (62)

161

JOHN STEINBECK and EDWARD F. RICKETTS

Doc's laboratory is a veritable extension of the tide pool. As a supplier of marine specimens, Doc sells "the lovely animals of the sea, the sponges, tunicates, anemones, the stars and buttlestars, and sun stars, the bivalves, barnacles, the worms and shells, the fabulous and multi-form little brothers, the little moving flowers of the sea, nudibranchs and tetrabranchs. . . ." (15). His kindness extends to every form of animal life, so that though his profession demands that on occasion he kill specimens for research, he kills only out of necessity, since "he could not even hurt a feeling for pleasure" (16).

Doc is not only a highly competent marine biologist with a fundamental understanding of relational patterns in the "Great Organism of Life." He is also the "fountain of philosophy and science and art" on the Row. In addition to the many aquaria in his laboratory which hold an infinite variety of sea creatures, there is "a great phonograph" with hundreds of records lined up beside it, ranging from Benny Goodman to the Brandenburg Concertos. And on the walls are pinned reproductions of Daumiers, Titians, Picassos, Dalis, and Grahams (presumably Ellwood Graham[5]).

Doc is "a lonely and set-apart man" (a quality Steinbeck detected in Ricketts as well[6]), but at the same time he is the chief advisor to Mack and the boys, those "no-goods" and "blots-on-the-town" who are among the most enjoyable characters in any Steinbeck novel. "Mack and the boys," says Steinbeck, "are the Virtues, and Graces, the Beauties of the hurried mangled craziness of Monterey" (9); beloved children of "Our Father who art in Nature" who "dine delicately with the tigers, fondle the frantic heifers, and wrap up the crumbs to feed the sea gulls of Cannery Row" (9). Doc calls Mack and the boys "your true philosophers," and he sounds much like Ricketts discussing the ill effects of material gain to the psyche when he insists that

In a time when people tear themselves to pieces with ambition and nervousness and covetousness, they are relaxed. All of our so-called successful men are sick men, with bad stomachs, and bad souls, but Mack and the boys are healthy and curiously clean. They can do what they want. They can satisfy their appetites without calling them something else. (88)

Like the gentle if indolent Indians of Baja California whose laziness Ricketts believed was the proper state of mind for a contemplation of oneself in relation to the world, Mack and the boys "know everything that has ever happened in the world and possibly everything that will happen" (88). When Doc suggests that "they will survive in this particular world better than other people" (88), he reiterates Ricketts' faith in the survival quotient of simple people who, though poor and hungry and plagued by toothaches, do not kill themselves over things which do not concern them and so live longer and richer lives than their more prosperous neighbors who are enslaved by the products of their own technology.

"Everywhere in the world there are Mack and the boys," suggests Doc; the "sale of souls to gain the whole world is completely voluntary and almost unanimous—but not quite. . . . I've seen them in an ice-cream seller in Mexico and in an Aleut in Alaska" (89). Here again, Steinbeck is faithful to his model, since in his "Thesis and Materials for a Script on Mexico," Ricketts discusses in detail his experiences with a sidewalk ice-cream seller in Puebla who gave his wares to customers who had no money, never doubting that they would return to pay if ever they had the money. Ricketts states that if the ice-cream seller tried to conduct business with Americans along these lines, he "would have to adopt a C.O.D. policy . . . or else he'd have to retire bankrupt from his business, with an attitude of cynicism toward the 'honest' nordamericanos to boot."[7]

The spirit of goodwill shared by the leading denizens of Cannery Row pervades the entire novel. But the Row's unique flower of friendship reaches its apex during the famous party in Doc's laboratory which is one of the "most riotous parties in American literature."[8] And on the morning after the affair, Doc, who is still immersed in the mood of the previous evening, reads aloud from the Sanskrit poem, "Black Marigolds," as he intuitively breaks through to a realization that he has savored "the hot taste of life."

> Even now
> I know that I have savored the hot taste of life

> Lifting green cups and gold at the great feast.
> Just for a small and a forgotten time
> I have had full in my eyes from off my girl
> The whitest pouring of eternal light—
>
> (123)

Ostensibly then, Steinbeck says in *Cannery Row* that man can savor "the hot taste of life" if he pursues a free and uninhibited existence. But there is some question whether Steinbeck regards this approach to life as a tenable solution to man's quest for meaning in an increasingly rapacious world. For while Cannery Row is a self-contained island populated by "saints and angels and martyrs and holy men," the type of behavior practiced by the Row's denizens would be inadmissable anywhere else in the world. And whenever any of the characters ventures beyond the Row's sheltered confines, he encounters suspicion and resentment.

In one instance, Steinbeck draws upon an actual event in Ricketts' life and writes that when Doc was a student at the University of Chicago he decided to take a walking trip through the southeastern United States. Doc found that the people he met could not understand why he wanted to roam about the woods like a vagabond.[9] And although Doc "tried to explain. He said he was nervous and besides he wanted to see the country, smell the ground and look at grass and birds and trees, to savor the country, and there was no other way to do it save on foot" (64), the people were unable to share his enthusiasm, and they disliked him.

They scowled or shook and tapped their heads, they laughed as if they knew it was a lie and they appreciated a liar. And some, afraid for their daughters or their pigs, told him to move on, to get going, just not to stop near their place if he knew what was good for him. (64)

Later in the novel, when Doc travels down the California coast on a collecting expedition, he is beset by an unlikely assortment of perverse hitchhikers, rude waitresses, and bounty hunters. Similarly, Mack and the boys have had distressing experiences outside the Row. Mack came to the Row in a state of utter dejection, since everything he had ever done before had gone wrong. He tells Doc that he sought out the uninhibited, clowning life of the

Edward F. Ricketts on a walking tour of the American Southeast, 1920

Row in order to flee the "serious world" which destroys clowns: " 'Same thing ever' place 'til I just got to clowning. I don't do nothin' but clown no more. Try to make the boys laugh' " (82).

It might be argued that Steinbeck's apparent approval of the indolent life-styles of Mack and the boys is evidence that in *Cannery Row* he "steps stage-front to proselytize his readers" about the virtues of escape.[10] Certainly, Steinbeck enjoyed contemplating the retreats of the scientist and the loafer. But his vision of America was not so naive as to blind him to the inevitable transciency of those life-styles. When Malcolm Cowley observed that the novel might be a "poisoned cream puff" thrown at "respectable society," Steinbeck replied that if Cowley read *Cannery Row* again, "he would see how very poisoned it was."[11] Indeed, Steinbeck indicts what we call the "civilized world," and he correspondingly applauds life on the Row. But he reveals paradoxically (and this is the novel's real venom) that although Doc is a fountain of science, art, and philosophy, and although Mac and the boys are "the Virtues, the Graces, and the Beauties," they live insular lives and are themselves surrounded on all sides by an ever-expanding commercial society which will one day make those life-styles untenable.[12] The party is over—"the hot taste of life" has been savored—and there is nothing left but nostalgia. *Cannery Row* ends with Doc wiping "his eyes with the back of his hand. . . . And behind the glass the rattlesnakes lay still and stared into space with their dusty frowning eyes" (123).

Fontenrose has identified parallels between the characters of *Cannery Row* and those of *In Dubious Battle*. "Mack of *Cannery Row* looks like a deliberate burlesque of Mac in *In Dubious Battle*," and "each Mac[k] stands in complementary relation to Doc; each is a man of devices, and Doc is the objective non-teleological observer."[13] "The Party is definitely rejected and we are invited to a party," notes Fontenrose, since Steinbeck believes that "our sad, lonely condition can be alleviated only by moments of great joy, parties, and love affairs, when we savor 'the hot taste of life.' "[14] Because of its transient nature, however, the party is not much better than the Party. Moreover, both Docs are lonely, set-apart men, who, while able to break through to momentary insights of great understanding, are in the end sustained only by their melancholy. And even apart from Steinbeck's social convictions about the weak survival quotient of the non-teleological visionary amid the chaos of the modern world, this is essentially how the novelist saw Ricketts: as a searching but troubled man, walled off a little who tried but never for more than an instant succeeded in "crashing through into the light." On the basis of Ricketts' world-view as expressed in his own writings, one might argue that Steinbeck's portrait is inaccurate and unfair. But while this argument is valid, it simply is not relevant to a study of Steinbeck's fiction. For this is the way Steinbeck saw his closest friend, and this is the way he portrayed him in *In Dubious Battle* and again in *Cannery Row*.

But while Steinbeck's portrait of his Ricketts-figure in *Cannery Row* closely resembles his treatment of Doc Burton in *In Dubious Battle*, there is a marked difference between the forces with which each must contend. Burton is defeated by the iron teleologies of the partisan Party leaders who confuse ends and means and refuse to take the time to listen to Doc's high-falutin ideas. Doc in *Cannery Row*, however, is plagued by materialistic Americans who are blind to the ecological truths of nature and to the organismic structure of life, but who, because of their unremitting possessiveness and sheer numbers, may ultimately inherit the entire world. Indeed, says Doc, in a verbatim restatement of a passage characteristic of Ricketts' thought patterns in *The Log from the Sea of Cortez*,

The things we admire in men, kindness and generosity, openness, honesty, understanding and feeling are the concomitants of failure in our system. And those traits we detest, sharpness, greed, acquisitiveness, meanness, egotism and self-interest are the traits of success. And while men admire the quality of the first they love the produce of the second. (89)[15]

What distinguishes *Cannery Row* from *In Dubious Battle* and from nearly all of Steinbeck's earlier fiction is the novelist's implicit willingness to accept Ricketts' long-held views about the destructive nature of "that factor of civilization we call progress." Of course, Steinbeck had always waged war against shortsighted propagandists whose political schemes for change are attended by a loss of vision. But with the exception of the *Log*, in which he allowed Ricketts to express his own views on material progress, he consistently championed meaningful change and regarded Ricketts' non-teleological appreciation of what is as socially irresponsible. In *Cannery Row*, however, Steinbeck admits that the marine biologist may have been right all along; that despite the truth of Smuts' dictum that "purpose is the highest, most important activity of the free, creative mind," in America this sense of purpose has made us a nation of vipers. The one significant distinction between Steinbeck's handling of Doc Burton and his treatment of the Doc of *Cannery Row* is that whereas the novelist blames Burton for being unable to convert his insight into something of social meaning, Doc, although as set-apart a man as Burton, is never blamed at all. Unlike Burton, Doc is an heroic figure; the best that man can hope to become in the imperfect universe in which he lives.[16]

By 1945, John Steinbeck's world had changed perceptibly. And what he saw in postwar America strongly mitigated against his lofty philosophical idealism. Returning to a fully industrialized California which could no longer be a parent to the kind of agrarian reform he posited in *The Grapes of Wrath*, a California in which the Rotarian creed had become the admired model of social behavior, Steinbeck, in his works following *Cannery Row*, not only questioned and attacked material self-interest, but even grew skeptical of man's ability to "grow beyond his work" and "emerge ahead of his accomplishments."

Ironically, Steinbeck's changing perspective is largely responsible for the inferior quality of much of his later writing. For Steinbeck's best works are distinguished by his organismically based belief in man's inherent capacity for achieving greatness of mind and deed (as an individual and as part of a moving phalanx) in conjunction with a Rickettsian understanding of cosmic wholeness and a faith in man's ability to break through to a vision of this unity. When, however, the novelist became convinced of the ubiquitous nature of man's self-interested drive for material wealth,

Intimations of a Wasteland

Steinbeck the philosophical visionary gradually became either Steinbeck the conventional moralist exhorting man to choose goodness over evil, or Steinbeck the wasteland prophet lamenting the inevitable demise of the good man in a corrupt world.

Among Steinbeck's more adroit examinations of human nature in the context of his growing conviction about the ever-increasing nature of man's pursuit of wealth and power is *The Pearl*. Based upon a story he had heard during his expedition with Ricketts to the Gulf of California about a poor Mexican fisherman who found a fabulous pearl which he thought would guarantee his future happiness, but which almost destroyed him before he threw it back into the sea, Steinbeck worked hard on this fable, rewriting it several times. It was finally published in 1947, but went largely unnoticed, and it was not until six years later that the novelist cautiously affirmed that *The Pearl* was finally "gathering some friends."[17]

In contrast with the bawdiness of *Cannery Row*, *The Pearl* is a simple, lyrical tale which Steinbeck called "a black and white story like a parable."[18] It is a parable about the search for happiness and the nature of man's need to choose between the inherently benign natural life and the frantic, self-oriented modern world. At the crux of Steinbeck's theme in *The Pearl*, however, is not only a statement about the choice between simplicity and luxury, but also his conviction that human nature makes it impossible for man to choose what Ricketts called "the region of inward adjustments" (characterized by "friendship, tolerance, dignity, or love") until he has attempted to succeed in "the region of outward possessions."[19] At the end of *The Pearl*, Kino, the poor fisherman, realizes the destructive nature of material wealth and hurls the pearl back into the Sea of Cortez, but Steinbeck simultaneously shows his inability to make this decision until his drive for wealth and status has ended in tragedy and disappointement. For unlike Ricketts, who believed that the simple Indians of the Gulf would disparage the quest for material wealth if untouched by the greed of their northern neighbors, Steinbeck writes in *The Pearl* that "humans are never satisfied, that you give them one thing and they want something more."[20] And he insists, paradoxically, that this "is one of the greatest talents the species has and one that has made it superior to animals that are satisfied with what they have" (25). *The Pearl* is Steinbeck's parable of the human dilemma; it is a study of the agony involved in man's recognition of the vanity of human wishes.

At the beginning of Steinbeck's fable, Kino is a poor but mildly satisfied pearl fisherman. A devoted husband and father, his song is the "Song of the Family," which rises "to an aching chord that caught the throat, saying this is safety, this is warmth, this is the *Whole*" (5). He is a man who, like the contented Indians of the Gulf depicted by Ricketts in his Sea of Cortez journal, enjoys a "deep participation with all things, the gift he had from his people" (51).

He heard every little sound of the gathering night, the sleepy complaint of settling birds, the love agony of cats, the strike and withdrawl of little waves on the beach, and the simple hiss of distance. And he could smell the sharp odor of exposed kelp from the receding tide. (51)

But despite his sense of participation with the land and with his family, Kino is victimized by his poverty and exploited because of his ignorance. "He was trapped as his people were always trapped and would be until . . . they could be sure that the things in the books were really in the books" (30). When, therefore, Kino finds "the pearl of the world," he sees in it an end to the poverty and exploitation which heretofore he has been forced to accept. Gradually, the "Song of the Pearl" merges with the "Song of the Family," Steinbeck points out, "so that the one beautified the other" (24). And Kino envisages a day when he will be able to afford to send his child to school so that "one of his own people could tell him the truth of things" (35). Kino tells his wife, Juana, "This is our one chance. Our son must go to school. He must break out of the pot that holds us in" (37).

But Kino's thinking about the future becomes cloudy; his vision becomes as hazy as the mirage of the Gulf. "There was no certainty in seeing, no proof that what you saw was there or was not there" (15). And Kino looks down into the surface of his fabulous pearl and forms misty, insubstantial dreams that will never come true. For "in this Gulf of uncertain light there were more illusions than realities" (20).

As a member of a village of pearl fishermen, Kino is a member-unit in the organism of the greater community of La Paz. Steinbeck describes the town organismically as "a thing like a colonial animal. A town has a nervous system and a head and shoulders and feet. A town is a thing separate from all other towns, so that there are not two towns alike. And a town has a whole emotion" (22). Thus, when Kino finds his great pearl, the organism of the town stirs to life and an interest develops in Kino—"people with things to sell and people with favors to ask" (23).

The essence of pearl mixed with essence of men and a curious dark residue was precipitated. Every man suddenly became related to Kino's pearl, and Kino's pearl went into the dreams, the speculations, the schemes, the plans, the futures, the wishes, the needs, the lusts, the hungers, of everyone, and only one person stood in the way and that was Kino, so that he became curiously every man's enemy. (23)

No one resented Kino as long as he was an impoverished fisherman. But Kino stirred the fantasies of the townspeople, and upset the equilibrium of the organism.

If every single man and woman, child and baby, acts and conducts itself in a known pattern and breaks no walls and differs with no one and experiments in no way and is not sick and does not endanger the ease and peace of mind or steady unbroken flow of the town, then that unit can disappear and never be heard of. But let one man step out of the regular thought or the known and trusted pattern, and the nerves of the townspeople ring with nervousness and communication travels over the nerve lines of the town. Then every unit communicates to the whole. (39)

When he senses the greed of the envious villagers, Kino, who "had broken through the horizons into a cold and lonely outside" (28) (Steinbeck's choice of words is significant here), hardens and "his eyes and his voice were hard and cold and a brooding hate was growing in him" (37). And as attempts are made first to cheat him of his wealth and later to steal his pearl, the "Song of the Pearl" becomes a "Song of Evil" as Kino fights to save himself, his family, and his newfound wealth. Kino admits that "This pearl has become my soul. . . . If I give it up I shall lose my soul" (62).

Gradually, Kino realizes that while he has irrevocably lost one world, he has not gained another. He insists that because "I am a man," "I will fight this thing" and "win over it," and he drives "his strength against a mountain" and plunges "against the sea" (56). But Kino's hopes are destroyed, for as Juana, his ostensibly suppliant but strong and knowing wife (like Ma Joad, Juana is "pure Briffault"), realizes, "the mountain would stand while the man broke himself"; "the sea would surge while the man drowned in it." At the same time, Juana knows that it is the striving that makes Kino a man, "half insane and half god, and Juana had need of a man" (56).

Kino saves his pearl from those who would steal it, but he pays dearly for it with the destruction of his house and canoe, and ultimately with the death of his baby. Finally, Kino begins to see the pearl as a "grey, malignant growth," and he chooses the "region of inward adjustments" over the "region of outward possessions" by throwing the pearl back into the Gulf. And though he has lost his canoe, his home, and his child, and so is even poorer than before, his choice has been made possible only because he has "gone through the pain" and "come out on the other side" (80). Kino's story is the parable of the human condition; a parable of that two-legged paradox, man, growing accustomed to "the tragic miracle of consciousness," struggling, and finally succeeding, to forge the design of his microcosmic history.

While Ricketts' ideas about the inherent virtues of the simple, natural life serve as a thematic substratum on which Steinbeck builds his parable, the novelist's chief concern in *The Pearl* is with how man's failure to "participate" in "the region of inward adjustments" can lead to complete personal and social disintegration. In his next novel, *The Wayward Bus* (1947), Steinbeck moves even further from Ricketts' patterns of thought to probe the effects of materialistic self-interest on a widely diverse group of individuals, related only in that they are all victims of the self-centeredness which, for Steinbeck, more than anything else characterized the power drives in postwar American society.

The Wayward Bus is an allegory of modern life in which a random collection of men and women on a bus bound from one main California highway to another, are forced to re-examine their own lives and inspect the manner in which they interact with their fellow men. During the course of their trouble-filled journey, they destroy or at least partly redeem themselves, as they attempt or refuse to redefine their thinking and rechannel their behavior.

Thematically, the impact of Ricketts' world-view on *The Wayward Bus* is negligible. On the other hand, early in the novel Steinbeck does employ the marine biologist's unique manner of seeing as fictional method in a way he had not done since *Of Mice and Men*. In his story of Juan Chicoy and the eight passengers on his bus (named Sweetheart) bound from Juan's cafe at Rebel Corners to San Juan de la Cruz, the novelist delineates his characters with the objectivity of a scientist studying bugs under a microscope. Unlike *The Pearl*, in which Steinbeck exhibits compassion for Kino's plight, and in contrast with *Cannery Row*, where he stirs his readers' emotions with his gentle portraits of Doc and Mack's group of vagabonds, Steinbeck feels little warmth for Juan and his fellow travelers, who are consistently involved in absurd struggles, trivial power plays, and foolish self-deceptions.

As Antonia Seixas points out, the characters in *The Wayward Bus* are all "type-specimens," components as well as products of our civilization.

Elliot Pritchard is the type-specimen business man; his wife, Bernice, is the type-specimen "Lady," sweet, gentle, and terribly powerful, with the unconscious craftiness of the weak and lazy who must live by rules and force those rules on all around them. There is Horton, the traveling salesman, whose best-selling item is the "Little Wonder Artificial Sore Foot." There are the adolescents, Pimples Carson, apprentice mechanic, and Norma, the homely, pathetic waitress.[21]

But while Steinbeck describes the flawed lives of his main characters in objective detail, he never says how or why they got that way. In other words, he seems to be saying, "Here is a typical group of *homo Americanus.* See, this is how they look, this is how they act."[22]

At this point, however, the similarity between Ricketts' objective, non-teleological way of seeing and Steinbeck's pattern of fictional reality ceases. For while Steinbeck may be more interested in how his type-specimens look and act than in their respective pasts, he is deeply concerned about their futures. In short, what begins as a non-teleological account of something that happened turns into a conventional morality play (the novel's epigraph is a quotation from *Everyman*) in which Steinbeck, angered by men and women who are unconcerned with the lives of their fellow men and who have cut themselves off from any meaningful contact with the "region of inward adjustments," specifically structures the allegorical pattern of the novel in order to drive Sweetheart's driver and passengers to penitence.

Since most of the novel's action takes place in and around Juan Chicoy's bus, it is tempting to regard Sweetheart as an organism, the constitutent parts of which are Juan and his passengers. But from the outset, Juan and the other travelers are such self-interested people leading such fragmented lives that they are unable and unwilling to key-into their organismic sphere of being. In contrast with this self-directed group of "pilgrims," Steinbeck creates as a backdrop a lush and fertile nature, the beauty of which only the most insensitive can ignore.

In the deep spring when the grass was green on fields and foothills, when the lupines and poppies made a splendid blue and gold earth, when the great trees awakened in yellow-green young leaves, then there was no more lovely place in the world. It was no beauty you could ignore by being used to it. It caught you in the throat in the morning and made a pain of pleasure in the pit of your stomach when the sun went down over it. The sweet smell of the lupines and of the grass set you breathing nervously, set you panting almost sexually. And it was in this season of flowering and growth, though it was still before daylight, that Juan Chicoy came out to the bus carrying an electric lantern. Pimples Carson, his apprentice-mechanic, stumbled sleepily behind.[23]

Juan and Pimples (and the other wayward travelers) "stumble sleepily" through life and disdain not only their fellow passengers but also the beauty of the natural order. The characters' struggles with themselves and with each other multiply; tensions erupt into near-violence. And the "little wind" that blows in the passengers' faces, bringing "the smell of lupine and the smell of a quickening earth, frantic with production" (8) goes unnoticed.

During the journey to San Juan de la Cruz, Sweetheart is detoured off the main highway by high floodwaters which have washed out a bridge spanning the San Ysidro River. Here Steinbeck fuses his Everyman allegory with the Old Testament Flood motif in that events which occur along the seldom-used and dangerous back road to San Juan force Sweetheart's driver and passengers to re-examine themselves and reassess their relationships with their fellow travelers.[24]

When Juan, who for some time had been trying to find a way to abandon his passengers, allows Sweetheart to swerve into a ditch, the irritable travelers step off the bus below a tall yellow cliff. As they look up, they see at the very top "in great faint letters . . . the single word REPENT. It must have been a long and dangerous job for some wild creature to put it there with black paint, and it was nearly gone now" (160). The travelers climb to shelter in "three deep, dark caves" in the cliff below the sign, and it is in these caves that Steinbeck's Everyman theme is worked out. Deprived of all material comforts and without their driver, who has ostensibly gone to seek help, the passengers face themselves and one another squarely for the first time in the novel.

Seven of Juan's passengers undergo measurable alterations of character. All but the pernicious Mr. Van Brunt (who refuses to repent and dies in his own darkness) arrive at a somewhat fuller self-understanding and a recognition of their responsibilities toward their fellow "pilgrims." Juan Chicoy's shift in outlook is the most dramatic. Juan, who fled from the bus to an abandoned barn, suddenly gives up his illusory dream of escaping to the hills of Mexico. He returns, rallies his charges, and together, they dig Sweetheart out of the mud and travel on toward San Juan de la Cruz. As the bus resumes its journey, the passengers peer out the windows and see "a little rim of lighter sky around the edge of a great dark cloud over the western mountains" (212). The rain clouds lift, and the evening star comes into view, shining "clear and washed and steady" on a renewed earth.

Steinbeck's Everyman allegory is simply not believable. His portrayal of nature (as in *The Moon Is Down*) is too schematic, and his characters are flat and one-dimensional. Most importantly, their repentances seem facile and essentially meaningless. Juan does come back to dig Sweetheart out of the mud. But his return is not marked by any genuine sense of commitment, but rather by a vague feeling of involvement which really amounts to little more than resignation. In short, *The Wayward Bus* is a weak novel because Steinbeck all but abandons the broad ecological and organismal substructure which gave the actions of such characters as Jim Casy, Tom Joad, and even Mayor Orden and Kino, a genuine locus of meaning. There is no character, who, by breaking through to a knowledge of the deep thing, makes the "education of the heart" philosophically satisfying. Sweetheart lumbers on into San Juan, but one feels that her passengers, though momentarily shaken from their petty self-interest, lack any sense of purpose and so will return to the hypocritical beliefs and shallow dreams which characterize the world of which they are products and victims. Essentially motionless, Juan and his passengers never really key-into a moving phalanx of any kind. They do not "grow beyond their concepts" because they have no concepts. And they cannot "emerge ahead of their accomplishments" because they have accomplished little. In short, the characters in *The Wayward Bus* really do no more than the animals Steinbeck and Ricketts observed in the tide pools of the Sea of Cortez: SURVIVE. And this, the novelist seems to say, perhaps without consciously recognizing it, is the tragedy of man's wayward pilgrimage through the wasteland of modern life.

In late May 1951, while Steinbeck was hard at work on *East of Eden*, he reflected back a few years and noted that before he met his wife Elaine and started serious work on his new novel, "every life force was shriveling. Work was non-existent. I remember it very well. The wounds were gangrenous and mostly I just didn't give a dam[n]."[25] Steinbeck's early postwar fiction reflects the growing infection which led to these gangrenous wounds. The novelist had returned from the war to a vastly changed America. He tried first (in *Cannery Row*) to recapture a sense of the past, only to realize that neither the dropout nor the scientific-philosophic visionary could long survive the onslaught of civilization. Then, in *The Pearl*, he employed an old legend to explain the modern dilemma of man's drive to better himself and the concomitant woe which attends the craving. Finally, in *The Wayward Bus*, Steinbeck focused directly on the specimen-types who people the modern world and attempted with little artistic success to drive these characters to penitence.

Gradually, Steinbeck was becoming a novelist without a vision. His organismic view of man and the world, and his belief in the manner in which individuals can key-into a moving phalanx to work toward common human goals seemed increasingly ludicrous in a society of splintered, self-directed Americans. Simultaneously, Steinbeck apparently became convinced that Ricketts' understanding of the deep thing, of the fundamental unity of all life in a cosmic whole was meaningless in a world in which most men and women were too preoccupied with their own interests to seek that knowledge. Most importantly, *The Pearl* and *The Wayward Bus* are Steinbeck's first full-length works in a decade in which there are no Ricketts philosopher-figures whose ideas help to directly voice or ironically reflect that unique view of man and the cosmos which characterizes the novelist's greatest writing.

Laying Down
the Ghost

*T*here was very little communication between Steinbeck and Ricketts during the period in which *The Wayward Bus* was written and published. Geography contributed to this separation, for living in New York, far from Ricketts and Monterey, Steinbeck was moving in new circles among people whose company he found increasingly meaningful. It was also at about this time that his marriage to Gwendolyn Conger deteriorated, and with the uncertain future of his two young sons much on his mind, Steinbeck evidently had little time to communicate with his old friends in California. John Steinbeck had become a New Yorker, and while he retained fond memories of good times on the Monterey Peninsula, he sensed as early as 1947 that he could never go home again.

It was in this spirit that he sought new vistas for his literary expression. During the summer of 1947, Steinbeck traveled through Russia with photographer Robert Capa, and with Capa wrote *A Russian Journal* (1948) shortly after their return. With the exception of some sardonic remarks about how the stifling of individual initiative in the collective Soviet state resulted in political and economic inefficiency, there is virtually no trace of the

178

more important aspects of Ricketts' world-view in *A Russian Journal*. Instead, Steinbeck directs most of his interest to the rich, fertile countryside of Georgia where "there was a good smell of green things all over," and on the "lively and friendly" farmers "divided into battalions" as they harvested their cucumber crop.[1] Steinbeck notes that "each family had its house and a garden and an orchard where there were flowers, and where there were large vegetable patches and beehives" (74). And he almost seems to suggest that the Georgian and Ukrainian farmers have achieved what Ma Joad and the other dispossessed Oklahoma tenant farmers were denied. Certainly, Steinbeck's affection for the small Russian farmers living close to the soil reflects his belief that while not so "successful" as the Elliot and Bernice Pritchards of modern America, their life-styles are certainly more appealing.

Across the world from where Steinbeck and Capa were touring the Russian countryside, Ed Ricketts was hard at work on plans for "The Outer Shores." Following his discharge from the Army, Ricketts made extensive collecting trips to Vancouver Island and the Queen Charlottes during the summers of 1945 and 1946, and he spent much of 1947 planning for a third and final trip with Steinbeck in June of 1948. Steinbeck had shown some interest by agreeing to write the foreword to the second edition of *Between Pacific Tides*, which was scheduled for publication late in 1948. And Ricketts, who sent the records of his earlier trips to Steinbeck in New York, thought of "The Outer Shores" as a northern sequel to *Sea of Cortez*.[2]

Steinbeck's actual reluctance to spend several weeks poking around in the tide pools of the Queen Charlotte Islands has already been discussed. Having completed preliminary work on "a giant novel" tentatively titled "Salinas Valley," Steinbeck may have felt that an interruption of the type the marine biologist had in mind would impede his drive for artistic independence.

In retrospect, there is a bitterly ironic note in the fact that Steinbeck's hesitancy to collaborate with Ricketts on "The Outer Shores" was attributable to his concern that a renewed participation with the marine biologist's thinking would prove detrimental

179

to his art. For Ricketts' death just weeks before the trip was scheduled to commence shattered Steinbeck's emerging literary independence and resulted in his even deeper involvement with the marine biologist's ideas about man and the world.

Steinbeck flew from New York to California as soon as he received news of Ricketts' accident, but arrived shortly after Ricketts' death on May 11. He stayed in Monterey only long enough to clear up some of Ricketts' personal affairs, to recover Ricketts' journals and some fragments of their correspondence, and to visit old friends. Initially, Steinbeck found it very difficult to adjust to the fact of his friend's death, and his disbelief turned first to anger and then to a deep sense of loss. But gradually, as the impact of the immediate thing dulled, Steinbeck developed a great feeling of life again as if a kind of harness had been removed which forced him to stand on his own two feet as a writer. Steinbeck wrote to Ritch and Tal Lovejoy only two weeks after Ricketts' death and spoke of himself as a writer growing new tissue; of having an energy restored that would drive him to work as he had not worked in many years. He told the Lovejoys that although he had to stop and go through all of his memories of Ricketts and of their friendship, he would do it all once and then let go forever.

Despite his intentions, the future proved that Steinbeck could not let go so easily. For although he continued to work on "Salinas Valley," which he finally completed late in 1951 as *East of Eden*, his four other major works written between 1948 and 1954 reflect his rekindled absorption with the person and/or ideas of his closest friend. In retrospect, the five years following Ricketts' death were for Steinbeck a period of literary convalescence and separation, and it was not until he finished work on *Sweet Thursday* that he could lay down the ghost once and for all.

In his first works written after Ricketts' death, *Burning Bright* and "About Ed Ricketts," Steinbeck junked reality in order to portray (first in fiction, and then in a direct tribute) his affection for Ricketts and for Ricketts' way of seeing. As time passed, however, the novelist found himself again able to deal critically with Ricketts' world-view (*Viva Zapata!*). Finally, in *Sweet Thurs-*

day, Steinbeck severed the cords completely by stating that the hard facts of modern existence made Ricketts' life-style utterly intractable.

"About Ed Ricketts" has already been referred to in sufficient detail. It is important to note, however, that in writing this sixty-page tribute which prefaces Viking's 1952 edition of the narrative section of *Sea of Cortez*, Steinbeck supports fact with fiction, and his portrait of Ricketts is less an authentic assessment of the marine biologist's significant contributions to the literature of the seashore (Steinbeck never mentions *Between Pacific Tides*) than it is a sincere statement of Steinbeck's unique affection for a man whose influence the novelist felt "deeply and permanently." "Maybe some of the events are imagined. And perhaps some very small happenings may have grown out of all proportion in the mind" (x). And yet, Steinbeck writes, this is the only kind of biographical account he was qualified to write in 1951 about a man who "will not die" . . . who "is always present even in the moments when we feel his loss the most" (xi). And in the troubled ending of his portrait of Ricketts, Steinbeck concedes his uncertainty "whether any clear picture has emerged" (lxvii). In fact, the only real conclusion Steinbeck does reach in "About Ed Ricketts" is that "thinking back and remembering has not done what I hoped it might. It has not laid the ghost" (lxvii).

Ricketts' ghost turns up as a potent force in *Burning Bright* (1950), Steinbeck's first work of fiction written after the marine biologist's death. Composed in the winter of 1949–1950, *Burning Bright* is structurally and thematically one of Steinbeck's weakest books, and its failure as art was the inevitable result of the novelist's attempt to lift a story involving a fundamental aspect of Ricketts' character "to the parable expression of the morality play."[3] Unlike his earlier and more successful ventures in the play-novelette (*Of Mice and Men* and *The Moon Is Down*), *Burning Bright* is less a work of fiction than a piece of abstract philosophical theory which Steinbeck works out through an imaginary dialogue between himself and Ricketts.

The plot of *Burning Bright* deals with sterility and concerns the inability of a fifty-year-old man (Joe Saul) to father a child by his young and very beautiful wife (Mordeen). Mordeen knows her husband is sterile, and because she is deeply in love with him and desperately wishes to give him the child he wants so badly, she commits adultery with Victor, Saul's insensitive assistant, and soon becomes pregnant. Eventually, Joe Saul learns of his sterility from a doctor and guesses what his wife has done. The remainder of the action in *Burning Bright* deals with Saul's gradual acceptance (upon advice from his close associate, Friend Ed) of the product of Mordeen's adultery, a decision heralded by his triumphant assertion of the unity of all men:

"I know," he said. "I had to walk into the black to know—to know that every man is father to all children and every child must have all men as father. This is not a little piece of private property, registered and fenced and separated. Mordeen! This is *the Child*."[4]

On one thematic level, *Burning Bright* has much in common with *The Pearl* and *The Wayward Bus*. Steinbeck's concern with the injurious effects of self-interest is apparent in his depiction of Joe Saul as a "lineless, faceless Everyone" (21) who triumphs over his own weakness when he successfully renounces his "crawling, whining ego" (121). And the villain of the story is Victor, a man whose orientation is "the self-centered chaos of childhood."

Victor's unfortunate choice it was always to mis-see, to mis-hear, to misjudge. He read softness into her [Mordeen] because of the softness of her voice, when she was only remembering. His was the self-centered chaos of childhood. All looks and thoughts, loves and hatreds, were directed at him. Softness was softness toward him, weakness was weakness in the face of his strength. He preheard answers and listened not. He was full colored and brilliant—all outside of him was pale. (35)

Steinbeck, then, asserts as his central premise in *Burning Bright* that the individual ego is less important than the species as a whole. And like Kino and Juana in *The Pearl* who "had gone through pain and come out on the other side," Joe Saul "went away into an insanity" and only then could return to realize that "it is the race, the species that must go staggering on" (129), that despite "all our horrors and our faults, somewhere in us there is a shining" (130). Indeed, *Burning Bright* is so much a parable about the destructive nature of self-interest, that Steinbeck places the story "in the hands of three professions which have long and continuing traditions, namely the Circus, the Farm and the Sea."[5] At the same time, he uses what he calls "a kind of universal language not geared to the individual actors or their supposed crafts but rather the best I was able to produce."[6]

Burning Bright was soundly condemned by theatrical and literary reviewers, and the stage production closed after just thirteen performances. Richard Rodgers, who with Oscar Hammerstein produced the play, has acknowledged "it was dead the first night," and that while Steinbeck was angry about the more insensitive reviews, he was philosophical about its failure (RR/RA, 3/23/71).[7] One reason for the failure of Steinbeck's play-novelette is its unconventional language, a discordant mass of archaisms and trite poetic diction. Even more problematical is Steinbeck's transposition of abstract character types from circus to farm to sea. For in attempting to universalize his thematic construct, the novelist unrealistically forced the story's organization. Steinbeck had demonstrated in several of his earlier works that the way to depict the whole is to begin with concrete characters and stay with them until the universal shines through. (In his preface to *The Forgotten Village*, as seen above, the author noted that "from association with this little personalized group, the larger conclusion concerning the racial group could be drawn with something like participation" [5].) But in *Burning Bright*, Steinbeck, who, his widow has speculated, was too colloquial a writer to write symbolist fiction (ES/RA, 3/24/71), abandons the idea of the personalized group and ends up climbing the bare wall of philosophical abstraction.

When Steinbeck discussed his dramatic intentions in *Burning Bright*, he pointed out that he wanted his audience "to leap a gulf of unreality and to join the company in creating a greater reality," but he simultaneously conceded that "for some people I suppose we made the jump too long." Still, reflects the novelist, unwilling to condemn his own method, "it was gratifying to see how many did make the leap into participation."[8]

JOHN STEINBECK and EDWARD F. RICKETTS

Although it is apparent that Steinbeck's decision to avoid concrete and believable characters was the result of his desire to universalize his parable, a close look at the two leading spokesmen for Steinbeck's central thesis in *Burning Bright* reveals that there may have been another serious consideration behind Steinbeck's decision to avoid the personalized group. Surely, "[J]oe [S]aul is [J]ohn [S]teinbeck and Friend [Ed] is [Ed] Ricketts" (ES/RA, 12/26/72). And while the story line in *Burning Bright* concerns sterility, Steinbeck's play-novelette is at the same time a memoir of the unique intellectual relationship between himself and the marine biologist. One of the most interesting things about *Burning Bright* is the manner in which Steinbeck carefully integrates what, in 1950, he regarded as the most important aspect of Ricketts' personality into his own attack on the evils of human pride. And just as Steinbeck freely confessed (in "About Ed Ricketts") that Ricketts helped teach him how to see and live, it is Friend Ed who teaches Joe Saul that "what seemed the whole tight pattern is not important" (128).

At the conclusion of "About Ed Ricketts," Steinbeck reflects that "the great talent that was in Ed Ricketts, that made him so loved and needed and makes him so missed now that he is dead" was "his ability to receive, to receive anything from anyone, to receive gracefully and thankfully and to make the gift seem very fine" (lxiv). Receiving, Steinbeck notes he learned from Ricketts, demands "a fine balance of self-knowledge and kindness" (lxv). It also "requires a self-esteem to receive—not self-love but just a pleasant acquaintance and liking for oneself" (lxv). "Once Ed was able to like himself," Steinbeck remembers, "he was released from the secret prison of self-contempt. Then he did not have to prove superiority any more by any of the ordinary methods, including giving. He could receive and understand and be truly glad. . . ." (lxvi). Most importantly, "Ed's gift for receiving made him a great teacher" (lxvi).

A close inspection of the dialogue between Joe Saul and Friend Ed in *Burning Bright* reveals that what Joe Saul really learns from Friend Ed is the lesson of how to receive; how to accept a child from a woman whose love, as Friend Ed points out, "is so great that she could do a thing that was strange and foul to her and yet not be dirtied by it" (122). When Joe Saul first learns of his sterility, he believes that because "My line, my blood, all the procession of the ages is dead" (118), he can no longer live with himself. It is then that Friend Ed attacks Saul's "crawling, whining ego" and his decision to "vomit" on a "gift of love given you such as few men have ever known" because of an "ugly twisted sense of importance" (121). Friend Ed tells Joe Saul that "in your smallness you had not the graciousness to receive this gift" (122), and he teaches Saul that "it is so easy a thing to give—only great men have the courage and courtesy and, yes, the generosity to receive" (123).

I don't know what you'll do, Joe Saul. But I would hope that some greatness might be left in you. They say that crippled men have compensations which make them stronger than the strong. I could wish that you would know and understand that you are the husband and father of love. The gift you have received is beyond the furthest hope of most men. It's not that you should try to excuse and explain. You should— you must—search in your dark crippled self for the goodness and the generosity to receive. (123)

Just as Steinbeck was at first uncertain of his ability to go on alone after Ricketts' death, Joe Saul pleads with Friend Ed (who has his "sailing order") not to leave him on his "particular dark ocean." "Don't leave me, Friend Ed. For God's sake, don't leave me alone! I'm afraid. I don't know what to do!" (123). Gradually, though, Joe Saul gathers the strength to carry on alone, and while he fears "a new and unknown road," he does receive "gracefully and thankfully" the product of his wife's adultery. Free from the need to prove his superiority to anyone, Joe Saul emerges from his "secret prison of self-contempt," and he realizes that while he once thought that "my blood must survive—my line," now "it's not so." "The baby is alive," says Saul triumphantly, "this is the only important thing" (129).

Steinbeck chose as his epigraph for *Burning Bright* the first stanza of Blake's "Tyger" in order to illustrate his celebration of the miracle of life; that "despite man's cruelty, violence, weakness and wickedness, some life force had framed him in 'fearful symmetry.' "[9] And in the process of discovering his own fearful symmetry, Joe Saul learns the central precept of Ricketts' cosmic vision: that because "every man is father to all children and every child must have all men as father," "all that lives is holy." Of course, Steinbeck has problems in delineating this thesis, since the proposition that all men are brothers does not seem to include Victor, who, from the standpoint of the principle of natural selection, is a disruptive mutant who must be destroyed to preserve the whole.[10] On the other hand, if we see beneath the prophet's robes of Friend Ed the real humanity and holistic vision of Ed Ricketts, then perhaps we can accept as thematically consistent his disposal of Victor in that he is like Doc in *Cannery Row* who can "kill anything for need but he could not even hurt a feeling for pleasure." As Warren French points out, this idea is really congruent with the novelist's theories about universal brotherhood, but whether or not it is acceptable to the individual reader of *Burning Bright* is strictly another matter.[11]

And so, in conjunction with his very serious interest in the problem of sterility and his continuing moral concern with the disintegrative effects of self-interest, *Burning Bright* is laced through with the presence of the ideas and personality of Ed Ricketts. One might even argue that there is as much Ricketts in *Burning Bright* as there is in *Cannery Row*, and that *Burning Bright* fails where *Cannery Row* succeeds because a warm and genuine personality (Doc) is replaced by a robed prophet in a clown's suit.

Because of the failure of Steinbeck's language and his reliance upon "faceless" characters who voice abstract philosophical concepts, one must conclude that *Burning Bright* is among Steinbeck's least successful works. But from the standpoint of the impact on the novelist's fiction of the ideas and person of Edward F. Ricketts, *Burning Bright* is as important a work as anything Steinbeck had written since *The Grapes of Wrath*. The integration of Ricketts' personality and ideas with Steinbeck's theme in *Burning Bright* proves the novelist's final contention in "About Ed Ricketts" that "association with him [Ricketts] was deep participation with him, never competition."

Although *Burning Bright* was Steinbeck's first work of fiction to be published after Ricketts' death, it was written after the novelist had completed a significant portion of the story for his screenplay of *Viva Zapata!* which Elia Kazan made into one of 20th Century-Fox's more successful movies of 1952. Steinbeck began work on *Viva Zapata!* shortly after Ricketts' death and completed it in May 1950. As Lisca notes, the novelist was particularly concerned that Fox would follow his screenplay closely. He wrote a special introduction to the shooting script so that the "producer, director and cameraman would understand what it was about, and he even went on location with Twentieth Century-Fox to supervise the actual filming."[19]

His only political work written after World War II, *Viva Zapata!* represents for Steinbeck a return to earlier themes and subject matter. The novelist had been vitally interested in the life and career of the Mexican revolutionary, Emiliano Zapata, for some time before he began work on his filmscript, and Richard Albee recalls that "John first learned about Zapata at my home in Hollywood, as early as 1931 or 1932, from [Reina Dunn,] the Mexican-American daughter of an American reporter who 'covered' Zapata and wrote a rather crummy book about him" (Albee-RA, 5/9/71). It is doubtful that Steinbeck acquired much significant information about Zapata from H. H. Dunn's *The Crimson Jester* (1933), but he did learn a good deal about the Mexican freedom fighter from conversations with Dunn's daughter.

The materials of *Viva Zapata!* resemble those of *In Dubious Battle* and *The Grapes of Wrath*. Steinbeck did learn from Dunn's work that like the dispossessed Oklahoma tenant farmers, the Mexican-Indian peasants under Zapata's command had been deprived of their land by absentee landlords. And the novelist must have been moved by Dunn's reportage of a speech by one of Zapata's followers, "We come from the soil. We must have that soil again. It belongs to us Indians, not to the white planters, not to the halfbreed *caciques*, but to us who have lived on it since before the beginning of the centuries."[13] In this spirit, Steinbeck depicts Zapata and his followers as agrarian reformers, and when a sympathetic small landowner named Don Nacio tells a large planter named Don Garcia that because the Indians have lived on the land "since before the Conquest," "they are really the true owners," he speaks for the landless Zapatistas who, like the Joads in *The Grapes of Wrath*, believe that being born on the land, working on it and dying on it "makes ownership, not a paper with numbers on it."

In Steinbeck's script, Zapata wins his revolution only to be corrupted by the misuse of power. Suddenly, just as he is becoming as tyrannical as the dictators he helped to overthrow, Zapata realizes what he has become, and he rectifies his errors, at the cost of his life. And in death, he becomes a mythic figure from whom all oppressed people can take strength.[14]

Robert Morsberger has written a highly compelling analysis of *Viva Zapata!* in which, through an examination of Steinbeck's handling of the story's contrasting political doctrines in terms of Camus' distinction between the rebel and the revolutionary, he observes that Steinbeck sympathized with Zapata the rebel and "a man of individual conscience," in contrast with Fernando, the revolutionary, who is an example of the kind of man who uses a people's grievances for his own ends. Morsberger notes that Steinbeck's depiction of "the conflict between creative dissent and intolerant militancy" has its roots in *In Dubious Battle* and *The Grapes of Wrath*, and he concludes that the real strength of *Viva Zapata!* lies in the author's firm warning against the misuse of power, not only to the forces of right-wing reaction but equally to the extremists of left-wing revolution.[15]

Steinbeck's Zapata is above all a man of his people. Like Tom Joad in *The Grapes of Wrath*, Zapata has no real expertise in theories of revolution, but he sympathizes deeply with the plight of his people and he maintains a strong personal relationship with the land of his birth. And like Tom, who at first wants only to "lay his dogs down one at a time," Zapata does not want "to be the conscience of the world. I don't want to be the conscience of anybody."[16] But Zapata cannot ignore the hard facts of political and economic oppression, and when he strikes out against the Mexican Rurales and frees a peasant whose only crime has been to crawl through a fence at night to plant some corn, Zapata touches off a mass movement, of which he is destined to become the leader and symbol. Suddenly need turns to concept and concept to action. The phalanx forms as men and women swarm from the Mexican countryside to key-into the new movement behind Emiliano Zapata. The landless Zapatistas are much like the united migrant families in *The Grapes of Wrath* in that they "obey impulses that register only faintly in their thinking minds," and "do what they have to do" in order to achieve an equitable program of land reform. Zapata and his followers defeat the repressive forces of President Diaz, and Zapata believes "the fighting is over" (63). But instead of leading to peace and reform, Zapata's rebellion is spoiled by the insurgency of doctrinaire revolutionaries who inaugurate a series of political betrayals which eventually lead to the death of Zapata himself.

Through the character of Fernando Aguirre, a fervent young man with a typewriter which he calls "the sword of the mind," Steinbeck presents a political version of the individual whose self-interest blinds him to a recognition of the brotherhood of man. In many respects, Fernando resembles Mac and Jim of *In Dubious Battle*, though Fernando's inhuman self-interest distinguishes him from the selfless if equally inhuman Party leaders (and this, of course, makes Fernando a more modern version of the villain in the light of Steinbeck's concern with the evils of self-interest in *The Pearl, The Wayward Bus,* and *Burning Bright*). Like Jim Nolan, Fernando moves in "a straight line," and his absolutist revolutionary logic permits him to commit any atrocity that seems expedient.

Most significantly, it is Fernando who demands the excecution of the sensitive humanist, Pablo, whom he wrongly suspects of treason after some of Zapata's forces are ambushed. A man of vision who "in his patience and wisdom, resembles Anselmo in *For Whom the Bell Tolls*,"[17] Pablo is clearly the Ricketts-figure in Steinbeck's screenplay. It is he whom Zapata sends to "look deeply into the eyes of Madero" (the first leader of the fight against Diaz) and report what he sees. And it is Pablo who defends the well-intentioned but politically inept Madero as "a good man" who "wanted to build houses and plant fields" (88) after Fernando has condemned Madero as an enemy, an action Pablo simply cannot understand.

> PABLO. But you're his emissary, his officer, his friend . . .
> FERNANDO. I'm a friend to no one—and to nothing except logic . . . This is the time for killing. (71)

Like Doc Burton, who opposes the Party's use of force as a solution to political problems, Pablo refuses to accept Fernando's thesis that violence is valuable for its own sake. He pleads that if only "we could begin to build—even while the killing goes on. If we could plant while we destroy . . ." (88). And when Fernando accuses him of treason to the "cause," Pablo cautions Zapata against tyranny and begs him not to forget the real needs which drove him to rebellion. Pablo sounds a good deal like Doc Burton when he attacks the empty teleology of blind political partisanship.

> Our cause was land—not a thought, but corn-planted earth to feed the families. And Liberty—not a word, but a man sitting safely in front of his house in the evening. And Peace, not a dream—but a time of rest and kindness. The question beats in my head, Emiliano. Can a good thing come from a bad act? Can peace come from so much violence (He now looks directly into Emiliano's immobile eyes)? And can a man whose thoughts are born in anger and hatred, can such a man lead to peace? (88–89)

But despite his clarity of vision, Pablo is executed, and Steinbeck again shows how political expediency undermines the insight of the sensitive visionary. For just as Mac has "no time to mess around with [Burton's] high falutin ideas," there is no place in Fernando's revolution for Pablo's ideas about peace and land reform. Once again, a Ricketts-figure is defeated by a world that cannot tolerate undistorted vision. And once again, Steinbeck proves Ricketts' adage (as articulated by Doc in *Cannery Row*) that "the things we admire in men, kindness and generosity, openness, honesty, understanding and feeling are the concomitants of failure in our system. And those traits we detest, sharpness, greed, acquisitiveness, meanness, egotism and self-interest are the traits of success" (89).

Steinbeck does affirm, however, that although the sensitive soul cannot survive the deceptions and intrigues of the political revolutionary, the strong-minded social activist who is thoroughly committed to the real needs of his people can deny his betrayers. Gradually, Zapata comes to understand the distorted nature of Fernando's "principle of successful rule" in which "there can be no opposition" (101). He learns what Steinbeck and Ricketts discovered in their games of "speculative metaphysics"; that "opposition is creative and restriction is non-creative. The force that feeds growth is therefore cut off."[18] And helped by reminders from his people, Zapata realizes the corrupting nature of absolute authority, and "in the name of all I fought for" (55), he relinquishes his power in order to take "it back where it belongs, to thousands of men" (106).

Zapata returns to his native Mexican hills and initiates a program of planting and building. He works alongside the once-landless peasants who with his help have keyed-into a moving phalanx which has given them a sense of purpose and direction. And he learns that because his followers are now a free, creative people, they no longer need him nor anyone else to lead them. And when Zapata's wife, Josepha, who fears her husband may be ambushed, asks him what will happen to the people if he is killed, Zapata replies,

EMILIANO. *They've* changed. That is how things really change—slowly through people. They don't need me any more.
JOSEPHA. They have to be led.
EMILIANO. But by each other. A strong man makes a weak people. Strong people don't need a strong man. (121)

And so, when Zapata is killed after being trapped by the troops of Carranza and Obregon, his followers know that the spirit of Zapata can never die.

YOUNG MAN. They'll never get him. Can you capture a river? Can you kill the wind?

LAZARO. No! He's not a river and he's not the wind! He's a man— and they still can't kill him! . . . He's in the mountains. You couldn't find him now. But if we ever need him again—he'll be back. (127–128)

Like Jim Casy, Tom Joad, Mayor Orden, and Juan Diego, all of whom are committed to work for the needs of their people, Emiliano Zapata is the creative rebel who suffers because of his conscience. He is one of those "great personalities of history [who] stamps upon their social period their creative faith."[19] And by recording Zapata's drive for land reform and his final renunciation of the power that corrupts, Steinbeck recreates one of the most turbulent phases of Mexican history to convey his belief in at least one man's enduring capacity for greatness of mind and deed.

With regard to the impact of Ricketts' ideas about man and the world on Steinbeck's screenplay, one might argue that because *Viva Zapata!* does not contain the same kind of Ricketts-based philosophical substratum as *In Dubious Battle* or *The Grapes of Wrath* (the emphasis on holistic thinking, the doctrine of breaking through, etc.), Zapata's actions lack a metaphysical base and his (and Pablo's) speeches about leadership and land reform are superficial platitudes left over from Weedpatch and the Torgas Valley. But what would have happened to Steinbeck's screenplay if the author chose to portray Zapata riding through the Mexican hills gazing at the stars and muttering about the "holy sperit" and the "whole shebang"? *Viva Zapata!* is historical fiction, and while, through the use of characters like Pablo and Zapata, Steinbeck was able to integrate those facets of Ricketts' world-view with his own notions about agrarian reform and phalanx need which most successfully interpreted history, he anchored these statements firmly within the context of the screenplay's action. Extraneous soliloquies were omitted. And this is a major reason why *Viva Zapata!* succeeds whereas works like *The Moon Is Down* and *Burning Bright* fail. Pablo and Zapata differ from Doctor Winter and Mayor Orden and from Friend Ed and Joe Saul in that they simply do not have the time to play "speculative metaphysics." *Viva Zapata!* is one of Steinbeck's finest creations. Still politically and socially relevant, it is a work in which the author maintains complete control over his materials as he combines the most fundamental aspects of his own and Ricketts' way of seeing and so interprets creatively one of the most fascinating moments in Western history.

Steinbeck's employment of Ricketts-like characters and diverse aspects of Ricketts' way of seeing in *Burning Bright* and *Viva Zapata!*, and his unsuccessful attempt in "About Ed Ricketts" to go through the "memories, anecdotes, quotations and events" and then let go forever, reflect his inability (between 1948 and 1952) to lay down the ghost. However, during this period he completed work on *East of Eden*. The bulk of Steinbeck's work on what he called "my big novel" in which he planned "to use every bit of technique I have learned consciously,"[20] took place between January and November of 1951 after he had freed himself of his other professional commitments.

There is very little of Ed Ricketts in *East of Eden*. Although Steinbeck does on occasion rely on aphoristic bits of philosophical wisdom which recall Ricketts' way of thinking, this novel is essentially Steinbeck's attempt to resolve those complex moral issues which had been bothering him for nearly a decade.

During his last year of work on *East of Eden*, Steinbeck noted that he thought "that this might be my last book"; that although in the past "I have written each book as an exercise, as practice for the one to come," "there is nothing beyond this book—nothing follows it."[21] But by the time he finished *East of Eden*, Steinbeck knew there was something very important to follow; that while he had successfully shelved the ghost of Ed Ricketts during the composition of *East of Eden*, that ghost was not yet buried. And so, only months after *East of Eden* was finished, Steinbeck began work on what, from the standpoint of the impact of the person and ideas of Edward F. Ricketts on the novelist's fiction, is one of the most important works in his entire canon, *Sweet Thursday* (1954).

The earliest reviews of *Sweet Thursday* reflect a complete mis-understanding of what, for the reviewers, was simply a repeat performance of *Cannery Row*. Edward Weeks, writing for *Atlantic Monthly*, called it "good fun."[22] The reviewer for *Nation* affirmed that Steinbeck had "returned to the never-never world of 'Cannery Row'" with "unpretentious but relaxing" results; "The book was designed to go nicely with a highball in a warm sun and it does."[23] More discerning critics, who found *Cannery Row* a charming, entertaining tale despite the presence of Steinbeck's poison cream puff, were perplexed by the tone of *Sweet Thursday*. Robert Boyle called it "a grade-B potboiler" and a "sentimental mishmash,"[24] while Ward Moore objected to the "overpowering odor of sugar" in that "Cannery Row is no longer softened by a transmuting haze of artistry—it is tidied up and prettified beyond recognition."[25]

Moore points to the central problem with *Sweet Thursday*: Steinbeck's sentimental rendering of what once were delightfully picaresque materials. For despite Steinbeck's own statement that *Sweet Thursday* "is a romance based on my own folklore" so that its authenticity is irrelevant,[26] there is something deeply troubling about the novel's creamy sweetness and its cheerful affirmations.

Sweet Thursday is certainly not a repetition of *Cannery Row*, and it is, at least on the surface, a sentimental novel. Steinbeck wrote his new book with the theater in mind; by mid-1953 he was working on a new short novel "which would be converted into a musical for the sponsors of *Guys and Dolls*."[27] Rodgers and Hammerstein were interested in *Cannery Row* and *Sweet Thursday* (they even considered combining the two). And Elaine Steinbeck recalls that Steinbeck wrote *Sweet Thursday* thinking it might be staged as musical comedy (ES/RA, 3/24/71). Entitled *Pipe Dream*, the Rodgers and Hammerstein adaptation of *Sweet Thursday* went into production during the fall of 1955, and Steinbeck attended many of the rehearsals (RR/RA, 3/23/71). The play opened at the Shubert Theatre in December, and while it was hardly an instant popular success, it did survive the season, running for a total of 246 performances. *Pipe Dream* does contain a memorable song or two (particularly "All Kinds of People" and "Everybody's Got a Home but Me"), but Steinbeck's materials were terribly sentimentalized and his leading characters failed to come off as real people. It is even slightly painful to look into the Rodgers and Hammerstein version of the Great Tide Pool where "shrimps 'n' limpets 'n' snails 'n' eels," "the damndest collection o' creeps you ever seen," are "fightin' each other/ 'N eating each other,/ 'N lousin' up the sea."[28]

Doc is the central figure in the denouement of Steinbeck's sentimental plot, and he is the most unauthentic Ricketts-character in any Steinbeck novel, a fact which has troubled virtually everyone interested in the relationship between the two men. Ward Moore notes that Doc lives, despite Ed Ricketts' death, but he has become "the beneficiary of hovering solicitude" and the "recipient of anxious endowments."[29] Lisca, puzzled by Steinbeck's characterization of Doc in *Sweet Thursday*, speculates that Steinbeck either has deliberately set out "to destroy or depreciate his former mask," or he has "lost contact with the original, vital purpose of his mask or *persona* and is unaware of the violence done to the figure of Doc."[30] Elaine Steinbeck has unequivocally denied that her husband set out to demean Ricketts in *Sweet Thursday*, (ES/RA, 3/24/71). However, the Doc of that novel is not only unlike the Doc of *Cannery Row*, but his behavior sharply conflicts with that of his real-life prototype.

It is true, of course, that Steinbeck always portrayed Ricketts not precisely as he was but as the novelist saw him. In "The Snake," *In Dubious Battle*, *The Moon Is Down*, *Burning Bright*, and *Cannery Row*, Steinbeck exercised his artistic privilege to either heighten or foreshorten various aspects of the original. But the Doc of *Sweet Thursday* scarcely resembles Ed Ricketts at all. And unless Steinbeck had simply forgotten everything about the marine biologist in the year or two since completing "About Ed Ricketts" (which is most unlikely), it is doubtful that he would denigrate the memory of his closest friend without good reason.

The first question, then, that must be answered with regard to Steinbeck's thematic intentions in *Sweet Thursday* is simply, Who is this Doc who is best described as "a one-dimensional character resembling no scientist, living or dead"?[31] Superficially at least, he is still the marine biologist of *Cannery Row* who lives and works at his Western Biological Laboratory on the Monterey wharves. But whereas the earlier Doc was passionately devoted to his study of the faunal life in the coastal tide pools, the Doc of *Sweet Thursday* is listless and seems indifferent toward his work. Having returned from the war, during which he "served out his time as a tech sergeant in a V.D. section,"[32] Doc has lost interest in the marine specimens he collects and preserves. He is "no longer capable of the sustained attention required for his work. He takes every excuse to malinger and is genuinely relieved when his specimens die."[33]

The real Doc spent the postwar years at work on conservation problems related to the depletion of the sardine industry in Monterey, and he initiated research for his new book about marine life on the northern Pacific Coast. But the Doc of *Sweet Thursday* malingers because of a gnawing feeling of discontent with himself, and he begins to question his purpose in life.

The end of life is now not so terribly far away—you can see it the way you see the finish line when you come into the stretch—and your mind says, "Have I worked enough? Have I eaten enough? Have I loved enough?" All of these, of course, are the foundation of man's greatest curse, and perhaps his greatest glory. "What has my life meant so far, and what can it mean in the time left to me?" (14)

On occasion, Doc still goes out to the Great Tide Pool, but as he works among the rocks, his thoughts are elsewhere.

And sometimes, starting to turn over a big rock in the Great Tide Pool— a rock under which he knew there would be a community of frantic animals—he would drop the rock back in place and stand, hands on hips, looking off to sea, where the round clouds piled up white with pink and black edges. And he would be thinking. What am I thinking? What do I want? Where do I want to go? (15)

At the center of Doc's dissatisfaction with himself and beneath his self-questioning is his biting loneliness, so that while in *Cannery Row* Doc is as self-sufficient a man as can be found in any Steinbeck novel, in *Sweet Thursday* he seems almost parceled into segments. Moreover, only one segment of him finds any satisfaction in the marine fauna which occupied him so completely in the earlier novel.

And there would be three voices singing in him, all singing together. The top voice of his thinking mind would sing, "What lovely little particles, neither plant nor animal [plankton] but somehow both—the reservoir of all the life in the world, the base supply of food for everyone. . . . " The lower voice of his feeling mind would be singing, "What are you looking for, little man? Is it yourself you're trying to identify? Are you looking at little things to avoid big things?" And the third voice, which came from his marrow, would sing, "Lonesome! Lonesome! What good is it?" (15)

When Ricketts abstracted Jung's "Psychological Types," he defined himself as an "intuitive-thinker," one who pursues "the function of intellectual cognition and the forming of logical conclusions" through the discipline of science, "especially in its pure aspects," in contrast with the more sentimental "intuitive-feeler," who is moved by subjective evaluations of "likes and dislikes, hate, fear, love, etc." And while the Doc of *Cannery Row* fits Ricketts' definition of himself as an intuitive-thinker, the Doc of *Sweet Thursday* is an intuitive-feeler who concludes that "Thought is the evasion of feeling" which leads to a "walling up [of] the leaking loneliness" (15).

No longer able to regard all forms of life with understanding and sensitivity, Doc's interest in the study of marine invertebrates is now perfunctory. He has become what, in the *Log*, Steinbeck and Ricketts call a dry-ball, one of those scientists who are "the embalmers of the field, the picklers who see only the preserved forms of life without any of its principle" (29). Of course, Steinbeck and Ricketts ridicule the scientific specialist whose inquiries are limited to pedantic investigations of an unusual specimen which "may be of individual interest, but he is unlikely to be of much consequence in any ecological picture" (216). They do not mention any specific examples, but had they written the *Log* thirteen years later, they could have pointed to Doc's proposed paper about "Symptoms in Some Cephalopods Approximating

197

Apoplexy." In the *Log*, Steinbeck and Ricketts affirm that "the true biologist deals with life, with teeming, boisterous life, and learns something from it, learns that the first rule of life is living," and that the true scientist "must proliferate in all directions" (29). But the Doc of *Sweet Thursday* ignores the "teeming, boisterous life" and he does not proliferate at all.

On one occasion, Doc does attempt to fathom the great mysteries of life, but while his efforts seem genuine enough, they are ultimately futile. As he is studying the effects of apoplexy on octopi, Doc suddenly realizes that there may be physiological parallels between apoplectic octopi and human beings suffering from the same condition. Appropriately, Steinbeck remarks that "a flame was lighted in Doc."

> The flame of conception seems to flare and go out leaving man shaken, and at once happy and afraid. There's plenty of precedent of course. Everyone knows about Newton's apple. Charles Darwin said his *Origin of Species* flashed complete in one second, and he spent the rest of his life backing it up; and the theory of relativity occurred to Einstein in the time it takes to clap your hands. This is the greatest mystery of the human mind—the inductive leap. Everything falls into place, irrelevancies relate, dissonance becomes harmony, and nonsense wears a crown of meaning. (17)

Moreover, Steinbeck paraphrases Ricketts' doctrine that "intense struggle is one of the commonest concomitants to a great emergent" when he observes that "the clarifying leap" through which "everything falls into place" always "springs from the rich soil of confusion, and the leaper is not unfamiliar with pain" (17). Unlike Darwin, however, Doc does not break through the "rich soil of confusion," nothing "falls into place," irrelevancies do not relate. "I want to take everything I've seen and thought and learned and reduce them and relate them and refine them until I have something of meaning, something of use. And I can't seem to do it" (47).

Steinbeck portrays Doc as unable to make the "inductive leap" to which the novelist's other Ricketts-based figures aspire (Doc in *Cannery Row*, Doctors Winter and Burton, Friend Ed, etc.), and the new Doc, finding no real joy in his study of the tide pools,

Edward F. Ricketts in his laboratory, a photograph from
John Steinbeck's files. Steinbeck wrote on the back,
"This is Doc—in the basement—holding a small ray."

gradually rechannels his search for meaning toward more mundane
and less visionary objectives. The Doc of *Sweet Thursday* becomes
a new man who no longer embraces Ricketts' way of thinking, and
Steinbeck's depiction of his inability to achieve Ricketts' great
emergent represents the novelist's dirge over the destiny of the
Ricketts-like character in the modern world.

Ultimately, and with help from a strange seer and from an
unpublished novelist named Joe Elegant, Doc comes to believe
that a self-satisfying type of romantic love provides the solution
to his quest for meaning. He resolves his contradictory feelings
toward Suzy, the reluctant whore from Fauna's Bear Flag Cafe,
and proposes to her. The novel ends with Doc and Suzy driving

out of Monterey, with the reader knowing that Doc has collected his last "specimen." It is true that Ricketts became attached to a young woman named Alice just months before his death, and according to his own account, they drove to Las Vegas where they were married on January 2, 1948. (Actually, the wedding was performed in Barstow, California.) But in his journal account of his "wedding trip" through the Mojave desert, Ricketts did a good deal of serious speculating about "the idea of an ecological picture—if anything a toto-picture" concerning vectors and tensors and involving the strength of relationships between animals, food, and energy.[34] And certainly the Ed Ricketts who, after seeing the huge power lines spanning the desert from Boulder Dam to Priest Valley, wrote that "the high light of the trip aside from getting married" was "the hi-tension thing and its relation to human ecology"[35] bears no resemblance to the Doc of *Sweet Thursday* for whom the only "hi-tension thing" worth speculating upon is Suzy.

Interestingly, Steinbeck portrays Doc resolving his ambivalent feelings about Suzy by means of the non-teleological method of thinking. For just as he is about to conclude that Suzy is an illiterate girl with a violent temper who "has all the convictions of the uninformed" (155), his lower, deeper mind tells him that "Nothing's bad. It's all part of one thing—the good and bad. Do you know any man and woman—no matter how close—who don't have good and bad?" (156). Indeed, Doc employs non-teleological methodology to sanction his foray into romantic love—a strange but certainly significant application of Ricketts' mode of seeing.

But the most bitterly ironic application of Ricketts' world-view in *Sweet Thursday* (or in any Steinbeck novel, for that matter) occurs when the novelist uses the marine biologist's doctrine of breaking through in order to help Doc resolve his romantic dilemma. Early in the novel, Steinbeck notes that before the war, Doc "was able to turn affable and uncritical eyes on a world full of excitement."

He combined the beauty of the sea with man's loveliest achievement—music. Through his superb phonograph he could hear the angelic voice of the Sistine Choir and could wander half lost in the exquisite masses of William Byrd. He believed there were two human achievements that towered above all others: The *Faust* of Goethe and the *Art of the Fugue* of J. S. Bach. (13)

It should be pointed out that Steinbeck's choice of the *Art of The Fugue* and Goethe's *Faust* might well have been based upon an actual list Ricketts compiled on what he regarded as the greatest works by individual men. In fact, just months before he died, Ricketts told Antonia Seixas that Bach's Contrapunctus No. 19 in the *Art of the Fugue* "goes into that great thing which I think of as beyond life (and death), it speaks out of it, but no Bach could finish it, and he dies with it uncompleted on that magnificent shrieking high note" (EFR-AS, 2/4/48).

In ironic contrast with his real-life prototype, however, the Doc of *Sweet Thursday* goes to Bach's *Art of the Fugue* not to break through to "that great thing," but rather to gain the courage to propose to Suzy.

He went to his records and he found the *Art of the Fugue*. If I can't get courage from his greatness, he thought, I might as well give up. He sat unmoving while Bach built a world and peopled it and organized it and finally fought his world and was destroyed by it. And when the music stopped, as the man had stopped when death came to him, stopped in the middle of a phrase, Doc had his courage back. "Bach fought savagely," he said. "He was not defeated. If he had lived he would have gone on fighting the impossible fight."

Doc cried to no one, "Give me a little time! I want to think. What did Bach have that I am hungry for to the point of starvation? Wasn't it gallantry? And isn't gallantry the great art of the soul? Is there any more noble quality in the human than gallantry?" (161–162)

Doc identifies Bach's "gallantry" with his own romantic crisis; and then suddenly he stopped, and "he seemed to be wracked with inner tears."

"Why didn't I know before?" he asked. "I, who admire it so, didn't even recognize it when I saw it. Old Bach had his talent and his family and his friends. Everyone has something. . . .

Let me face this clearly, please! I need her to save myself. I can be whole only with Suzy." (162)

A confused and desperate Doc breaks through to the realization that he can be whole only with Suzy. In short, Doc's shift of interest from the tide pool to a reformed whore indicates that he has redefined the very essence of wholeness. The ecologically oriented marine biologist of *Cannery Row* who once lived comfortably in "the region of inward adjustments" has become a lonely and self-directed sentimentalist who has terminated his search for meaning in nature, believing that in Suzy his search for order will be complete.

From the standpoint of Steinbeck's theme in *Sweet Thursday*, it is vital to recognize that the change in Doc is closely linked to an analogous change in what was once "the poem, the stink, and the grating noise" of Cannery Row. For the Row is no longer the teeming center of life it was in Steinbeck's earlier novel.

The canneries themselves fought the war by getting the limit taken off fish and catching them all. It was done for patriotic reasons, but that didn't bring the fish back. . . . The pearl-gray canneries of corrugated iron were silent and a pacing watchman was their only life. The street that once roared with trucks was quiet and empty. (1)

There has been a new era born in Monterey in which the entire order of things has been mutated or destroyed.

There were prodigies and portents that winter and spring, but you never notice such things until afterward. On Mount Toro the snow came down as far as Pine Canyon on one side and Jamesburg on the other. A six-legged calf was born in Carmel Valley. A cloud drifting in formed the letters O-N in the sky over Monterey. Mushrooms grew out of the concrete floor of the basement of the Methodist Church. Old Mr. Roletti, at the age of ninety-three, developed senile satyriasis and had to be forcibly restrained from chasing high-school girls. The spring was cold and the rains came late. Vellela in their purple billions sailed into Monterey Bay and were cast up on the beaches, where they died. Killer whales attacked the sea lions near Seal Rocks and murdered a great number of them. . . . And last, but far from least, the Sherman rose developed a carnation bud. (12)

"Everything is changed, Doc, everything," mutters Mack. And Doc's reply, "Maybe I'm changed too" (11), reflects the dismay and the disappointment of a man who has returned to a moldy laboratory ("dust and mildew covered everything" [1]) and to a lifeless Cannery Row.

Laying Down the Ghost

Steinbeck defined the organismal basis of life in *Cannery Row* when he wrote that "the word is a symbol and a delight which sucks up men and scenes, trees, plants, factories, and Pekinese" into "a fantastic pattern" that converts chaos into cosmos (8). "The word" in that novel makes Lee Chong more than a Chinese grocer; it transforms Mack and the boys into "the Virtues, the Graces, the Beauties," children of "Our Father who art in nature"; and it makes the Great Tide Pool a microcosmic emblem of the cosmic whole.

Despite appearances, the Row in *Sweet Thursday* is still an organism, the parts of which are inextricably bound up with one another. Steinbeck writes that "To a casual observer Cannery Row might have seemed a series of self-contained and selfish units, each functioning alone with no reference to the others." But the "fact is that each was bound by gossamer threads of steel to all the others—hurt one, and you aroused vengeance in all. Let sadness come to one, and all wept" (37). But in defining the commensal and symbiotic relationships between the units which make up the organism of the "new" Cannery Row, Steinbeck alters his symbols. "The word" illumines nothing; the Great Tide Pool is lifeless; Mack and the boys are no longer "the Virtues and the Graces," but coarse and rather unpalatable vagabonds; and Lee Chong has left the Row altogether. Significantly, Joe Elegant notes that the old symbols no longer furnish meaning and insight into life, that even Doc's paper (itself a more modern symbol than "the word" of *Cannery Row*) is inadequate: "The symbol is the paper he wants to write, but that in itself has impurities. . . . His symbol is false" (145). Unfortunately, the symbol that Elegant proposes to substitute for the paper is not "the word," but romantic love, which offers Doc a good deal of sentiment, but not the "hot taste of life" he once sought in the Great Tide Pool.

Additional evidence of Steinbeck's deep-seated despair in the novel is the source of the gospel of romantic love. This solution to Doc's "leaking loneliness" is advanced not by Steinbeck, but by those characters whom the novelist clearly dislikes. It is suggested by the crackpot seer who resembles the strange old man

203

Joseph Wayne found at the coast in *To a God Unknown*, but who has shifted the ground of his metaphysic "from mystic concepts of the unity of all life to the doctrine of romantic love, which he prescribes for Doc."[36] It is suggested by Joe Elegant, the pathetic author of moody books full of "dark rooms" with "cryptic wallpaper" and "decaying dreams."[37] And it is suggested by Old Jingleballicks, a fictional edition of an individual who, in "About Ed Ricketts," Steinbeck recalls was one of those few people whom Ricketts did not like.[38]

It is these men, not one of whom appears in the word-ordered cosmos of *Cannery Row*—who advocate and finally effect Doc's liaison with Suzy. It is Jingleballicks who arranges for Doc to leave the Row altogether in favor of a research post in the Cephalopod Research Center at the California Institute of Technology. It is they, in short, who hurl the cosmos of Cannery Row into chaos. In sharp contrast to every other Ricketts-based character in Steinbeck's fiction, Doc acts less in *Sweet Thursday* than he is acted upon. He is a casualty of the change which has come over Cannery Row and so is not Steinbeck's persona, but only his victim, and his fate seems less tragic than pitiable.

There is no question but that on the surface *Sweet Thursday* is a sentimental novel. The crucial issue in terms of Steinbeck's theme, however, is that the source of this sentimentality resides less in the author than in several of his characters, none of whom function as Steinbeck's spokesmen. In other words, in this novel Steinbeck stands further from the action than he did in *Cannery Row*. He shows how, in an age of corrupt values and distorted perspectives, his characters seek refuge in what they regard as a bit of saving sentiment. *Sweet Thursday* is an ironic, bittersweet novel, for beneath its "good clean fun" is Steinbeck's lament over the death of an era he loved and the demise of a man whom he deeply admired.

In the light of Steinbeck's overall thematic objectives in *Sweet Thursday*, it seems clear that he had not lost touch with the personality of Ed Ricketts. Certainly, Steinbeck knew that Ricketts, unlike the Doc of his novel, had not lost interest in his work.

When he came to Monterey after Ricketts' death, he took custody of Ricketts' journals, and after perusing them, told Floris Hartog that at some future time he might consider editing the unpublished record "of the best mind I have ever known" (JS-FPH, 7/3/48).

And yet, in even Steinbeck's more authentic portraits of Ricketts, the novelist seems bothered by what (in "About Ed Ricketts") he saw as a transcendent sadness in his love—something he missed or wanted, "a searching that sometimes approached panic" (liii). And so, while Steinbeck has always portrayed his Ricketts-figures as intellectually self-sufficient individuals, he has simultaneously shown (even in *Cannery Row*) that because they are "walled off a little" in their private quest to break through to the deep thing, they stand at a distance from the realities of contemporary life and so are vulnerable when put in circumstances demanding a degree of social adjustment. The world Steinbeck portrayed in *Sweet Thursday* placed a high premium on social adjustment, so that (as Jingleballicks tells Doc) while it is true that the "only creative thing we have is the individual," in order to participate in the good things of life "the individual must become part of the group and thus lose his individuality and his creativeness" (122).

Unable to retain his intellectual or emotional self-sufficiency, Doc surrenders to one of the most destructive groups in any Steinbeck novel that quality which so distinguished his predecessor in *Cannery Row*. And though one might regard Doc's capitulation to romantic love as Steinbeck's "testament of acceptance," the novelist's bitterly ironic treatment of capitulation makes it clear that Steinbeck was no more satisfied with Doc's decision than, for example, Herman Melville approved of Starry Vere's verdict that Billy Budd must hang. Throughout Steinbeck's fiction, from *In Dubious Battle* to *Burning Bright*, Steinbeck's Ricketts-based characters either strive to maintain their cosmic, non-teleological vision (even at the cost of their lives) or, through the novelist's skillful management of theme, they convert non-teleological perception into meaningful social action. But the Doc of *Sweet Thursday* lives in a world in which there are no satisfactory outlets for Ricketts' unique brand of creative self-expression. And facing the prospect of personal oblivion, Doc chooses a life with Suzy in what seems Steinbeck's eulogy on the destiny of the Rickettsian visionary amid the harsh reality of the modern world.

Steinbeck laid down the ghost once and for all in *Sweet Thursday*, but the future proved that he paid quite a price in the endeavor. For his portrayal of Doc's demise suggests a mildly analogous pattern in the remainder of his own writing. The Steinbeck after *Sweet Thursday* who cut himself off from further fictional access to Ricketts' person or his world-view is no more the Steinbeck of *In Dubious Battle* or *The Grapes of Wrath*, than Doc the bridegroom, is Doc the holistic scientist who seeks the "hot taste of life" in the Great Tide Pool. *Sweet Thursday* ends with Doc and Steinbeck finally parting company. Doc and Suzy head south to La Jolla and ultimately to Cal Tech where Doc will probably accept the research post arranged by Jingleballicks. Steinbeck turns east toward New York and Paris, where he will write a series of relatively inconsequential books which are best described as footnotes in relation to his career as a whole.

Travels
with Steinbeck

*I*f *East of Eden* isn't good," Steinbeck said in 1952, "then I've been wasting my time. It has in it everything I have been able to learn about my art or craft or profession in all these years."[1] This is how John Steinbeck saw his biggest novel, which began as the "story of my country and the story of me," but which in the course of composition was gradually transformed into a sprawling study of good and evil in the world (through a fictional representation of the Cain-Abel story) and an affirmation of free will by which the individual can purposefully assert his moral impulse.

Although it is not difficult to understand the novelist's enthusiasm about his epic study of three generations of two families (the Trasks and the Hamiltons), his insistence that *East of Eden* contains "everything I have been able to learn about my art or craft or profession in all these years" demands a closer critical look. In this work in which there is very little of Ed Ricketts' personality or ideas about man and the world, Steinbeck's examination of man's dual capacity for good and evil leads the novelist to muddle and seriously obscure the real value of one of the most fundamental notions implicit in Ricketts' way of seeing.

207

This, of course, is the gospel of non-teleological thinking, about which Steinbeck had long held ambivalent feelings. For years, he had valued the non-teleological point of view as fictional method—as a way of seeing characters and events. And he had portrayed sympathetically those characters who can free their perceptions from their preconceptions and so see situations as a whole and without bias. At the same time, Steinbeck saw in Ricketts' method of thinking, which is concerned with what *is* instead of what *could be* or *should be*, and which dismisses traditional distinctions between good and evil, an excuse for maintaining the status quo.

Steinbeck's postwar writings reveal an increasing concern with man's capacity for self-interest and suggest that the novelist had come to believe that whatever is is anything but right. In a letter to Pascal Covici written during the composition of *East of Eden*, Steinbeck maintains it is the duty of the writer "to lift up, to extend, to encourage"[2]: "how any negative or despairing approach can pretend to be literature I do not know. It is true that we are weak and sick and ugly and quarrelsome but if that is all we ever were, we would millenniums ago have disappeared from the face of the earth, and a few remnants of fossilized jaw bones, a few teeth in strata of limestone would be the only mark our species would have left on the earth."[3]

John Steinbeck becomes a moralist in *East of Eden*, and he develops as the central theme of his novel the thesis that man can rule over sin. The vehicle Steinbeck employs to convey his theme is the Hebrew word *timshel*, and through the character of Samuel Hamilton, modeled on the novelist's maternal grandfather, for whom Steinbeck cherished a good deal of fondness, the author defines the *timshel* as meaning "Thou mayest" and so heralds what he regards as man's greatest glory: his ability to choose good over evil.

"Thou mayest rule over sin," Lee. That's it. I do not believe all men are destroyed. I can name you a dozen who were not, and they are the ones the world lives by. It is true of the spirit as it is true of battles—only the winners are remembered. Surely most men are destroyed, but there are others who like pillars of fire guide frightened men through the darkness. "*Thou mayest, Thou mayest!*" What glory![4]

The entire structure of *East of Eden*, in which Steinbeck's characters are "symbol people" who are clothed "in the trappings of experience so that the symbol is discernible but not overwhelming,"[5] fulfills the novelist's thesis that man can rule over sin. As Joseph Wood Krutch points out, "lest we might possibly fail to see that upon this point the whole meaning of the book is intended to depend, its last sentences are 'Adam looked up with sick weariness. . . . His whispered word seemed to hang in the air: *Timshel!* His eyes closed and he slept.' "[6]

In *East of Eden*, John Steinbeck has made good and evil, right and wrong, moral absolutes. And it seems we have come a long way from Jim Casy's conclusion in *The Grapes of Wrath* that "there ain't no sin and there ain't no virtue," and from Dr. Burton's refusal in *In Dubious Battle* to put on the blinders of good or bad because they might hamper his vision.[7] Of course, Burton's high-falutin ideas about right and wrong went nowhere, just around in a circle, and in *The Grapes of Wrath*, Steinbeck transformed Casy into a teleological activist who gives his life to ensure the triumph of good over evil. But it is nevertheless true that in both novels Steinbeck affirms that the non-teleological method of seeing is valuable in that it can expose distorted perspectives (Uncle John's possessive interest in sin in *The Grapes of Wrath*, Mac and Jim's blind political partisanship in *In Dubious Battle*), as long as the non-teleological principles of understanding-acceptance are applied to the quest for worthwhile social goals.

In *East of Eden*, Samuel Hamilton and Lee, the Chinese servant-philosopher, who together decipher the meaning of the *timshel*, see men and situations non-teleologically. At one point in the novel, Lee tells Samuel that "You are one of the rare people who can separate your observation from your pre-conception. You see what is, where most people see what they expect" (142). But Lee and Samuel do not employ this ability to see what *is* in order to achieve social justice (as is the case with Casy in *The Grapes of Wrath*); rather, they use their insights to preach the moral gospel of "Thou mayest." Lee, defined by Steinbeck as "a philosopher," a kind and thoughtful man who is "in the book because I need him,"[8] forces Caleb Trask to face his guilt so that he can choose good over evil. And Samuel, whom Steinbeck wished to make "into one of those pillars of fire by whom little and frightened men are guided through the darkness,"[9] rouses Adam Trask from his moral lethargy. As Samuel puts it, I "forced him to live or get off the pot" (274). And so, what Steinbeck seems to be doing in *East of Eden* is employing *is* thinking for the purpose of affirming a moral principle about the absolute nature of good and evil. He is using the non-teleological method to prove a restrictive teleological thesis—a convenient approach perhaps, but one that is not philosophically satisfying.

Taken as a whole, Steinbeck's authorial role as a moralist in *East of Eden* severely constricts the range of his vision. According to the terms of his argument, the "never-ending contest in ourselves of good and evil" goes on in each individual, never in the group. And thus in this novel, Steinbeck places the responsibility for salvation squarely on the shoulders of the individual. In much of his earlier fiction, of course, the novelist carefully formulated a workable and balanced formula for how the group can work toward meaningful goals without harm to the individual, so that in the best of groups (or phalanxes), the individuality of the unit-men is aggrandized rather than subverted. But in *East of Eden*, Steinbeck, for whom morality had eclipsed biology as a way of seeing, largely ignores the importance of the group while lauding the virtues of individual man.

And yet, though Steinbeck's interest has shifted from Ricketts and biology to morality and individual ethics, the novelist on occasion does rely upon his knowledge of biology as an important source of metaphor and simile. He describes the vicious Cathy Ames (Trask) as a psychic monster, "produced by 'a twisted egg or a malformed gene.' "[10] And he depicts the army as a group that does not tolerate individual differences in its members, absorbing them into itself.[11] More importantly, Steinbeck patterns Samuel Hamilton after several of his earlier heroes, particularly Joseph Wayne in *To a God Unknown* and Jim Casy in *The Grapes of Wrath*. Like Wayne and Casy, Samuel lives close to and loves the land. And while his acreage is "harsh and dry. There were no springs, and the crust of topsoil was so thin that the flinty bones stuck through," Samuel has no regrets about having purchased his barren parcel of land. When Adam Trask tells him to abandon his "dust heap," Sam replies:

> "I love that dust heap," Samuel said. "I love it the way a bitch loves her runty pup. I love every flint, the plow-breaking outcroppings, the thin and barren topsoil, the waterless heart of her. Somewhere in my dust heap there's a richness." (263)

And like Casy, Samuel is a man of insight and understanding who spreads the principles of his perceptions and whose message survives his own death.

Despite these surface similarities, however, there is a basic dissimilarity between Sam and his earlier counterparts which involves a definition of their differing conceptions of world order. For while Joseph's love of nature seems a fitting prerequisite for his self-sacrifice to preserve the natural order, and whereas Casy's love of man and the land and his perception of cosmic unity leads to his conclusion that (in Tom's words) "all [men must] work together for our own thing—all farm our own lan'" (571), there seems no logical connection between Samuel's love for his dust heap and his insistence that "thou mayest rule over sin." And this is precisely why, from the standpoint of Steinbeck's stance as a moralist, *East of Eden* ultimately fails. Steinbeck's problem is a metaphorical one: he cannot sustain a Christian doctrine using biological or agrarian metaphors. The extensive emphasis Steinbeck places on Samuel's love for his dust heap is irrelevant in a novel concerned with the affirmation of free will.

East of Eden is a book with many virtues. When, for example, one considers the implications of Steinbeck's notions about the nature of evil, parallels emerge between *East of Eden* and the most important works of Hawthorne and Melville. At the same time, Steinbeck's novel fails for a variety of reasons: for the failure of its language; for Steinbeck's inability to weave together his two plot lines; and mainly for the incongruous application of a set of old ideas (which grew largely out of the novelist's friendship with Ricketts) in a novel about man's struggle to choose good over evil.

Although in *East of Eden* Steinbeck deals with settings and subject matter drawn largely from his California past, he had become, during his years of work on this novel, a full-fledged New Yorker. Elaine Steinbeck has noted that by the early 1950's Steinbeck decided not to return to Monterey, but rather focused his love of things rural on Sag Harbor, which he came to regard as a sort of "Cannery Row East" (ES/RA, 3/24/71). In 1953, he wrote a short piece for the *New York Times Magazine*, "The Making of a New Yorker," in which he exclaims, "My God! I belong here. Isn't this wonderful?"[12] Later in the same piece, Steinbeck reflects that "I can work longer and harder without weariness in New York than anyplace else."[13]

Steinbeck also developed an affinity for Europe during the 1950's, and Mrs. Steinbeck recalls that for a brief time at least, Steinbeck considered moving to London (ES/RA, 3/24/71). Much of Steinbeck's writing during the late fifties took place and is set abroad. In 1959, he spent eleven months in England researching Thomas Mallory, and he even did some writing on the Arthurian legends which has not been published. It was during these years that he intensified his moral concerns, and according to Adlai Stevenson, who visited the Steinbecks at their cottage in Somerset in June 1959, the novelist was even talking about the Arthurian legend in terms of "its symbolism of the recurrent need in times of confusion and doubt for moral authority and direction. He talked of its meaning for us today, of the everlasting struggle between simple goodness and clever evil, and the hunger for purity and ennobling purposes after intervals of corruption of the spirit of man."[14] There was, in short, little room in Steinbeck's new Arthurian world for Pilon, Danny, and Torelli's thirty-nine-cent wine.

Out of Steinbeck's trips to the Continent came such minor pieces as "How to Fish in French," "Vegetable War" (a critique of English cooking of Brussels sprouts), and "Yank in Europe," a defense of the behavior of American tourists in Paris. There was also a delightful short story entitled "The Affair at 7 Rue de M—," which chronicles his son John's bizarre struggle to elude a cancerous blob of bubble gum.

The one full-length work which resulted from his stay in Europe is *The Short Reign of Pippin IV* (1957), a lighthearted moral fable which, as the dust jacket announces, tells the story of "what happens to a retiring middle aged astronomer suddenly drafted to rule the unruly French; of his teen-age glamour-struck daughter and her American swain, son of the Egg King of Petaluma, California; and of sundry members of the ancient nobility, art dealers, nuns, guards, gardeners, politicians, and plain people."

The Short Reign of Pippin IV is a sapless and languid novel. Rather than representing "a perceptible change for the better" in Steinbeck's writing,[15] this work testifies to the novelist's inability to portray a complex urban society as successfully as he once depicted the rural confines of the Salinas Valley; the transatlantic leap robbed him of the natural idiom which characterizes his best writing.

There is scant evidence of Ricketts' ideas in *The Short Reign of Pippin IV*, and what there is appears to have been included almost as an afterthought. At one juncture King Pippin encounters a strange old man fishing for old statues in the reedy water of a moat with a long-tined rake. The old man tells Pippin that throwing the statues into the moat as well as recovering them are acts which are neither good nor bad, and he concludes, in Ricketts-like fashion, that "There's just people—just what people do."[16] Why Steinbeck included this episode is unclear, since it bears no apparent relationship to and even seems to contradict the main thread of the novel's moral fabric.

In the course of his story about Pippin's inner struggle to seek a foundation on which to build a proper code of behavior, Steinbeck does level a number of satiric jabs at modern American society reminiscent of *Cannery Row* and *Sweet Thursday*. But they are vague and insubstantial in that Steinbeck substitutes surface humor for a sensitive and delicate handling of satiric materials. In short, Steinbeck's subtle depiction of the effects of the new order in *Sweet Thursday* gives way to a superficial assault on that order in a work which seems less a novel than an extended piece of Sunday supplement journalism.

In discussing the anticipated reception of *The Short Reign of Pippin IV*, Steinbeck acknowledged it "would have a very limited audience."[17] But he consciously sought a far wider reading public in his next and final novel, *The Winter of Our Discontent* (1960), which marks his return to serious fiction. Set in the imaginary New England community of New Baytown, *The Winter of Our Discontent* is an analytical and occasionally piercing study of the moral vacuum in modern America by a writer who seemingly had begun to question his former belief in man's ability to choose good over evil. In *The Winter of Our Discontent*, man's fall from grace is caused by his complete subservience to the dollar, which has occasioned the replacement of all meaningful codes of morality and human decency with the far more lucrative fast-buck philosophy.[18]

As is the case with *The Short Reign of Pippin IV*, there is virtually nothing in Ricketts' world-view which informs the thematic line of *The Winter of Our Discontent*. The characters in this novel are motivated by a new principle which unifies their shallow lives. Unaware of "the word" of *Cannery Row* and even of the romantic love of *Sweet Thursday*, the world Steinbeck depicts in *The Winter of Our Discontent* is organized only by the devotion its denizens pay to the all-powerful dollar. Money becomes, in fact, the *élan vital* of New Baytown life, and Steinbeck, in a stroke of savage irony, endows the dollar with mock-religious significance as it orders the lives of the book's misdirected characters. The main fortress of New Baytown life is Mr. Baker's bank with its "sacred" vault before which a "Mass" is performed every workday morning.

I followed him [said Ethan Allen Hawley, the book's protagonist and narrator] and it was just as Joey [the bank teller] said—like a religious ceremony. They practically stood at attention as the clock hand crossed nine. There came a click and buzzing from the great steel safe door. Then Joey dialed the mystic numbers and turned the wheel that drew the bolts. The holy of holies swung stately open and Mr. Baker took the salute of the assembled money. I stood outside the rail like a humble communicant waiting for the sacrament."[19]

Mr. Baker's bank is the locus of meaning in a corrupt world, a symbol of sterility in Steinbeck's version of the wasteland. Impenetrable to attack (even Ethan cannot rob it), it exists, a catholic as well as a secular force. The story commences on Good Friday and ends just after the Fourth of July, dates which express corruption in Christian and patriotic ethics.[20] And in describing how June becomes July, Ethan despairingly states that

> The light-rimmed boundary of the east was July, for June had gone away in the night. July is brass where June is gold, and lead where June is silver. July leaves are heavy and fat and crowding. Birdsong of July is a flatulent refrain without passion, for the nests are empty now and dumpy fledglings teeter clumsily. No, July is not a month of promise or of fulfillment. Fruit is growing but unsweet and uncolored, corn is a limp green bundle with a young and yellow tassel. The squashes still wear umbilical crowns of dry blossom. (217)

Six-legged cows, dead sea lions, carnation buds germinating from Sherman roses, and passionless birdsongs from empty nests and limp green corn: Steinbeck's vision of decay in *The Winter of Our Discontent* is an East Coast equivalent of that in *Sweet Thursday*.

There are occasional glimpses of hope in *The Winter of Our Discontent*, particularly at the end of the book when Ethan struggles to avoid compromising with the adulterated society in which he lives. Like Joseph Wayne in *To a God Unknown*, Ethan seeks a retreat, a place (which for him is a cave near Long Island Sound) where he can inspect his life while "sitting cross-legged in a niche like a blinking Buddha" (48). The result of Ethan's "taking stock," however, bears little similarity to Joseph's communion with nature in the forest of Our Lady, for Ethan chooses a set of values precisely opposite to those embraced by Wayne. Whereas Joseph renounces false idols and becomes one with the land and the rain, Ethan flees water (the high tide that threatens his place) and returns to the corrupt world from which he had sought escape.

The end of *The Winter of Our Discontent* seems to indicate that Steinbeck the moralist had run out of steam. For a decade he had steadfastly refused to chant the destruction of man's spirit, and he had written *East of Eden* and, to a lesser extent, *The*

Short Reign of Pippin IV, to champion man's ability to choose the virtuous life. But first by indirection (*Sweet Thursday*) and then by direct statement, Steinbeck's vision of the wasteland unsettled his moral horizon. For there are no "timshels" in *The Winter of Our Discontent*, just Ethan Hawley's pathetic desire to go home. "I had to get back," claims Ethan. "Else another light might go out" (298). And despite claims of his own salvation, Ethan is wholly unconvincing. Firmly entrenched in the world of Mr. Baker's bank vault, Ethan's "light" is opaque and inconsequential, and it would prove futile for him to attempt to attain a brighter light which Steinbeck, the frustrated moralist, can no longer provide.

Despite the darkening of the novelist's fictional genius, which is apparent from the fact that he wrote neither another novel nor any more short stories after *The Winter of Our Discontent*, Steinbeck was active as a journalist and traveler during the last eight years of his life. And whatever may have been responsible for his silence as a writer of fiction, it was not because he had run out of things to say. His interest in science, long in hibernation, surfaced when he accompanied scientist Willard Bascom on an expedition to examine a piece of the earth's core at the Project Mohole experimental drilling site 150 miles off the coast of Lower California. Steinbeck wrote a long account of his travels with "the elite and motley crew" of Cuss I for *Life*, and he ended his report with the hope of being invited back "when the new ship sails toward new wonders in about two years."[21] Elaine Steinbeck recalls that her husband very much wanted to go on an expedition to the Great Barrier Reef[22] (ES/RA, 3/24/71), and early in 1965, he thought about accompanying his friend Bascom on a research expedition to South Africa.

In his last years, Steinbeck's interest swung from science back to politics, and he became an advocate of the American military presence in Southeast Asia—much to the chagrin of his liberal admirers. Elaine Steinbeck and Robert Wallsten have indicated that Steinbeck gradually altered his views about the Vietnam War (ES and RW/RA, 12/26/72), and in August 1967, the novelist wrote Elizabeth Otis that the people running the war do not understand what they have undertaken and are gradually drawing America into a quicksand. Steinbeck affirms that we can never win this war (or any war) in traditional terms; rather we will engage ourselves so completely that we will be neither willing nor able to withdraw. Finally, Steinbeck calls the South Vietnamese leaders corrupt and ill-sighted, and he condemns the Vietnamese elections as a ploy to get money from the American congress (JS-EO, 8/31/67). Unfortunately, because of a serious and prolonged illness during which Steinbeck was in severe and continued pain, the novelist was unable to retract publicly his earlier views on the Vietnam War (he wrote nothing during the last year of his life except some random letters); there are no published statements by him which reflect a diminishing support of the hawkish national leadership.

In addition to his Vietnam articles and some other minor pieces he wrote for the dailies and for the Sunday supplements, Steinbeck wrote two full-length works of nonfiction during the 1960's which reflect his new life-style as a traveler-journalist. The first, *Travels with Charley in Search of America* (1962), is the written record of Steinbeck's journey across the United States with his French poodle, Charley, and is an assortment of selected incidents leading to often serious reflections about various facets of the American experience. A best seller with a wide range of popular appeal, *Travels with Charley* is written in the same vein as *The Log from the Sea of Cortez*, but it lacks the power and depth of vision of the Steinbeck-Ricketts volume. Steinbeck's final book is *America and Americans* (1966), a brief narrative about Steinbeck's America interlaced with some unusually fine photographs, which have the salutary effect of diverting attention away from the author's cliché-ridden prose.

Travels with Charley and *America and Americans* have been disregarded by the critics, partially because of their newness but also because of their structural weaknesses, the worst of which are Steinbeck's marked tendency toward sentimentality and his growing dependence on flat, stylized diction. Nevertheless, the two books should not be ignored, for beneath their obvious defects, they contain important reflections on an America about which Steinbeck wrote for years with hope and finally with a deep sense of anguish. Moreover, there is a substantial scattering of Ed Ricketts' ideas in *Travels with Charley* and *America and Americans.* And there are some curious parallels in tone and subject matter between Steinbeck's travelogues and Ricketts' postwar writings which suggest that the two had not grown so far apart intellectually as Steinbeck, the moralist of the 1950's, seemingly indicated.

As the survey of Ricketts' writing has shown, the marine biologist was for many years a dedicated environmentalist. His concern for the ecological balance of life is manifest not only in his direct attacks on man's indiscriminate raping of nature, but is implied in his metaphysical conclusions about the relational unity of all existence. But nowhere in his writings are Ricketts' ecological concerns more apparent than in his postwar writing and research on the depletion of the California sardine, which he regarded as a prime example of the shortsightedness of man's commercial spirit. Similarly, in *Travels with Charley*, Steinbeck, who traveled alone since "two or more people disturb the ecologic complex of an area,"[23] saw example after example of how commercialism, "the complicated systems of American business," routed the once benign order of things. Traveling through Seattle for instance, Steinbeck notes everywhere a "frantic growth, a carcinomatous growth. Bulldozers rolled up the green forest and heaped the resulting trash for burning. I wonder why progress looks so much like destruction" (162). Throughout *America and Americans,* Steinbeck laments the "nonsensical spoilage of the battle-ruined countryside" by a land of people whose "ability to conserve has not grown with our power to create" (130). And in *Travels with Charley*, he notes with little pleasure the more spectacular aspects of nature which the government has fenced off and isolated from the natural order as a whole. The national park, says Steinbeck, is enclosed like a freak, a "wonderland of nature gone nuts" (146).

It was largely through Ricketts' eyes that Steinbeck learned how to see natural beauty and how to intuit from nature fundamental truths about the relational unity of all life. And Steinbeck's simple appreciation and mystic reverence for nature is more in evidence in *Travels with Charley* and *America and Americans* than in any of his works since *Sea of Cortez*. However, Steinbeck's delineation of his feeling for nature is often watered down by an ornate style. On one occasion in *Travels with Charley*, he describes the Aurora Borealis as it "hung and moved with majesty in folds like an infinite traveler upstage in an infinite theatre" (44). Later in the narrative, there is a passage describing the California redwoods which reads more like a commercial guidebook than like the Steinbeck of *Cannery Row* and *Sea of Cortez*.

> The redwoods, once seen, leave a mark or create a vision that stays with you always. No one has successfully painted or photographed a redwood tree. The feeling they produce is not transferable. From them comes silence and awe. It's not only their unbelievable stature, nor the color which seems to shift and vary under your eyes, no, they are not like any trees we know, they are ambassadors from another time. (168)

Steinbeck affirms his feelings of religious solemnity before these stateliest of nature's monuments, but his statements include many of the stock phrases of the picture postcard. "The emotion we felt in this grove," Steinbeck writes in *America and Americans*, "was one of awe and humility and joy" (130). And in *Travels with Charley*, he states that one feels a "cathedral hush," a "remote and cloistered feeling" while standing beside "the godlike thing" (171).

But there are descriptive passages in *Travels with Charley* which, because they capture a Ricketts-like sense of wonder about nature as a symbol of cosmic order, do reflect the genuine spirit of awe and wonder which accounts for the particular excellence of the narrative section of *Sea of Cortez*. For example, during his discourse on life in the Mojave desert which makes up the finest chapter in *Travels with Charley*, and which brings to mind Ricketts' 1948 journal entries about how the Mojave reflects "the ideas of an ecological picture—if anything a toto-picture," Steinbeck senses a "living presence" in the desert that convinces him it is the birthplace of the unity of all life.[24]

> At night in this waterless air the stars come down just out of reach of your fingers. In such a place lived the hermits of the early church pierc-

219

ing to infinity with unlittered minds. The great concepts of oneness and of majestic order seem always to be born in the desert. (189–190)

Steinbeck stands in the desert and points a rifle at two coyotes which, he notes, we are taught to regard as chicken-stealing vermin. Suddenly, though, he stops and asks himself, "Why should I interfere?" (188). He realizes "In the delicate world of relationships, we are tied together for all time" (189), and he opens two cans of dog food and leaves them for the coyotes as a votive.

There is also one passage about the redwood groves in *Travels with Charley* which recalls a genuine feeling of "presence" in nature.

And there's a breathing in the black, for these huge things that control the day and inhabit the night are living things and have presence, and perhaps feeling, and, somewhere in deep-down perception, perhaps communication. I have had life-long association with these things. (Odd that the word "trees" does not apply.) (171–172)

Steinbeck declines to explain rationally "the great concepts of oneness and majestic order" in the desert or his feeling of "communication" with the giant redwoods. In fact, he suggests in *Travels with Charley* that "It would be pleasant to be able to say of my travels with Charley, 'I went out to find the truth about my country and I found it. . . .' I wish it were that easy" (185). But, reflects Steinbeck, "I discovered long ago in collecting and classifying marine animals that what I found was closely intermeshed with how I felt at the moment" (185). And, in a statement that specifically recalls Boodin's dictum (as quoted in the *Log*) that "the laws of thought are the laws of things," Steinbeck insists that "external reality has a way of being not so external after all" (185). And indeed, it is in those passages where external reality is not totally external (and in which he recaptures the spirit of Ricketts' mode of seeing) that Steinbeck is at his best in *Travels with Charley* and *America and Americans*.

Despite the fact that Steinbeck employs many of the ideas he and Ricketts once shared about man and the world, the novelist makes it clear in *Travels with Charley* that participation in the

John Steinbeck on 17 Mile Drive, Monterey Peninsula, about 1965

present makes a return to the past impossible. Coming to the West Coast, Steinbeck anticipated his arrival:

> The Pacific is my home ocean; I knew it first, grew up on its shore, collected marine animals along the coast. I know its moods, its color, its nature. It was very far inland that I caught the first smell of the Pacific. When one has been long at sea, the smell of land reaches far out to greet one. And the same is true when one has been long inland. I believe I smelled the sea rocks and the kelp and the excitement of churning sea water, the sharpness of iodine and the under odor of washed and ground calcareous shells. Such a far-off and remembered odor comes subtly so that one does not consciously smell it, but rather an electric excitement is released—a kind of boisterous joy. (161)

But when he arrives in Monterey and Salinas, about which he had not written anything since *Sweet Thursday* (except a short piece for *Holiday* about Salinas[25]), the author finds his old haunts hardly recognizable. "I remember Salinas, the town of my birth, when it proudly announced four thousand citizens. Now it is eighty thousand citizens and leaping pell mell on in a mathematical progression . . . with no end in sight" (174). Visiting Cannery Row, which, through his books, he helped to make into a tourist attraction, Steinbeck is told by Johnny Garcia, an old *paisano* friend, that the new people "are rich people. They plant geraniums in big pots. Swimming pools where frogs and crayfish used to wait for us" (180). The pilchards have all been caught, and the Row's former residents are either dead or gone.

> "Ed Ricketts, Whitey's Number One and Two, where's Sonny Boy, Ankly Varney, Jesus Maria Corcoran, Joe Portagee, Shorty Lee, Flora Wood, and that girl who kept spiders in her hat?"
> "Dead—all dead," Johnny moaned. (181)

And to Steinbeck returning home from a long sojourn in New York and Europe, the realization of the death of the old order becomes crystallized in a sense of irretrievable loss. "Tom Wolfe was right. You can't go home again because home has ceased to exist except in the mothballs of memory" (183).

Interfused with Steinbeck's nostalgia for a lost past in *Travels with Charley* and, to a lesser extent, in *America and Americans*, is a vigorous attempt to make sense out of nonsense by predictions that good will come out of chaos after all. This attitude occurs most frequently in *America and Americans*, where Steinbeck masses vague prophecies which suggest that although man has often tripped over his own feet, he will someday overcome his self-made obstacles.

> We have not lost our way at all. The roads of the past have come to an end and we have not yet discovered a path to the future. I think we will find one, but its direction may be unthinkable to us now. (142)

It is significant, however, that such questions as precisely where we will find the path to the future or what direction the path will take are never really answered.

On one occasion in *Travels with Charley*, Steinbeck suggests with incredible optimism that the current pendulum which has desecrated the natural order and turned man to urban centers will swing back so that the swollen cities will "rupture like dehiscent wombs and disperse their children back to the countryside" (65). One wonders, however, whether Steinbeck really believes this or whether he is merely confusing the countryside with the suburb.

Nevertheless, unlike so many of his contemporaries, Steinbeck never totally gave up on the world, and he always regarded himself as a novelist of affirmation. Frederic Carpenter has called him an "American Dreamer," and a central theme in Steinbeck's fiction, from his first novel (Morgan's dream of weath and empire) to his last (Hawley's search for his moral self) has been man's search for the "happy valley." But particularly in his later novels, the search for paradise is combined with the opposite theme of paradise lost which creates irreconcilable contradictions. One need only consider Doc's choice of a substitute paradise in *Sweet Thursday* or Ethan Hawley's decision to compromise with corruption in *The Winter of Our Discontent* to see that in later life, Steinbeck chose to interpret reality by exposing a rapacious, materialistic society which destroys the simple human virtues. It is only in selected instances (usually in his prewar fiction) that Steinbeck, armed with Ricketts' notions about man's ability to break through to understanding, shows man mastering his inner and outer conflicts and achieving a paradise of the mind and heart.

223

JOHN STEINBECK and EDWARD F. RICKETTS

Steinbeck gradually shifted the specific objectives in his search for meaning, but although in each of his last novels he seemed to detect less and less worth affirming, he never abandoned the pursuit. As late as 1965, he wrote in one of a series of columns for the Sunday supplements, that he would never surrender to the popular disease of acute literary pessimism: "I don't have to be 'in' or 'op,' and I don't have to view our times with professional despair."[26] Still sounding a good deal like the biologist of *Sea of Cortez*, Steinbeck chides his countrymen for our follies and corruptions, and always for the old reasons: for our blindness, our predilection for nonsense, our failure to perceive relation and intuit the whole. "Why are we lost in a cloud of nonsense?" asks Steinbeck. "I think it is because we see it only a little bit at a time, and don't relate it to the whole."[27]

Steinbeck's plunge into the confines of traditional morality (with its heavy emphasis on the role of the individual in the search for salvation) in *East of Eden* and *The Short Reign of Pippin IV*, and his journey down the avenues of nostalgia in *Travels with Charley* and *America and Americans*, forced him to abandon many of his own and Ricketts' ideas about man and the world. And deprived of a comprehensive philosophical base, Steinbeck's final efforts to enlarge his "longer valley" in a continued search for purpose and meaning lack range and power. But with the exception of a few statements about the Vietnam War in which he seems to conclude that all that lives is not holy, that all things are not one thing, Steinbeck's last works of nonfiction indicate that it was the force of Ricketts' ecological and holistic vision that kept the dream alive.

Steinbeck and Ricketts: An Epilogue

*H*ow does one determine precisely the extent of the impact of one human being upon another, particularly when the two individuals under consideration are as complex as John Steinbeck and Edward F. Ricketts? How can one be certain where each idea germinated, and how can one know who really influenced whom? Steinbeck says in "About Ed Ricketts" that "very many conclusions Ed and I worked out together through endless discussion and reading and observation and experiment. We worked together, and so closely that I do not know now in some cases who started which line of speculation since the end thought was the product of both minds" (xlv). But he flatly contradicts himself a page later when he affirms that in pure creativeness, "there are no true collaborations. The creative principle is a lonely and an individual matter" (xlvi). And so all one really learns from Steinbeck is that we are not likely to get any clear-cut answers from him on the subject.

Virtually everyone personally acquainted with Steinbeck and Ricketts who is willing to talk about the friendship between the two maintains that Ricketts' influence on Steinbeck was pervasive and that it permeates most of the novelist's early fiction. A very

225

few, like Tony Berry, captain of the *Western Flyer,* suggest that Ricketts' impact as a scientist on Steinbeck was negligible, that although Ricketts was a trained biologist, Steinbeck was equally enthusiastic about collecting faunal specimens and really learned little from Ricketts. But most acquaintances of Steinbeck and Ricketts, as well as most Steinbeck critics, attribute all of the novelist's interest in science to Ricketts. And some, like Jack Calvin, even go so far as to assert that "without Ed, John would never have emerged from the crowded ranks of second raters" (JC-RA, 7/14/69).

There are reasonable explanations for this tendency on the part of those who knew both men to credit Ricketts for being the genius behind Steinbeck's view of man and the world. For one thing, Ricketts was a biologist and Steinbeck was not, though there are few who would deny the genuine nature of Steinbeck's interest in the animals of the littoral. For another thing, Ed Ricketts was a brilliant man and an expert on many subjects who eagerly shared his thoughts without any show of intellectual bravado. But despite the vitality of his thinking, Ricketts wrote poorly and could not get most of his original work published. Of course, *Between Pacific Tides* and *Sea of Cortez* reached print, but the appeal of the former has been limited largely to professional oceanographers, and the presence of Steinbeck's name on the title page of *Sea of Cortez* has obscured the identity of his lesser known collaborator. And so, feeling that Ricketts was ignored in his own time, his friends simply want him to have his day. Ed Ricketts was one of those unique human beings endowed with a special blend of personality and intellect who affected people deeply and permanently, and those who knew both men and knew the depth of their friendship have justifiably, they feel, concluded that Steinbeck's success as a writer was due in large part to that friendship.

The findings of this study lend considerable support to the claims of those who believe that the true measure of Ricketts' influence on Steinbeck's life and writing has been unduly minimized. Steinbeck's affection for Ricketts was so great that on one occasion he permitted the partial distortion of his own views to

John Steinbeck upon his receiving the
Nobel Prize for Literature, 1962

provide Ricketts with a format for his ideas (*Sea of Cortez*). He even considered embarking on a project for which he had little or no enthusiasm ("The Outer Shores"), simply to avoid hurting his friend's feelings. We now know the extent of Ricketts' involvement in the writing of the narrative section of *Sea of Cortez*, and we know that he wrote the vitally important essay on non-teleological thinking which has lived an underground existence for more than three decades.

From a careful investigation of character, theme, and metaphor in Steinbeck's fiction, we know that Ed Ricketts had a titanic impact on the novelist's work. He appears as a major character in one guise or another in at least a half dozen of Steinbeck's books. Moreover, Ricketts' passion for holistic and ecological thinking, his associational beliefs about the behavior of men and animals in groups, his doctrine of breaking through, and his disdain for the self-oriented acquisition of material wealth provided Steinbeck with many of his central thematic tenets. No, it hardly seems coincidental that Steinbeck's fictional genius declined after Ricketts' death. Rather, it seems apparent that the train that killed Ricketts set off a series of reactions that helped kill Steinbeck as a serious novelist.

At the same time, we know now that Steinbeck's interest in science antedated his friendship with Ricketts, and that his belief in the organismal conception of life which figures so prominently in his greatest novels can be traced to his experience at the Hopkins Marine Station and to his reading of organismal biology and philosophy. Certainly, Ricketts fanned Steinbeck's interest in things scientific; he provided a needed stimulus for Steinbeck's curiosity. But to say that all of Steinbeck's concern with science in general and with marine biology in particular came directly from Ricketts is to distort the facts.

We know also that Steinbeck and Ricketts disagreed on a number of issues, and that the measure of Ricketts' influence on Steinbeck can best be shown through an examination of their intellectual differences. For example, despite his reliance on Ricketts' non-teleological approach to life as fictional method and metaphor, Steinbeck could not accept the social implications of Ricketts' gospel of *is* thinking. They disagreed on the issue of human progress; Steinbeck's teleological dedication to man's pursuit of a better life forced him to reject what he regarded as Ricketts' quietistic belief in an understanding-acceptance approach to life. And while the novelist shared Ricketts' belief in the creative importance of the individual, his intense social consciousness, manifest in his carefully developed argument of phalanx, shows that (in his best works) he also recognized the importance of the group as an agent of meaningful social change.

Above all, Ricketts was in large measure a set-apart man, cut off and detached from much of the world about him. But John Steinbeck was a product of his time. And just as we are a fluid society, always running and never content with what we have, Steinbeck was a writer in motion. His phalanxes are moving phalanxes, and virtually all of the protagonists in his fiction (even those who are motivated by greed and self-interest) are portrayed in pursuit of a dream. And when the novelist does depict characters in stasis (Doc Burton, Danny and his *paisanos*, Doc and Mack and the boys), he does so to show the weak survival quotient of those who resist the flow of civilization.

Steinbeck is at his best as a writer, not when he fictionalizes a given set of Ricketts' precepts about man and the world, or when he totally ignores Ricketts' world-view, but rather when he examines critically what he regards as the virtues and flaws in Ricketts' vision and integrates the marine biologist's way of seeing with his own commitment to human progress.

Despite the occasional excesses in Steinbeck's fictional employment of Ricketts' person and ideas, which had the effect of undermining his art (*The Moon Is Down, Burning Bright*), there is no doubt but that the overall force of Ricketts' personality was largely responsible for Steinbeck's success as a writer. The virtues of those books in which there is no trace of the marine biologist's person or ideas (*Cup of Gold, The Short Reign of Pippin IV, The Winter of Our Discontent*) are slim. This is not said to minimize Steinbeck's genius. For despite the novelist's insistence that "in pure creativeness there are no collaborations," it is clear that the artist rarely operates in a vacuum. And with Ricketts' world-view accessible to him, we may be thankful that Steinbeck chose not to write all his books in isolation.

By analyzing the range and depth of Ricketts' impact on Steinbeck's fiction, one may see Steinbeck's accomplishments as a writer with fresh perspective. The novelist's philosophy of life is not tenth-rate, and his social and political material is not worn and obsolete. In his best works, Steinbeck fused science and philosophy, art and ethics, by combining the broad-visioned and compelling metaphysic of Edward F. Ricketts with a personal gospel of social action. In his own time and with his own voice, John Steinbeck defined and gave meaning to the uniquely complicated nature of the human experience.

NOTES

Notes

Steinbeck and Ricketts: An Overview

1. Arthur Mizener, "Does a Moral Vision of the Thirties Deserve a Nobel Prize?" *New York Times Book Review*, December 9, 1962, p. 45.

2. Joseph Fontenrose, *John Steinbeck: An Introduction and Interpretation* (New York: Holt, 1963), p. 96. Several critics have been unwilling to accept the idea that Steinbeck's philosophy of life is deficient. Accordingly, they have attempted to rescue the novelist by variously systematizing his beliefs as moralistic, behavioristic, or humanistic. See Woodburn O. Ross, "John Steinbeck: Naturalism's Priest," *College English* (May 1949), and "John Steinbeck: Earth and Stars," *Studies in Honor of A. F. R. Fairchild* (Columbia: University of Missouri Press, 1946). Both articles are reprinted in *Steinbeck and His Critics*, eds. E. W. Tedlock, Jr., and C. V. Wicker (Albuquerque: University of New Mexico Press, 1957), pp. 206–215, 167–182. Also see Frederic I. Carpenter, "John Steinbeck: American Dreamer," *Southwest Review*, XXVI (July 1941), 454–467, and Lester Jay Marks, *Thematic Design in the Novels of John Steinbeck* (The Hague: Mouton, 1969).

3. One of two published accounts of Ricketts is by Steinbeck, the personal sketch entitled "About Ed Ricketts" which precedes the Viking Compass 1951 republication of the narrative portion of *Sea of Cortez*. Quotations from "About Ed Ricketts," when noted, are identified by page number in the text. The other, by Joel W. Hedgpeth, is a more objective account of Ricketts as a man and a scientist: "Philosophy on Cannery Row," in *Steinbeck: The Man and His Work*, eds. Richard Astro and Tetsumaro Hayashi (Corvallis: Oregon State University Press, 1971), pp. 89–129.

4. Lawrence R. Blinks of the Hopkins Marine Station suggests that Ricketts may have been influenced by the great botanist, Henry Chandler

Cowles, who was at Chicago at the time and was working with the same kinds of ideas on plants (LRB/RA 10/8/70).

During one break from his studies, and following a disappointment in love, Ricketts took a long walking trip through the southeastern United States and published a short account of it entitled "Vagabonding Through Dixie," *Travel*, XLV (June 1925), 16–18, 44, 48. Steinbeck writes about Ricketts' walking trip in "About Ed Ricketts" and *Cannery Row*, but doesn't mention Ricketts' article.

5. This note appears on the inside cover of Ricketts' "New Series Notebook No. 2," which, with "New Series Notebooks No. 3 and No. 4," is housed in the library of the Hopkins Marine Station, Pacific Grove, California.

6. Edward F. Ricketts, "Contents of PBL Destroyed Nov. 1936," p. 6. This is an unpublished list of personal possessions lost in the fire of 1936.

7. Hedgpeth, "Philosophy on Cannery Row," p. 104. Also see pp. 125–127 for a detailed bibliographical history of *Between Pacific Tides*. Hedgpeth completely revised the book for its fourth edition (1968).

8. John Steinbeck, "Foreword," *Between Pacific Tides*, 3rd ed., by Edward F. Ricketts and Jack Calvin, revised by Joel W. Hedgpeth (Stanford: Stanford University Press, 1952), p. vi.

9. Edward F. Ricketts and Jack Calvin, *Between Pacific Tides* (Stanford: Stanford University Press, 1939), p. viii.

10. Joel W. Hedgpeth, "Preface," *Between Pacific Tides*, 4th ed., by Edward F. Ricketts and Jack Calvin, revised by Joel W. Hedgpeth (Stanford: Stanford University Press, 1968), p. 1.

11. Ricketts and Calvin, *Between Pacific Tides*, 1st ed., p. vii.

12. Ricketts and Calvin, *Between Pacific Tides*, 4th ed., p. 60.

13. *Ibid.*, p. 206.

14. Hedgpeth, "Preface," p. 1.

15. Steinbeck, "Foreword," p. vi.

16. Edward F. Ricketts, "Suggested Outline for Handbook of Marine Invertebrates of the San Francisco Bay Area," MS., n.d., p. 2.

17. Edward F. Ricketts, pencilled notes in the San Francisco Bay Area Handbook file. Ricketts often referred to Steinbeck as "Jon" and sometimes "Jn."

18. *Ibid.*

19. Edward F. Ricketts, "Essay No. 2," MS. in the San Francisco Bay Area Handbook file, n.d., p. 1.

20. Edward F. Ricketts, "Zoological Preface," MS. dated variously January 7 and August 27, 1940, in the San Francisco Bay Area Handbook file. Novalis and the whole issue of what Ricketts meant by "homesickness, the wish to be everywhere at home," plays a crucial role in his worldview.

21. *Ibid.*, p. 4.

22. *Ibid.*, p. 11.

23. Edward F. Ricketts, "Morphology of the *Sea of Cortez*," MS., n.d.

24. John Lyman, "Of and About the Sea," *American Neptune* (April 1942), p. 183.

25. Joel W. Hedgpeth, "The Scientific Second Half of *Sea of Cortez*," San Francisco *Chronicle*, "This World" section, December 14, 1941, p. 26.

26. Peter Lisca, *The Wide World of John Steinbeck* (New Brunswick: Rutgers University Press, 1958), p. 183.

27. Fontenrose, *John Steinbeck*, p. 85. Also see Clifton Fadiman, "Of Crabs and Men," *New Yorker* (December 6, 1941), p. 107; Sterling North's review in the Chicago *Daily News*, December 10, 1941, p. 28; and Scott Newhall, "John Steinbeck's Chioppino of Biology and Philosophy," San Francisco *Chronicle*, "This World" section, December 14, 1941, p. 26.

28. Edward F. Ricketts, "Memorandum from Steinbeck-Ricketts to Pat Covici and to the Editorial Board of Viking," August 25, 1941. It should also be pointed out that another member of the crew, Horace (Sparky) Enea, kept an informal diary of the trip, parts of which were published in the Monterey *Peninsula Herald*.

29. Ricketts, "Morphology of the *Sea of Cortez*." A close acquaintance of Steinbeck and Ricketts has known the facts behind the writing of *Sea of Cortez* for years, but her words have gone unheard by critical ears. Beth Ingels, who reviewed the book for the Monterey *Peninsula Herald*, noted that "in the course of the book it becomes obvious where Steinbeck leaves off and Ricketts begins." "*Sea of Cortez*: New Picture of Steinbeck," Monterey *Peninsula Herald*, December 6, 1941.

30. In the conclusion of his book, Lisca comments that Ricketts had much to do with the essay on non-teleological thinking (*Wide World*, p. 291). Why Lisca disregards this in his discussion of *Sea of Cortez* is unclear.

31. In a later letter, Ricketts told Campbell that Henry Miller had also read and "praised very highly the essay on non-teleological thinking" (EFR-Ca, 12/31/41).

32. Besides Ricketts, Steinbeck, and Carol Steinbeck, the crew consisted of Tony Berry (captain), Ratzi Coletto, Sparky Enea, and Hall (Tex) Travis. According to Berry, the charter price for the *Western Flyer* was $2,500.

33. Graham recalls that Steinbeck spent long hours on the narrative and took his work extremely seriously (EG/RA, 10/8/70). Graham's original sketch for the finished oil is reproduced on the dust jacket of Astro and Hayashi, *Steinbeck: The Man and His Work*.

34. With regard to the "borrego" hunt, it is interesting that both men refer to a certain Sr. Gilberto Baldibia, a teacher, who, with rancher Leopoldo Pérpuly and customs official Manuel Madinabeitia, took Steinbeck and Ricketts into the mountains inland from Puerto Escondido. Ricketts and Steinbeck identically misspelled his name, which is Valdivia (GV/RA, 3/23/72). This misspelling raises the possibility that Steinbeck simply transcribed the entire incident from Ricketts' earlier account. At this writing, Srs. Valdivia and Madinabeitia live in La Paz, Sr. Pérpuly in Loreto. And Madinabeitia recalls with pleasure his evening with two of the most fascinating human beings he ever encountered (MM/RA, 3/23/72).

35. Edward F. Ricketts, "Verbatim Transcription of Notes of Gulf of California Trip, March–April, 1940," MS., n.d., p. 18.

36. *Ibid.*

37. See Stanley Hyman, "Some Notes on John Steinbeck," *Antioch Review*, II (June 1942), reprinted in Tedlock and Wicker, *Steinbeck and His Critics*, pp. 152–166.

38. At one point, Steinbeck noted that the book "is a good clearing-out of a lot of ideas that have been working on me for a long time." See Lewis

Gannett, "Steinbeck's Way of Writing," *The Portable Steinbeck*, rev. ed. (New York: Viking Press, 1946), p. xxv.

39. See Ricketts, "New Series Notebook No. 2," p. 203.
40. Actually, Ricketts' plans for a cold-water *Sea of Cortez* date to 1942, when he wrote: "My study of the marine invertebrates has divided itself geographically into three divisions. The first, on the animals of the US and Canada, appeared as 'BPT.' A second, the appendix to 'Sea of Cortez,' extended the range to the south. . . . The third part (now far in the future; Japan's threats in the Dutch Harbor are looking after that!) will deal with the Aleutians, Gulf of Alaska, Bering Sea, etc." (EFR-SUP, 2/11/42).
41. See Hedgpeth, "Philosophy on Cannery Row," p. 114.
42. Edward F. Ricketts, "The Outer Shores," MS. transcription from field notes in 1947 and 1948, p. 143.
43. John Steinbeck, *Journal of a Novel* (New York: Viking Press, 1969), p. 57.
44. *Ibid.*, p. 4.
45. Ricketts, "The Outer Shores," p. 28.
46. Sir Arthur Eddington, *The Nature of the Physical World* (Ann Arbor: University of Michigan Press, 1958 [Ann Arbor Paperbacks]), p. 353.
47. Ricketts, "The Outer Shores," p. 26.
48. Steinbeck, "About Ed Ricketts," p. xiii.

A Morphology of Breaking Through

1. Ricketts, "Verbatim Transcription," p. 38.
2. Ricketts, "The Outer Shores," p. 26.
3. Eddington, *Physical World*, p. 210.
4. Ricketts, "Essay No. 2," p. 1.
5. Ricketts, "The Outer Shores," p. 108.
6. Ricketts, "Zoological Preface," p. 4.
7. John Steinbeck and Edward F. Ricketts, *The Log from the Sea of Cortez* (New York: Viking Press, 1962 [Compass]), p. 60. All further citations from the *Log* refer to this edition and are identified by page number in the text.
8. See Frederick Bracher, "Steinbeck and the Biological View of Man," *Pacific Spectator*, II (Winter 1948), 14–29. Reprinted in Tedlock and Wicker, *Steinbeck and His Critics*, pp. 183–196.
9. John Steinbeck and Edward F. Ricketts, *Sea of Cortez* (New York: Viking Press, 1941), p. 300.
10. William Emerson Ritter, *The Natural History of Our Conduct* (New York: Harcourt, 1927), p. 4.
11. Jacob Boehme, *The Signature of All Things* (London: Fernhill, 1969), p. 91.
12. Edward F. Ricketts, "A Spiritual Morphology of Poetry," MS. dated July 1939, p. 4.
13. Ricketts, "The Outer Shores," p. 3.
14. *Ibid.*, p. 14.
15. Ricketts, "Verbatim Transcription," p. 14. Sr. Madinabeitia recalls that the group spent the night at this oasis above the waterfall, and he remem-

bers how much Ricketts enjoyed throwing little pebbles into the pools below and listening for echoes (MM/RA, 3/23/72).

16. Ross, "John Steinbeck: Naturalism's Priest," pp. 211–212.
17. Ricketts, "Zoological Preface," p. 4. There is evidence to suggest that Ricketts found Carlyle's translation in the preface of Maeterlinck's *On Emerson and Other Essays* (New York: Dodd, 1933). In an informal list entitled "2nd Hand Book Desiderata, as of July, 1938," Ricketts mentions Maeterlinck's work. He does not refer to Carlyle's translation of Novalis anywhere in his works.
18. Edward F. Ricketts, "The Philosophy of Breaking Through," MS., Mexico City, 1940 draft, p. 7.
19. *Ibid.*, pp. 1–2.
20. *Ibid.*, p. 3.
21. *Ibid.*, p. 4.
22. *Ibid.*, p. 7.
23. *Ibid.*, p. 9.
24. Ricketts, "New Series Notebook No. 2," p. 95. Later in the same notebook, Ricketts observes that "the deep thing" is "almost completely hidden away from us" so that often "the only thing we can know is projection" (p. 222). Both notebook entries were made sometime in 1944.
25. Edward F. Ricketts, "Non-Teleological Thinking," MS. subtitled, "Non-teleological, relational or 'is' thinking, as contrasted to the more usual cause-effect methods. An inductive presentation." March 1941 draft, typed by Antonia Seixas, p. 19.
26. In a letter to Pat Covici, Ricketts admitted that he had used the term *teleology* in "a special sense" (EFR-PC, 9/28/41).
27. Ricketts, "Non-Teleological Thinking," p. 3.
28. *Ibid.*, p. 17.
29. *Ibid.*, p. 16.
30. *Ibid.*, pp. 17–18.
31. In the *Log*, for example, Ricketts (and Steinbeck) observe that the Indians of the Gulf "seemed to live on remembered things, to be so related to the seashore and the rocky hills and the loneliness that they are these things" (75).
32. Edward F. Ricketts, "Ideas on Psychological Types, Abstracted and Diagrammed from Jung's Essay; 'Psychological Types,' " MS., n.d.
33. Ricketts, "A Spiritual Morphology of Poetry," p. 8.
34. *Ibid.*
35. *Ibid.*, p. 11.
36. *Ibid.*, p. 12.
37. *Ibid.*
38. *Ibid.*, p. 14.
39. *Ibid.*, p. 16.
40. *Ibid.*, p. 9.
41. Ricketts, "New Series Notebook No. 4," p. 187.

Progress and the Organismal Conception

1. Edward F. Ricketts, "Fort Ord Journal," MS., entry for February 11, 1943.
2. William Emerson Ritter and Edna W. Bailey, "The Organismal Concep-

tion: Its Place in Science and Its Bearing on Philosophy," *University of California Publications in Zoology*, XXXI (1931), 307.

3. *Ibid.*
4. *Ibid.*, p. 308.
5. *Ibid.*, p. 349.
6. Ritter, *The Natural History of Our Conduct*, p. 5.
7. Interestingly enough, Ritter did a good deal of scientific research on the organismal life-style of pelagic tunicates in the region of Southern California.
8. W. C. Allee, *Animal Aggregations* (Chicago: University of Chicago Press, 1931), p. 354.
9. *Ibid.*, pp. 361–362.
10. W. E. Agar, *A Contribution to the Theory of the Living Organism* (Melbourne, Australia: Melbourne University Press, 1951), p. 2.
11. Ritter, *The Natural History of Our Conduct*, p. 41.
12. See Alfred North Whitehead, *Science and the Modern World* (New York: New American Library, 1925), p. vii.
13. Ritter and Bailey, "The Organismal Conception," p. 358. There is also some evidence that Ricketts was familiar with the work of Smuts, since in a letter to Joseph Campbell in which he discusses his theory of holism, Ricketts notes, "I use the term holistic in the same sense that Jan Smuts considers it in his essay 'Holism' in XIV Encyl. Brit." (EFR-Ca, 7/3/40).
14. Albee studied under Boodin at U.C.L.A. during the early 1930's, and he brought with him to the Monterey Peninsula the ideas of his mentor, whom he believes "may well have been the greatest metaphysical thinker America has produced, and one of the greatest in the world" (Albee-RA, 5/9/71).
15. John Dewey, "The Influence of Darwinism on Philosophy," reprinted in *American Thought: Civil War to World War I,* ed. Perry Miller (New York: Holt, 1954), pp. 223–224.
16. J. C. Smuts, *Holism and Evolution* (New York: Macmillan, 1926), p. 224.
17. *Ibid.*, p. 226.
18. *Ibid.*, p. 242.
19. *Ibid.*, p. 231.
20. *Ibid.*, p. 251.
21. Robert Briffault, *The Making of Humanity* (London: Allen & Unwin, 1919), p. 51.
22. *Ibid.*, p. 85.
23. John Elof Boodin, *Cosmic Evolution* (New York: Macmillan, 1925), pp. 34, 35.
24. John Elof Boodin, *A Realistic Universe* (New York: Macmillan, 1916), p. xviii.
25. John Elof Boodin, *The Social Mind* (New York: Macmillan, 1939), p. 14. Joseph Campbell remembers Steinbeck's interest in Boodin's work (Ca/RA, 4/1/71). Appropriately, Campbell has written, "the modern hero-deed must be that of questing to bring to light again the lost Atlantis of the coordinated soul," in *Hero with a Thousand Faces* (Cleveland: World, 1956 [Meridian Books]), p. 388.
26. Smuts, *Holism and Evolution*, p. 259.

27. Edmund Wilson, "The Boys in the Back Room," *Classics and Commercials* (New York: Random House, 1962 [Vintage]), pp. 19–56.
28. Lisca, *Wide World*, pp. 99–100.
29. John Steinbeck, *America and Americans* (New York: Viking Press, 1966), p. 143. All further citations from *America and Americans* refer to this edition and are identified by page number in the text.
30. John Steinbeck, *The Grapes of Wrath* (New York: Viking Press, 1958 [Compass]), pp. 204–205. All further citations from *The Grapes of Wrath* refer to this edition and are identified by page number in the text.
31. Steinbeck's critics have refused to acknowledge the teleological cast of the novelist's thinking. Some have noted what they regard as a dichotomy in Steinbeck's thinking, his failure to reconcile the cold observation characteristic of "his" non-teleological approach to life with the human elements in his fiction (see Ross, "John Steinbeck: Earth and Stars," p. 178). Others have simply called Steinbeck a non-teleologist and insisted that his fictional ideal is the "biologist-hero who applies Steinbeck's non-teleological methods of observation to the several complex relationships and, acting as a kind of chorus, comments on the whole picture" (Marks, *Thematic Design*, p. 25).
32. Ricketts, "The Philosophy of Breaking Through," p. 7.
33. Ricketts was particularly moved by Novalis' *Hymns to the Night*, in which Novalis affirms that night is the path to inner being, the way to poetry, to creation.
34. Edward F. Ricketts, untitled MS. on German and Japanese patterns of culture, hereafter identified as "Essay on Germany and Japan." Written in August 1942, p. 12.
35. Ricketts, "The Philosophy of Breaking Through," p. 16.
36. Ricketts was well versed in the *Tao Teh King*. In a letter to Joseph Campbell, he mentions reading two new translations of that work (EFR-Ca, 12/16/39).
37. Edward F. Ricketts, "Thesis and Materials for a Script on Mexico," MS. dated 1940, p. 3. Hereafter referred to as "Anti-script."
38. *Ibid.*
39. *Ibid.*, p. 1.
40. *Ibid.*, p. 4.
41. Ricketts, "The Outer Shores," p. 18.
42. Ricketts, "Essay on Germany and Japan," p. 14.
43. Ricketts, "Anti-script," p. 3.
44. John Steinbeck, *The Forgotten Village* (New York: Viking Press, 1941), pp. 139, 141. All further citations from *The Forgotten Village* refer to this edition and are identified by page number in the text.
45. Ricketts, "Anti-script," p. 5.
46. Donald Weeks, "Steinbeck against Steinbeck," *Pacific Spectator*, I (Autumn 1947), 447–457.

The Argument of Phalanx

1. Ricketts, "Fort Ord Journal," entry for January 3, 1943.
2. Ricketts, "Zoological Preface," p. 11.
3. Ricketts, "Verbatim Transcription," p. 36.
4. Ricketts, "Anti-script," p. 4.

5. John S. Kennedy, "John Steinbeck: Life Affirmed and Denied," in *Fifty Years of the American Novel*, ed. Harold C. Gardiner; reprinted in Tedlock and Wicker, *Steinbeck and His Critics*, p. 124.
6. Lisca mentions Steinbeck's "phalanx theory" and even suggests that Ricketts "had a hand in formulating Steinbeck's group-man theories," which is apparent from a folder of notes he kept "for a study of phalanx literature." (*Wide World*, p. 291). Lisca doesn't document his assertion. Nowhere in any of Ricketts' essays, journals, or notebooks is there evidence that the marine biologist helped Steinbeck develop the "Argument of Phalanx."
7. Ritter and Bailey, "The Organismal Conception," p. 308.
8. Morton Beckner, *The Biological Way of Thought* (Berkeley: University of California Press, 1968), p. 187.
9. J. S. Haldane, *Mechanism, Life, and Personality*, 2nd ed. (New York: Dutton, 1923), p. 80.
10. Ritter, *The Natural History of Our Conduct*, p. 3.
11. John Steinbeck, "Argument of Phalanx," two-page MS., n.d., p. 2.
12. William Emerson Ritter, *The Unity of the Organism; or the Organismal Conception*, 2 vols. (Boston: Gorham Press, 1919), Vol. 1, p. 24.
13. Steinbeck, "Argument of Phalanx," p. 1.
14. *Ibid.*
15. *Ibid.*
16. *Ibid.*, pp. 1, 2.
17. John Steinbeck, "Some Thoughts on Juvenile Delinquency," *Saturday Review*, XXXVII (May 28, 1955), 22.
18. Boodin's theories of the role of the self in society resemble such group psychologies as Le Bon's "collective mentality" and Durkheim's "mental movements."
19. Boodin, *The Social Mind*, p. 430.
20. *Ibid.*, p. 177.
21. *Ibid.*, p. 557.
22. Smuts, *Holism and Evolution*, p. 253.
23. John Steinbeck, "The Leader of the People," *The Red Pony* (New York: Viking Press, 1965 [Compass)]), p. 180. All further citations from "The Leader of the People" refer to this edition and are identified by page number in the text.
24. Lisca, *Wide World*, pp. 105, 107.
25. Claude-Edmonde Magny, "Steinbeck, or the Limits of the Impersonal Novel," trans. Françoise Gourier, reprinted in Tedlock and Wicker, *Steinbeck and His Critics*, p. 221.
26. See W. F. Frohock, "John Steinbeck: The Utility of Wrath," in his *The Novel of Violence in America*, rev. ed. (Boston: Beacon, 1964), pp. 124–143.
27. John Steinbeck, "The Vigilante," *The Long Valley* (New York: Viking Press, 1956 [Compass]), p. 140. All further citations from *The Long Valley* refer to this edition and are identified by page number in the text.
28. Ritter and Bailey, "The Organismal Conception," p. 355.
29. See Baker Brownell, *The New Universe* (New York: Van Nostrand, 1926).
30. John Steinbeck, "Critics, Critics, Burning Bright," *Saturday Review*, XXXIII (November 11, 1950), 21.

31. Ralph Waldo Emerson, "Self-reliance," in *The Selected Writings of Ralph Waldo Emerson*, ed. Brooks Atkinson (New York: Random House, 1950 [Modern Library)], pp. 152–153.

From Men to Gods

1. JS-EO, 4/15/36, as quoted in Lisca, *Wide World*, p. 26.
2. F. W. Watt, *John Steinbeck* (New York: Grove, 1962), p. 26.
3. John Steinbeck, *Cup of Gold* (New York: Bantam, 1953), p. 44. All further citations from *Cup of Gold* refer to this edition and are identified by page number in the text.
4. Lisca, *Wide World*, p. 27.
5. JS-ROB, 2/11/33, as quoted in Lisca, *Wide World*, p. 39.
6. Lisca, *Wide World*, p. 39. Much of Lisca's account of the genesis of *To a God Unknown* derives from an early analysis of the novel by Harry Thornton Moore, *The Novels of John Steinbeck* (Chicago: Normandie House, 1939).
7. JS-MO, 5/8/31, as quoted in Lisca, *Wide World*, pp. 39–40.
8. The name is spelled Wane in Street's play, but Wayne in Steinbeck's novel.
9. Webster F. Street, "The Green Lady," MS., n.d., Act I, p. 3.
10. *Ibid.*, p. 1.
11. Webster F. Street, revision notes for "The Green Lady," MS., n.d.
12. *Ibid.*
13. JS-MO, 5/17/32, as quoted in Lisca, *Wide World*, p. 41.
14. JS-MO, 8/18/31, as quoted in Lisca, *Wide World*, p. 40.
15. Gannett, "Steinbeck's Way of Writing," pp. xi–xii. Joseph Campbell read much of *To a God Unknown* during the final stages of composition, and he recalls cautioning the novelist against excessive metaphysical speculation unclothed with a believable story line (Ca/RA, 4/2/71).
16. John Steinbeck, *To a God Unknown* (New York: Bantam, 1960), p. 4. All further citations from *To a God Unknown* refer to this edition and are identified by page number in the text.
17. Campbell, *Hero*, p. 81.
18. For interesting discussions of Joseph's role as Christ-figure and as Fisher-king, see Lisca, *Wide World*, pp. 45–46, and Fontenrose, *John Steinbeck*, pp. 15–16.
19. Lisca, *Wide World*, p. 43.
20. *Ibid.*, p. 49.
21. Ricketts, "The Philosophy of Breaking Through," p. 5.
22. *Ibid.*, p. 9.
23. *Ibid.*, p. 18.
24. *Ibid.*
25. Lisca writes that Steinbeck's preoccupation with ritual in *To a God Unknown* is evidence of the novelist's interest in "man's unconscious heritage of the experiences of his race," and he supports this thesis by quoting a passage from the *Log* about man's race-memory which in many ways explains Steinbeck's use of ritual in *To a God Unknown* (*Wide World*, p. 53). When, however, it is observed that the passage in the *Log* alluded to was written not by Steinbeck but by Ricketts, and not in

1941 but during a 1932 collecting expedition with Joseph Campbell in southeastern Alaska, the impact of Ricketts' world-view on *To a God Unknown* looms even larger.

The Pastures of Pleasure and Illusion

1. Gannett, "Steinbeck's Way of Writing," p. xii.
2. See Fontenrose, *John Steinbeck*, p. 20.
3. JS-MO, 5/8/31, as quoted in Lisca, *Wide World*, pp. 56–57.
4. Lisca, *Wide World*, p. 59.
5. Briffault, *The Making of Humanity*, p. 85.
6. John Steinbeck, *The Pastures of Heaven* (New York: Bantam, 1951), p. 18. All further citations from *The Pastures of Heaven* refer to this edition and are identified by page number in the text.
7. Ricketts, "The Philosophy of Breaking Through," p. 3.
8. Lisca, *Wide World*, p. 66.
9. Fontenrose, *John Steinbeck*, p. 27.
10. Steinbeck's critics are indecisive about the actual meaning of the curse, and Fontenrose even admits his uncertainty as to the novelist's attitude toward it. (Fontenrose, *John Steinbeck*, p. 21).
11. Warren G. French, *John Steinbeck* (New York: Twayne, 1961), p. 46.
12. *Ibid.*, p. 76.
13. Antonia Seixas, "John Steinbeck and the Non-teleological Bus," *What's Doing on the Monterey Peninsula*, I (March, 1947), reprinted in Tedlock and Wicker, *Steinbeck and His Critics*, p. 277.
14. John Steinbeck, *Of Mice and Men* (New York: Viking Press, 1963 [Compass]), p. 37. All further citations from *Of Mice and Men* refer to this edition and are identified by page number in the text.
15. Ricketts, "Non-teleological Thinking," p. 17.
16. *Ibid.*, p. 2.
17. T. K. Whipple, "Steinbeck: Through a Glass Though Brightly," *Study Out the Land* (Berkeley: University of California Press, 1943), p. 106.
18. Edith Ronald Mirrielees, *Writing the Short Story* (New York: Doubleday, 1929), p. 3. Evidence of Miss Mirrielees' influence on Steinbeck is noted by Webster F. Street in "John Steinbeck: A Reminiscence" (in Astro and Hayashi, *Steinbeck: The Man and His Work*, p. 39). Steinbeck himself acknowledged his indebtedness to Miss Mirrielees in his preface to the Compass edition of Mirrielees' *Story Writing* (New York: Viking Press, 1962), pp. vi–viii.
19. Frohock, "John Steinbeck," p. 128–129.
20. See Lisca, *Wide World*, p. 79.
21. Freeman Champney, "John Steinbeck, Californian," *Antioch Review* (Fall 1947), reprinted in Tedlock and Wicker, *Steinbeck and His Critics*, p. 144. Similarly, Edmund Wilson called the *paisanos* "cunning little living dolls that amuse us as we might be amused by pet guinea pigs, squirrels or rabbits" ("The Boys in the Back Room," p. 41).
22. John Steinbeck, *Tortilla Flat* (New York: Viking Press, 1963 [Compass]), p. 22. All further citations from *Tortilla Flat* refer to this edition and are identified by page number in the text.
23. Lisca, *Wide World*, p. 88. For other interesting comments about Steinbeck's handling of the *paisanos*, see Stanley Alexander, "The Conflict of

Form in *Tortilla Flat*," *American Literature,* XL (1968), 58–66, and Joseph Warren Beach, "John Steinbeck: Journeyman Artist," in his *American Fiction: 1920–1940* (New York: Macmillan, 1941), and reprinted in Tedlock and Wicker, *Steinbeck and His Critics*, p. 88.

24. Steinbeck, preface to Mirrielees' *Story Writing*, p. vi.
25. John Steinbeck, "The Snake," *The Long Valley*, p. 73.
26. Steinbeck, "About Ed Ricketts," pp. xxiii–xxiv.
27. Street, "John Steinbeck: A Reminiscence," pp. 39–40.
28. *Ibid.*
29. "The Vigilante" was first published as "The Lonesome Vigilante" in *Esquire*, October 1936.
30. John Steinbeck, "Johnny Bear," *The Long Valley*, p. 158.
31. Lisca, *Wide World*, p. 99.
32. John Steinbeck, "Flight," *The Long Valley*, p. 50.
33. John Steinbeck, "The Raid," *The Long Valley*, p. 107.
34. John Steinbeck, "The Chrysanthemums," *The Long Valley*, p. 23.
35. John Steinbeck, "The Harness," *The Long Valley*, p. 129.
36. John Steinbeck, "The White Quail," *The Long Valley*, pp. 38, 39.

In the Troubled Garden

1. JS-MO, 2/4/35, as quoted in Lisca, *Wide World*, p. 114. The book's brutality has disturbed many critics who feel that Steinbeck applauds or at least remains impartial toward the violent methods endorsed by Mac and Jim. See Wilson, "The Boys in the Back Room," pp. 40, 44.
2. John Steinbeck, *In Dubious Battle* (New York: Viking Press, 1963 [Compass]), p. 103. All further citations from *In Dubious Battle* refer to this edition and are identified by page number in the text.
3. Lisca, *Wide World*, p. 125.
4. *Ibid.*
5. Ricketts, "Non-Teleological Thinking," p. 3.
6. Steinbeck, "Argument of Phalanx," p. 2. In *In Dubious Battle*, Doc Burton expresses a desire to "know more about group-man, to know his nature, his ends, his desires. They're not the same as ours. . . . I simply want to see as much as I can, Mac, with the means I have" (132).
7. Steinbeck, "Argument of Phalanx," p. 1.
8. *Ibid.*, p. 2.
9. See Smuts, *Holism and Evolution*, p. 259.
10. French, *Steinbeck*, pp. 70–71.
11. Frederic I. Carpenter, "The Philosophical Joads," *College English* (January 1941), reprinted in Tedlock and Wicker, *Steinbeck and His Critics*, pp. 241–249.
12. Ricketts, "A Spiritual Morphology of Poetry," p. 16.
13. Ricketts, "The Philosophy of Breaking Through," p. 16.
14. Boodin, *The Social Mind*, p. 557.
15. French, *Steinbeck*, pp. 95–112.
16. Robert Briffault, *The Mothers* (New York: MacMillan, 1931), p. 23. Steinbeck's interest in Briffault's theory of the mother-role may be responsible in part for the unusual women characters in his fiction, particularly for the absence of sexually oriented female characters in most of his novels and short stories.

17. The best study of Steinbeck's agrarianism is Chester E. Eisinger, "Jeffersonian Agrarianism in *The Grapes of Wrath*," *University of Kansas City Review*, XIV (Autumn 1947), 149–154. Eisinger's article is reprinted in *The Grapes of Wrath: Text and Criticism*, ed. Peter Lisca (New York: Viking Press, 1972), pp. 720–728.
18. Herbert Kline, "On John Steinbeck," *Steinbeck Quarterly*, IV (Summer 1971), 84.
19. Lisca, *Wide World*, p. 168.
20. French, *Steinbeck*, p. 86.
21. Ricketts, "Anti-script," p. 1.
22. *Ibid*. Ricketts defines "the region of outward possessions" as "communication and transportation; education in the formal and usual sense, as emphasizing the acquisition of facts and skills, and in which the teaching is by rule, more or less impersonal, and in quantity production; sanitation, medicine and surgery."

Steinbeck and Ricketts Go to War

1. Ricketts, "New Series Notebook No. 2," p. 40.
2. Ricketts, "Essay on Germany and Japan," p. 1.
3. *Ibid*.
4. *Ibid*., pp. 14–15.
5. *Ibid*., p. 15.
6. *Ibid*.
7. Edward F. Ricketts, notebook memo, dated July 13, 1943.
8. Ricketts, "Fort Ord Journal," p. 1.
9. *Ibid*., p. 5.
10. *Ibid*.
11. *Ibid*., p. 6.
12. *Ibid*., p. 13.
13. *Ibid*.
14. *Ibid*., p. 17.
15. *Ibid*., p. 20.
16. *Ibid*., p. 21.
17. Ricketts, "Verbatim Transcription," p. 41.
18. *Ibid*.
19. See "About Ed Ricketts," pp. lx–lxii.
20. Steinbeck, "Argument of Phalanx," p. 1.
21. John Steinbeck, *Bombs Away* (New York: Viking Press, 1942), p. 5. All further citations from *Bombs Away* refer to this edition and are identified by page number in the text.
22. John Steinbeck, *Once There Was A War* (New York: Bantam, 1960), pp. 6, 2. All further citations from *Once There Was a War* refer to this edition and are identified by page number in the text.
23. Lisca, *Wide World*, p. 185.
24. "It was," Lisca notes, "the result of several conversations he [Steinbeck] had with Colonel William J. Donovan on ways of aiding resistance movements in Nazi-occupied countries" (*Wide World*, p. 186).
25. "Correspondence," *The New Republic*, CVI (May 4, 1942), 495, 607–608.
26. John Steinbeck, *The Moon Is Down* (New York: Bantam, 1964), p. 29.

All further citations from *The Moon Is Down* refer to this edition and are identified by page number in the text.

27. Ricketts, "Non-teleological Thinking," p. 7.
28. "The laws of thought parallel the laws of things" is, of course, a phrase from Boodin's *A Realistic Universe*, p. xviii. Interestingly enough, Steinbeck paraphrases this statement by Boodin in the unfinished preface he wrote in 1940 for the San Francisco Bay Area handbook.
29. The only one of Steinbeck's works before *The Moon Is Down* in which nature is portrayed schematically is *Cup of Gold*. Besides being the only Steinbeck novels written before the end of World War II that do not deal with life in California's agricultural valleys, *The Moon Is Down* and *Cup of Gold* each depict an indignant nature rising up to resist an intrusive band of invaders.

Intimations of a Wasteland

1. Gannett, "Steinbeck's Way of Writing," p. xxvi.
2. See Lisca, *Wide World*, p. 198.
3. John Steinbeck, *Cannery Row* (New York: Bantam, 1959), p. 2. All further citations from *Cannery Row* refer to this edition and are identified by page number in the text.
4. Fontenrose, *John Steinbeck*, p. 105.
5. In late October and early November of 1941, there was an exhibition of Graham's work at the Hotel Del Monte in Carmel. Ricketts reviewed Graham's show for the Monterey *Peninsula Herald* and noted that Graham captured "the deep thing, the inward sense of order being worked out." He considered Graham "one of the serious and significant painters of this region."
6. See in particular, Steinbeck's "About Ed Ricketts," p. liii.
7. Ricketts, "Anti-script," p. 11.
8. Lisca, *Wide World*, p. 215.
9. Curiously, Ricketts never mentions the distrust shown him that Steinbeck talks about in such detail. See "Vagabonding Through Dixie," pp. 16–18, 44, 48.
10. Lisca, "Escape and Commitment: Two Poles of the Steinbeck Hero," in Astro and Hayashi, *Steinbeck: The Man and His Work*, p. 84.
11. See Lisca, *Wide World*, p. 183.
12. The passage of time has more than confirmed Steinbeck's fears. The Row has been victimized by the very commercialism Steinbeck feared—and largely because of the fame of the novel. Many of the old canneries have been converted to restaurants and night spots, and the John Steinbeck Theatre stands across from what was once Lee Chong's grocery but is now a tourist bookshop. A million dollar shopping complex has recently been completed.
13. Fontenrose, *John Steinbeck*, p. 108.
14. *Ibid.*
15. See *The Log from the Sea of Cortez*, p. 96.
16. French, *Steinbeck*, p. 127.
17. John Steinbeck, "My Short Novels," *Wings* (October 1953), p. 8.
18. Gannett, "Steinbeck's Way of Writing," p. xxvii.
19. See Ricketts, "Anti-script," p. 1.

20. John Steinbeck, *The Pearl* (New York: Viking Press, 1965 [Compass]), p. 25. All further citations from *The Pearl* refer to this edition and are identified by page number in the text.
21. Seixas, "John Steinbeck and the Non-teleological Bus," p. 278.
22. *Ibid.*, p. 279.
23. John Steinbeck, *The Wayward Bus* (New York: Bantam, 1957), pp. 7–8. All further citations from *The Wayward Bus* refer to this edition and are identified by page number in the text.
24. Steinbeck has been criticized for his handling of the Everyman allegory. See Fontenrose, *John Steinbeck*, p. 110, and French, *Steinbeck*, p. 144. But considering that Steinbeck purposefully integrates the Everyman allegory with the Flood motif, these criticisms seem unwarranted. Steinbeck often uses mythical and allegorical references, but he is not the kind of myth-maker who patterns each novel on a specific myth. There are rare exceptions, particularly in *Tortilla Flat*, where the importance of Arthurian myth patterns determine the novel's theme and structure. But Steinbeck generally draws his allusions from diverse sources, mixes them together for thematic purposes, and emerges with a unique narrative which does not deserve criticism contesting his faithfulness to a specific source.
25. Steinbeck, *Journal of a Novel*, p. 95.

Laying Down the Ghost

1. John Steinbeck, *A Russian Journal* (New York: Viking Press, 1948), p. 171. All further citations from *A Russian Journal* refer to this edition and are identified by page number in the text.
2. That Ricketts planned to see a good deal of Steinbeck in 1948 is also apparent from his remarks to friends about plans to make *Cannery Row* into a film, using Pacific Biological Laboratory for the interior shots. Ricketts wrote Virginia Scardigli that once a "nuisance" lawsuit brought against Steinbeck (apparently by producer Berny Byrens) is resolved, the novelist will make *Cannery Row* into a movie "thru the Theatre Guild. . . . And it'll be very good" (EFR-VS, 4/9/48). It is possible that Steinbeck was not so interested in the *Cannery Row* film as Ricketts believed. Steinbeck had just completed a screenplay for *The Red Pony* and was considering another based on the life of Emiliano Zapata, so that he may have lost interest in the *Cannery Row* project long before actual plans for the filming were scrapped.
3. Steinbeck, "Critics, Critics, Burning Bright," p. 22.
4. John Steinbeck, *Burning Bright* (New York: Bantam, 1962), p. 130. All further citations from *Burning Bright* refer to this edition and are identified by page number in the text.
5. Steinbeck, "Critics, Critics, Burning Bright," p. 21.
6. *Ibid.*
7. Oscar Hammerstein defended his and Rodgers' role in producing the play: "We are very proud to have produced it because it's a play that should have been done" (New York *Times*, October 27, 1950, p. 24).
8. Steinbeck, "Critics, Critics, Burning Bright," p. 22.
9. Fontenrose, *John Steinbeck*, p. 115.
10. *Ibid.* Lisca, *Wide World*, p. 254.

11. French, *Steinbeck*, p. 151.
12. Lisca, *Wide World*, p. 249. The film was shot in the United States after the Mexican government, unenthusiastic about an American company making a movie about one of its most controversial historical figures, denied Fox permission to use Mexican locations.
13. H. H. Dunn, *The Crimson Jester* (New York: R. M. McBride, 1933), pp. 25–26.
14. See Lisca, *Wide World*, p. 249.
15. Robert Morsberger, "Steinbeck's Zapata: Rebel versus Revolutionary," in Astro and Hayashi, *Steinbeck: The Man and His Work*, p. 63. With the exception of Lisca's one-page summary of *Viva Zapata!*, there was not a single study of Steinbeck's screenplay during the first eighteen years after the film was produced, probably because the script was never published separately for perusal by the critics.
16. John Steinbeck, *Viva Zapata!* MS., shooting script final, May 16, 1951, 20th Century-Fox, p. 33. All further citations from *Viva Zapata!* refer to this script and are identified by page number in the text.
17. Morsberger, "Steinbeck's Zapata," p. 54.
18. Steinbeck, "About Ed Ricketts," p. xlvi.
19. Boodin, *The Social Mind*, p. 177.
20. Steinbeck, *Journal of a Novel*, p. 20.
21. *Ibid.*, p. 8.
22. Edward Weeks, "Suzy and the Octopus," *Atlantic Monthly*, CXCIV (August 1954), 82.
23. "A Minor Pleasantry," *Nation*, CLXXIX (July 10, 1954), 37. Even the usually perceptive Carlos Baker wrote that *Sweet Thursday* is a sequel to "the masses whose bridgework still permits them to relish salt-water taffy, Monterey style" ("After Lousy Wednesday," *New York Times Book Review*, June 13, 1954, p. 4).
24. Robert Boyle, "Boozy Wisdom," *Commonweal*, LX (July 9, 1954), 351.
25. Ward Moore, "Cannery Row Revisited: Steinbeck and the Sardine," *Nation*, CLXXIX (October 16, 1954), 327.
26. John Steinbeck, "Dreams Piped from Cannery Row," New York *Times*, November 11, 1955, p. 1.
27. Lisca, *Wide World*, p. 276.
28. Richard Rodgers and Oscar Hammerstein, *Pipe Dream*, Act 1, Scene 1.
29. Moore, "Cannery Row Revisited," p. 327.
30. Lisca, *Wide World*, p. 282.
31. Harvey Curtis Webster, " 'Cannery Row' Continued," *Saturday Review*, XXXVII (June 12, 1954), 11.
32. John Steinbeck, *Sweet Thursday* (New York: Bantam, 1956), p. 1. All further citations from *Sweet Thursday* refer to this edition and are identified by page number in the text.
33. Lisca, *Wide World*, p. 282.
34. Ricketts, "New Series Note Book No. 4," p. 218.
35. *Ibid.*
36. Lisca, *Wide World*, p. 283.
37. French suggests that Joe Elegant is a parody of Truman Capote, for whom Steinbeck never had much affection (*Steinbeck*, pp. 159–160). Jack Calvin, on the other hand, maintains that Elegant is based upon

Ritch Lovejoy, who died the year *Sweet Thursday* was published (JC/RA, 4/9/70).

38. The character of Old Jingleballicks is a composite of two stuffy marine biologists, neither of whom Ricketts liked much.

Travels with Steinbeck

1. John Steinbeck, quoted in Bernard Kale, "The Author," *Saturday Review*, XXXV (September 20, 1952), 11.
2. Steinbeck, *Journal of a Novel*, p. 115.
3. *Ibid.*, p. 116.
4. John Steinbeck, *East of Eden* (New York: Bantam, 1955), p. 274. All further citations from *East of Eden* refer to this edition and are identified by page number in the text.
5. Steinbeck, *Journal of a Novel*, p. 27.
6. Joseph Wood Krutch, "John Steinbeck's Dramatic Tale of Three Generations," *New York Herald Tribune Book Review*, September 21, 1955; reprinted in Tedlock and Wicker, *Steinbeck and His Critics*, pp. 304–305.
7. See Fontenrose, *John Steinbeck*, p. 124.
8. Steinbeck, *Journal of a Novel*, p. 73.
9. *Ibid.*, p. 115.
10. Fontenrose, *John Steinbeck*, p. 119.
11. *Ibid.*, p. 120.
12. John Steinbeck, "The Making of a New Yorker," *New York Times Magazine,* February 1 and 22, 1953, reprinted in *The Empire City*, ed. Alexander Klein (New York: Holt, 1955), p. 473.
13. *Ibid.*, p. 474.
14. John Steinbeck, "Our Rigged Morality," *Coronet*, XLVII (March 1960), 146.
15. French, *Steinbeck*, p. 165.
16. John Steinbeck, *The Short Reign of Pippin IV* (New York: Bantam, 1958), p. 116.
17. Steinbeck made this remark in a letter to C. V. Wicker, co-editor of *Steinbeck and His Critics* (see Lisca, *Wide World*, p. 288). As things turned out, the book sold well, largely because it was chosen as a Book-of-the-Month-Club selection.
18. *The Winter of Our Discontent* grew out of a short story by Steinbeck entitled "How Mr. Hogan Robbed a Bank," *Atlantic Monthly*, CXCVII (March 1961), 58–61. As Steinbeck enlarged the scope of the novel, the original story was pushed aside. This accounts for the minimal importance of the bank robbery in the longer work.
19. John Steinbeck, *The Winter of Our Discontent* (New York: Bantam, 1962), p. 211. All further citations from *The Winter of Our Discontent* refer to this edition and are identified by page number in the text. *The Winter of Our Discontent* is Steinbeck's first and only attempt at first-person narration.
20. See Fontenrose, *John Steinbeck*, p. 134.
21. John Steinbeck, "High Drama of Bold Thrust through Ocean Floor," *Life* (April 14, 1961), 110–118.
22. Mrs. Steinbeck has also noted her husband's burgeoning interest in the

American space program. In spite of his conviction that some of the money spent on space should go to solve problems on earth, he maintained a continuing curiosity about man's exploration of space (ES/RA, 3/24/71).

23. John Steinbeck, *Travels with Charley in Search of America* (New York: Viking Press, 1962), p. 6. All further citations from *Travels with Charley* refer to this edition and are identified by page number in the text.

24. It is unknown to most people that Webster Street accompanied Steinbeck from Monterey to Flagstaff, Arizona. Apparently Steinbeck was not worried that the two of them might disturb "the ecologic complex" of the Mojave.

25. John Steinbeck, "Always Something to Do in Salinas," *Holiday*, XVII (June 1955), 58. Steinbeck's remarks about Salinas in this short piece are harsh and disparaging. Steinbeck never really liked Salinas, not even in later life.

26. John Steinbeck, "Well, Max, Here's Why I'm a Columnist," *Seattle Times Sunday Supplement*, December 5, 1965, p. 1.

27. John Steinbeck, "Secretary of Nonsense Recommended," *Seattle Times Sunday Supplement*, December 12, 1965, p. 1.

INDEX

Index

253

Index

255

Index

Index

Vonnegut, Kurt, 149

Wallsten, Robert, 216
Western Flyer, 15, 226
Whitehead, Alfred North, 47

Whitman, Walt, 28, 35, 40
Wordsworth, William, 28

Zapata, Emiliano, 187. *See also*
Steinbeck, *Viva Zapata!*